Cultural Histories of the Material World

BARD GRADUATE CENTER
CULTURAL HISTORIES OF THE
MATERIAL WORLD

Cultural Histories of the Material World is a series centered on the exploration of the material turn in the study of culture. Volumes in the series examine the ways human beings have shaped and interpreted the material world from a broad range of scholarly perspectives and show how attention to materiality can contribute to a more precise historical understanding of specific times, places, ways, and means.

Peter N. Miller, Series Editor

Antiquarianism and Intellectual Life in Europe and China, 1500–1800
Peter N. Miller and François Louis, Editors

The Sea: Thalassography and Historiography
Peter N. Miller, Editor

Ways of Making and Knowing: The Material Culture of Empirical Knowledge
Pamela H. Smith, Amy R.W. Meyers, and Harold J. Cook, Editors

The Anthropology of Expeditions: Travel, Visualities, Afterlives
Joshua A. Bell and Erin L. Hasinoff, Editors

Ex Voto: Votive Giving Across Cultures
Ittai Weinryb, Editor

In Space We Read Time: On the History of Civilization and Geopolitics
Karl Schlögel
Translated by Gerrit Jackson

Cultural Histories of the Material World

Edited by Peter N. Miller

Bard Graduate Center

New York City

First published in the United States of America by the University of
Michigan Press, Ann Arbor, 2014. © 2014 University of Michigan.

First paperback edition published in 2019 by Bard Graduate Center,
New York City, by arrangement with the University of Michigan Press
and distributed by the University of Chicago Press. This book may be
purchased in quantity for educational, business, or promotional use.
For information, please e-mail marketing@press.uchicago.edu.

Printed in the United States of America

♾ This paper meets the requirements of ANSI/NISO Z39.48-1992
(Permanence of Paper).

28 27 26 25 24 23 22 21 20 19   1 2 3 4 5

ISBN-13: 978-1-941792-18-6 (paperback)

Library of Congress Cataloging-in-Publication Data
Names: Miller, Peter N., 1964- editor.
Title: Cultural histories of the material world / edited by Peter N.
  Miller.
Description: First paperback edition. | New York City : Bard Graduate
  Center, 2019. | Series: Bard Graduate Center cultural histories of the
  material world | "First published in the United States of America by the
  University of Michigan Press, Ann Arbor, 2014"–Title page verso. |
  Includes bibliographical references and index. | Summary: "This book
  considers how to study material culture from a historical perspective,
  and explores how studying material and materiality can enable new and
  different cultural historical perspectives. While gathering some of the
  most interesting thinkers in their respective fields, the contributions
  also examine material culture through a historiographical lens,
  considering how the field slipped between disciplines in the twentieth
  century, and how it has become more prominent inside and outside the
  academy in the last twenty years or so. The book builds on the recent
  proliferation of studies of materiality to offer a different,
  theoretically coherent approach to the topic"– Provided by publisher.
Identifiers: LCCN 2019022995 | ISBN 9781941792186 (paperback)
Subjects: LCSH: Culture–Philosophy.
Classification: LCC HM621 .C848 2019 | DDC 301.01–dc23
LC record available at https://lccn.loc.gov/2019022995

For Tony

A state of affairs (a state of things) is a
combination of objects (things).
It is essential to things that they should be
possible constituents of states of affairs.

—Wittgenstein, *Tractatus Logico-Philosophicus* 2.01–2.011

Contents

4. Future Histories

Preface to the Paperback Edition

I am delighted that *Cultural Histories of the Material World*, six years after its publication, is now beginning its life as a paperback. The book was planned as a small-plate special: lots of choices, no mutually exclusive tastes, nothing too filling. Included were historians, art historians, archaeologists, anthropologists, curators, and all manner of humanistic flavors in between.

Three years after the conference in 2010 that launched this book series—and provided the menu for this eponymous volume—the Bard Graduate Center in New York hosted another meeting, around the same table, to discuss what a project devoted to "cultures of conservation" might look like. It did not take long to realize that without the contributions of conservators and conservation scientists the "material" in these cultural histories would remain, if not entirely metaphorical, then certainly partially so. *Cultural Histories of the Material World* was published soon after this discussion, too soon after for its content to reflect this new realization.

If we were to have a second edition—if this preface were not only a matter of reissuing the book in paperback—we would want to bring these two projects together. How might we imagine conservation knowledge fitting into this volume? What we have here are a series of probes that use objects as historical evidence and launch from a variety of locations on the disciplinary and sub-disciplinary circumference. Every probe—every author—brings a unique way of seeing and feeling their way to an interpretation of the world that would have been impossible without the object in between. Conservators are historians of the object. Their presence somewhere out on that cultural historical arc ought to be perfectly obvious. (The underlying idea here I borrow from Ernst Gombrich's treatment of G. W. F. Hegel in *In Search of Cultural History*.)

And yet. We are still not there yet. Yes, in the intervening years, books have appeared such as Katja von Baum's *Let the Material Talk: Technology of Late-Medieval Cologne Panel Painting* (Archetype, 2014) which uses technical analysis to explore the art-making ecology of Cologne in the second half of the fifteenth century. But we still cannot easily imagine conservators and conservation scientists as comfortably lining up under the banner of *Cultural Histories of the Material World* as historians, art historians, archaeologists, and anthropologists do. Why? Let's take the example of *Let the Material Talk*. Conservation science is at the core of that project. It feeds the glowing hot furnace of technical art history. But, in fact, the book's questions remain firmly fixed around attribution and making—the "when," "what," "where," and "how" questions that animated yesterday's art history. The "why" that would lead into the wider and woolier fields of social and economic causation isn't even attempted. There are some exceptions: Marco Leona, Henry Smith, Yanbing Luo, and Elena Basso use conservation science to answer history's questions about nineteenth-century Japan (*Synthetic Arsenic Sulfides in Japanese Prints of the Meiji Period*), and Sanchita Balachandran merges the conservator with the anthropologist in her exploration of Indian bronzes in the Government Museum in Chennai (*The Development of a Conservation Consciousness at Angkor: A Study of the Colonial Politics of Archaeology*).

But with these scholars' pioneering work, we are still very much at the beginning of something. We are nowhere near realizing the full potency of the conservator as a historian of the object. For this to occur, the conservator will have to shift focus from the object to its people—or from its birth to its life. Of course these are gross generalizations! To be more precise, one would have to say that the shift in focus can be subtle and is by no means exclusive: namely, to use the object as a means to an end rather than only as an end in itself. The art object no less than the object of low aesthetic intentionality—or the "archaeological and ethnographic" object—can point us to other significant arenas. Up to now, because of the history and context for conservation training and practice, this broadening of scope is more the exception than the rule. But with forethought, a sense of ambition, as well as a shift in perspective, the conservator stands revealed as a scholar of material culture with a distinct set of powers.

To put it another way, the conservator does not need to know differently in order to be a cultural historian of the material world but only to self-define differently. Imagine what would be involved, on the example of Clifford Geertz, for the conservator to write a book of essays entitled "The Conservator as Author"? What would be involved in the self-presentation of the conservator? But, you are saying, isn't characterization also about institutional and disciplinary possibilities? And that is indeed correct. If conservators have not and do not think in terms of "the conservator as author," it is in good part because if they did so, they would not be published in the same places they are now and would not be read by the peers who vote on promotions and decide on grant applications. Which takes us back to this volume and this series. It is a place for just these sorts of explorations and new possibilities of writing, for new genres and for post-disciplinary re-creation. Its place in the ecology of learned journals and publications is proudly on the ever-expanding periphery, where it can contribute to the vital exercise of pushing old horizons so as to make possible the pulsing activity that we simply call creativity.

Peter N. Miller
Bard Graduate Center
Summer 2019

Series Editor's Preface

With this volume, the full scope of our ambitions for this book series is on view. Containing twenty-three contributions, ranging across the x, y, and z axes of time, space and discipline, what the reader encounters here is a collective project—not merely a collection of essays, but a statement about how scholars from different fields and continents of learning are now thinking about how the past can be studied through its material traces. Of course, we cannot here provide samples from every corner of the world, but we have hopefully given enough to show how rich is the potential for this new way of thinking.

We are, of course, not the first to notice this. But we are the first to give this movement, trend, tendency—even fashion—a name: *cultural histories of the material world*. What does this mean? What is its history? First off, there are many kinds of stories one could tell about the *material world*, this latter term referring to all things having some kind of physical form. This could include space, whether interior or exterior; structure, whether big or small; or thing, whether abiding, or only a vestige (in Latin, a *vestigium* is a footprint, the mark that remains made by something that is itself no longer present). A *cultural history* of the material world is, therefore, a story about materiality that is pointed toward issues that might extend well beyond the contours of anything material. A book about the circus could tell us something about views of animals, or notions of equality; another, about the discovery of fractal geometry, could tell us something about the relationship between drawing by hand and mathematical imaging, and between seeing and knowing; a third, about textiles and furniture, could bring us to questions of the role of women and the perceived values attached to different kinds of objects.

That all of these projects were undertaken as exhibitions at the Bard Graduate Center in New York tells us something else about *cultural histories of the material world*. The term is meant to make sense at a second order of intellectual processes or approaches, which might each occupy continuous parts of the spectrum of materiality, such as decorative arts, or material culture, or design history—but also those that are discontinuous, such as anthropology, archaeology, architecture, and the history of technology. There is no reason, in fact, why parallel research agendas or secondary literatures need communicate. And yet, to people interested in how materiality speaks to us, it is clear that there is a common *telos* to these varied learned initiatives. *Cultural histories of the material world* is the term we have chosen to designate it.

The essays in this volume emerged from a meeting held at the Bard Graduate Center in 2010 to launch the idea of this series. The contributors are all members of the editorial board (though not all members of the editorial board are contributors). Each was asked to write a short essay on what *cultural history of the material world* signaled to them. They were told to feel comfortable writing in whatever genre they liked: academic article, essay, belles lettres, memoir, conversation, even fiction. This breadth was sought precisely in order to model what we took to be the possible range of themes and styles for books in this series. Reading through this volume will, therefore, afford two simultaneous pleasures: the first, of reading fine scholarship written by scholars with something original to communicate and, the second, of seeing in the whole new possibilities for scholars and scholarship in the years to come.

Acknowledgments

I first met Sabine MacCormack when she chaired a search committee for a job I did not get. She sent me *Religion in the Andes* with the inscription, "Felix qui potuit rerum cognoscere causas." The next time I saw her, as I was going off for a year's fellowship, she told me that I should return having written the kind of book I could not have written before. Both of these anecdotes capture something essential about Sabine, and why her loss is so painful. She was passionately committed to discovering the truth—in the past and in the present, about strangers, about her friends, about herself—and she was actively hostile to the tyranny of convention and of the formulaic. The challenge of self-creation was dear to her, in her personal life and in her scholarly career, which spanned continents, chronologies, and disciplines. On the external editorial board of *Cultural Histories of the Material World,* she was helpful with suggestions and advice. At the meeting that launched the series, and which resulted in this book, she was a passionate advocate for serious but open scholarship. We—I—will miss her.

The conference out of which this book grew was held at the Bard Graduate Center in January 2010. I would like to thank Elena Pinto Simon, Graham White, Han Vu, Alex Phelan, and Ben Rosenthal for their help on the day, and Laura Grey and Kimon Keramidas on many days that followed. Daniel Lee and Vanessa Rossi were visitors then; they have since become an integral part of the team that produced this book and this series. It is a pleasure to thank all of them here. As always, I am indebted to the library and staff of the Bard Graduate Center, especially Heather Topcik, for a constant supply of reading material.

Tony Grafton has been friend, guide, and inspiration for twenty years now. If any one person could embody the ideal of precision and vision represented by this series, it would be him. This book is dedicated in his honor.

Introduction:
The Culture of
the Hand

Peter N. Miller

Rainer Maria Rilke looked at Rodin's sculptures and saw hands.

> Rodin has made hands, independent, small hands which, without forming part of a body, are yet alive. Hands rising upright, evil and irritated, hands whose five bristling fingers seem to bark like the five throats of a hell-hound. Hands in motion, sleeping hands and hands in the act of awaking; criminal hands weighted by heredity, and those that are tired and have lost all desire, lying like some sick beast crouched in a corner, knowing none can help them.[1]

This is dazzling. But Rilke is not casting about for a metonymic characterization of the relationship between "hands" and "wholes." No, he is on to something else. "Hands," he continues, "are a complicated organism, a delta in which much life from distant sources flows together and is poured into the great stream of action." For him, hands are real, and what they make is real. In fact, what they make is history. "Hands have a history of their own, they have, indeed, their own Culture."[2]

This book, and this series for which it is named, is devoted to the Culture of the Hand, on all the many levels gestured at, hinted at, or only implied by Rilke. One of the reasons why "culture" is so much better a word than the "civilization" used by the English translator of the Rodin book is that it gives us access to the very material level conveyed by the Latin term *cultura*—the human intervention upon nature—as well as to the conceptualizations that are the result of the equally effortful work of tending the spirit: *cultura animi*. Rilke's Culture of the Hand is, therefore, a way of defining human activity: training the hand, the works of the hand, the world made by many hands. This broad domain, in its many splendors, is the subject of this book: a book whose purpose is to show possibilities and teach questions, not to foreclose them or to preach answers.

For those of us interested in cultural histories of the material world, the twentieth century began in the 1880s, in Bonn, with Karl Lamprecht. This was the decade in which Aby Warburg was his student—later Marc Bloch devoted his most assiduous reading to Lamprecht, and Johan Huizinga engaged with Lamprecht at key stages of his career—and in which he cemented a relationship with Henri Pirenne.[3] But most of all, in this decade, Lamprecht launched projects which would define the next century's chief initiatives. He published a book on ornamental patterns in medieval incipits; he organized a collaborative "total history" of an illuminated manuscript, treating it as an artistic, political, economic, political, and material artifact; he published a four-volume study of the medieval Moselle region that blended geography, economy and law; and he launched himself into a multi-volume work on German history that he characterized in terms of cultural history.

Of course, if he is at all known today it is because of the two-decade-long polemic that broke out around him, and which centered on his practice as a scholar—the verdict was dim—and his endorsement of cultural history—then still a swear word among professional historians in Germany.[4] The *Lamprechtstreit*, like the contemporary Dreyfus Affair in France, divided teachers from students and colleagues from one another, forcing many who admired Lamprecht's originality to duck and cover, if not actively disavow any sympathy for his approach.

Yet, in a very real way, Lamprecht is the most important historian for the twentieth century, and in particular for those of us who tell stories with—as well as about—things. As the teacher of Warburg—and even if Gombrich went too far in making him the exclusive influence on Warburg at the expense of Usener—and as the promoter of Pirenne, who in turn inspired and was the godfather of the *Annales* (with Bloch and Febvre in turn serving as godfathers to Braudel, Le Roy Ladurie, Ginzburg, Davis, Glassie, and Darnton), Lamprecht stands behind the two most innovative schools of history in the twentieth century, or at least schools of cultural history, broadly understood.[5]

Our story, indeed, begins here. But it almost ends here as well. Because in 1929, the founding of the *Annales* marked the emergence of a material history with the culture shorn away, lest any flabby *Geistesge-schichte* debase the new coinage. Later that same year, Aby Warburg died in Hamburg. Over the next few years, the profile of his institute shifted away from the more anthropological, and material, contexts that so attracted its founder, to the intellectualized cultural history of *Hercules am Scheidewege* and *Studies in Iconology*. With this equal and opposite purging of the cultural from the material and the material from the cultural, Lamprecht's innovative synthesis mostly vanished from view. Where it remained active, in a clear example of Jürgen Kocka's notion of "ideological regression and methodological innovation," was in the increasingly racial Volks- and Landesgeschichte of the 1930s. Hermann Aubin, for example, began as a Lamprecht-inspired student of Landesgeschichte at Bonn, and wound up as the director of a Nazi ethnic demography institute at Breslau. (That he ended up back in Bonn, teaching through the 1950s and serving as a mentor to a new generation of spatial historians is a reminder that there can be two sides to every coin.)[6]

Over the course of the twentieth century, like Aristophanes's *ur*-hermaphrodite, these sundered perspectives sought, but never, or only too rarely, found each other. In the last decade or two, however, the gropings of material historians toward cultural explanations, and of cultural historians for materializations—perhaps best embodied in the turn to microhistory by social historians, histories of the book by literary scholars, antiquarianism by classicists and art historians, and the history of science by cultural historians—shows that the magnetism of Lamprecht's synthesis still works, even if invisibly, and at a great distance. This volume represents an explicit attempt at union on both the practical and theoretical levels: the essays do the work of joining cultural to material history, and the self-consciousness about this work, and about the perplexities and antinomies of the historical metanarrative with which they are in dialogue, is bound up with the desire of contributors to intervene in and repoint a historiography.

A genealogy of the relationship between culture and material would be a daunting undertaking, almost an encyclopedia of the West from the most ancient times—or even earlier, as Horst Bredekamp suggests in his essay—to the present. No one who has read through—or in antiquity, listened to—Cicero's discussion of the liberal versus the manual arts—one the province of the head and the free, the other that of the hand and the enslaved—can have any doubt of the depth of the valorization of the one, and depreciation of the other. This is an old but long-lasting perspective. It was still potent at the beginning of the twentieth century, when French and German scholars could debate their national superiority in terms of the supremacy of *Civilisation* or *Cultur*. The threat of the material and the quotidian loomed large over this debate: the French saw in *Cultur* the anthropological lowest common denominator; the Germans, in *Civilisation*, the banality of everyday practice. That the single most influential work of cultural history—Jacob Burckhardt's study of Renaissance Italy—still bears its late Victorian mistranslated title illustrates the gravitational pull exerted by these century-old perceptions. (It is, of course, "The *Culture* of the Renaissance in Italy," but Middlemore could not bear precisely Burckhardt's gesture at practice, rite, and as we might say today, *habitus*.)

The nineteenth century's problem with materiality is worth dilating upon. For while the ancient bias remains powerful, it is also deeply challenged. By the middle of the century there is a broad attempt to incorporate a wider range of evidence, including that of material remains and daily life, and new kinds of questions—including those that came to found the disciplines of anthropology, archaeology, folklore, and art history. No longer could these claims simply be ignored; having been made so forcefully, they now had to be rejected, equally forcefully. And they were.

This rejection, which coincided with the establishment of history as a modern university discipline, had the effect of setting back the history of historical scholarship by at least a half, if not a whole, century—and I mean by this the retarded rise of economic and especially social and cultural history, which was stillborn ca. 1860. The rejection reflected an insistence on the priority of history as practiced by professional academics over and against an insurgent popular practice; of the university over and against the local association and the museum; of the legitimacy of older, as opposed to more recent, history; and, of course, an underlying discomfort with materiality. The specter, too, that haunts this rejection, is that of Marx.

The revolutions of 1848 were not only, as Ryding and Dilly pointed out long ago in a brilliant article, the crucible of cultural history, they also launched the *Communist Manifesto*.[7] And from then on, even to our own day, talk of material history easily blurred in the listener's ear into historical materialism. Marx, then—even as he opened perspectives for some—became for others a tool for tarring. Of course, as anyone who has looked to Marx for a discussion of material culture knows full well, he makes no effort at all to show how material evidence tells us things about society that we do not already know. Marx was, indeed, a prophet of materiality—of the idea that the material matters—but he was not interested in exploring how it matters. Instead, he skips directly to the implications of production for broader questions of politics and economics. Indeed, what now passes for the study of material culture—close attention to the way in which things and people mutually interact—he classes, and dismisses, under the term "fetish." So, far from serving as a resource for those then, or since, interested in materiality, Marx doubly set it back: both in terms of a personal lack of interest, which he communicated to his followers, and in terms of the fear his political program inspired, which led others to condemn the whole prospect of material meanings. (Engels might represent a different set of possibilities, and a different genealogy.)[8]

The death of *Culturgeschichte* in the middle of the nineteenth century, and the botched attempt at revival by Lamprecht—bungled by doubts about his own scholarly credibility even more than by resistance to his questions—is a necessary backdrop to the project of this volume, for it helps explain why the last few decades of scholarship on things in the mainstream of the academy has so little precedent. Among professional art historians, whose training ought best to have prepared the way for an engagement with objects, material culture has labored under the burden of not being art. Nancy Troy begins her essay here with George Kubler's thought experiment about what art historians would have to do if they broadened their purview to include all man-made objects. This was clearly intended as a provocation, and as such, it has had some limited success—the appeal of visual culture conserves still some of its momentum.[9]

From the opposite end of the spectrum, archaeology, the science of objects *par excellence,* has until recently also little succeeded in bringing materiality to the center. Prehistory has served, from the start, as the model for academic archaeology, emphasizing both the interpretative *virtù* of a discipline able to conjure meaning from mute objects without contamination by texts, and the final liberation of professionals from the haunting paternity of the embarrassing, dilettantish premodern antiquary. Archaeologists' rejection of the mongrel, but richer, terrain of textual *plus* material evidence—what is often called "historical archaeology" to exclude the classical Greek and Roman periods, but which surely includes the ancient as well as modern worlds—effectively constituted the self-marginalization of materiality by its own priesthood, at least vis-à-vis the other humanities.

And so, here we are, now, with a volume whose contributors are drawn from history, art history, literature, music, archaeology, classics, folklore, and anthropology departments, and include professors and curators. They were charged to reflect on what a cultural history of the material world might look like from their particular vantage point, and to do so through a short text that could take the form of a loosely argued essay, a personal reflection, a closely argued case study, a manifesto, an exhibition or book review, or a short multimedia project. The goal was to produce a kaleidoscope of great power and beauty. The pieces that follow are just that: pieces. They offer small visions of what could be larger or grander research projects, or even career paths. There is no attempt here at comprehensiveness, nor even at coherence—only at insight. This is a book that can be read from cover to cover like a monograph with an argument—albeit sinuously articulated—or dipped into like a book of essays, each one of which stands on its own, and amidst its own constellation of questions.

This volume proposes that no one discipline owns material culture; rather, things, objects, or materials look different, pose different questions, and do different work depending on the world of presuppositions in which they operate. This volume also follows another of Rilke's premises. He explained that "Rodin knows that the body consists of so many stages for the display of life, of such life as in any and every part can be individual and great."[10] Objects, then, "stage" evidence just as texts do, just as images can, and just as performance does. One of these forms is not necessarily more eloquent, more perfect, more reliable than the others—only different in the way that different forms yield their content.[11]

However much attention had been paid to objects in various disciplines, at various times in the past, the development of a self-conscious discourse with material culture as its term of art is a function of the late 1960s and 1970s, and mostly in Anglo-Saxon scholarship. Echoes of this persist: at a recent Franco-American workshop on material culture and decorative arts, several of the French participants explained that when they heard "material culture" they saw "materialism." Yet, even the INHA—the French National Institute of Art History—now sponsors a position in "Arts et Culture Matérielle."[12] Questions as broad and wide as globalization are conducted in terms of the role and movement of things.[13] Even a tired term like "cultural studies" has sought reinvigoration through reaching out to material culture.[14]

The proliferation of studies of materiality in its many forms is now widely apparent. That so many of these are collective overviews, introductions, guides, or readers suggests both a great hunger for content but also an *olla podria* of methods, questions, fields, and horizons, with all that this implies.[15]

Our volume takes both this interest and this inchoateness for granted, and begins one step further along the curve: asserting to an audience already committed to materiality not to forget that before there was materiality there was material, and before people studied material culture they probably studied art. As Glenn Adamson explains, the rejection of decorative arts by material culture and design history—another cross-disciplinary way of being in the world of things—trades in connoisseurship and aesthetic identification with high style for a concern with evidence. In this move, an object's individuality is subsumed into its class typicality. This coincided, Adamson notes, with a shift to consumption studies and social-economic situatedness, and away from art, which must always be a unique experience—whether of consumption, or production. Is this, he asks, really a step forward? Or have certain important perspectives been lost in the process? Has this "material turn" represented something of a reductionism? Adamson notes that only in an art history, with its emphasis on arts did humanists receive training in materials and making, not to mention style analysis—all of which are needed if the maximum evidentiary value is to be extracted from artifacts, but which have been marginalized, often sneeringly, by those with an animus against the aesthetic (or at least a kind of Weberian unmusicality for the aesthetic impulse). One could add that Carlo Ginzburg's powerful 1995 *Art Bulletin* essay on the connoisseur as detective proved that there is no dichotomy, but only a continuity between object knowledge and the object as evidence for something outside the object.[16]

Philippe Bordes recalls for us that, once upon a time, this reminder that the object was not an either/or did not need to be articulated. Back then, people spoke quite unself-consciously about the *objet d'art*. Bordes asks us to view this taken-for-granted expression as instead a question posed. For him, the triumph of illusionistic art over costume (textiles) and jewels à la Burgundy, marks the start of the immaterial turn. The modesty of the materials involved (paper, canvas) only emphasized the power of artistic genius. The move to illusion was a move away from the materiality of the substance of the object, or even of what it was representing. One can hear in this argument much of what Thomas Campbell and Tristan Weddigen imply about what a history of art history would look like if tapestry, not painting, defined its standard practice.[17]

Bordes dares to suggest that the *objet d'art* is the most "consolidated expression of art" since it combines the immaterial and the material. If, however, the paintings which rose to head the canon in the Beaux-Arts system of the nineteenth century displaced materiality by mimesis, he worries that the late-twentieth-century swing of the dialectical pendulum toward the material—however valuable it has been—could, nevertheless, overcorrect and leave us only objects, with no art, but also no context. The challenge of a cultural history of the material world, as he outlines it, is to preserve the "twentieth-century rapprochement between form and material," and the gains in our understanding of the social context of art that is the "history" in art history.

Brigitte Bedos-Rezak puts Bordes's challenge in philosophical terms. She begins with the presumption that the linguistic turn ought not be simply negated by a material one, exchanging one incompleteness for another. Indeed, she notes, scholars have not gone much for "processual materialization of objects nor their ecological destiny." In fact, symbolism, as in the seals she writes about, remains a major focus of interest, which if not purely linguistic, is yet focused outward, on social phenomena. If formed materials, with the cultural processes built in, as opposed to raw materials on their own, seem the most common kind of historical data, she wonders whether a cultural history of the material world is not in fact a tautology. If all cultural histories are in some way materialized histories, then any separation between them—however heuristically provocative—is, in the end, only artificial. Her response, or proposal, is to focus on the clusters of meaning created by the intertwining of culture, history and material, avoiding pendulum swings between dualisms, or mere reductivism, or presentism, and acknowledging the multiple and always-changing identities of what we might call the "living" thing.

Ivan Gaskell, in his contribution, redirects the question. If history is about people, then a cultural history of the material world would refer to the ways people transform nature, or imbue it with meaning. Where Bedos-Rezak wants to navigate between the Scylla of ahistorical matter and the Charybdis of over-historicized materiality, Gaskell sees a radical opportunity: to dissolve the very notion of firm divisions between material, culture, and history. Relocating the Sudbury bow from Harvard's Peabody Museum of Anthropology to its Art Museum enabled him to tease out the many possible meanings that may be found in material depending upon its material context, which otherwise could be called its cultural history. The museum turns out to be a site of immense complexity because its intersecting identities as both material and cultural facilitate the possibility of fine-grained analysis. That Gaskell and Laurel

Thatcher Ulrich then pursued this idea through a series of courses that fed another exhibition, entitled "Tangible Things," highlights the enormous pedagogical possibilities of such a practice.[18] As he shows, relocation is revelation: in this particular case, it turns out that reputed owner of the Sudbury bow turns out not to have lived in Sudbury, and the event which the object commemorates seems never to have occurred.

Sabine MacCormack pushes this challenge out the door of the museum and into the human present. She reminds us that there are many, not just one, material worlds. The European model is founded on a distinction between the ability to do the work of making (*opus*), and the ability to conceptualize it (*ratiocinatio*). MacCormack, taking the example of Inés the Quechua, forcefully denies this dichotomy. But her point is even bigger. In extensive terms, the separation of *opus* and *ratiocinatio* cramps the possibility of a global vision because it assumes a universal conceptual landscape, which we know to be false. In intensive terms, like Momigliano's famous distinction between the antiquarian and the historian, this one presumes falsely that the creator at the rock face cannot also be the one to conceptualize and contextualize that creation. In thinking about this subject area, she implies, we might need also to rethink its conceptual foundations.

Still in the present, Daniel Miller uses the example of the history of Facebook to treat ethnographically the impact of a cultural artifact on individual people. In his in-depth treatment of "Nicole" and her relationship to this online world, we get a case study in the dynamic relationship between cultural history and biography. If the ethnographer's lens allows us to discover the historicity of a phenomenon generally viewed as timeless because of our own time, it also models for us the extent to which the meaning of a phenomenon is contingent upon its social life.

Lynn Meskell begins with a reflection on the impact of Miller's London School and the current romanticization of objects—their presentation as vehicles for biography, genealogy, or self-fashioning. Perhaps the most striking example of the power of this approach is the best-selling book, *The Hare with Amber Eyes* (2010).[19] What does not get accounted for now, however, according to Meskell, is the copresence of divergent qualities inhering in, and held together by, the object itself. This insight, which she traces to Hegel in the *Phenomenology of Spirit,* is then used as the basis for her attempt to elucidate, in the context of her digging at Çatalhöyük, the fully contextualized, synchronic meaning of an object. Staying with the object in one time and place becomes, for her, the model of a specifically archaeological interpretation. This idea that an object is part of a conversation with its surroundings translates Bedos-Rezak's vision of material as having "its own landscape of contingencies which affects both the objects' destinations and meanings" into the realm of archaeology.[20]

Among archaeologists, the past two decades have witnessed a long march away from a social science model toward the humanities. This invoked, first, the "post-processual," then the "interpretative," and now the "social." We might single out Ian Hodder, and then two of the contributors to this collection—Lynn Meskell and Michael Shanks—as leading examples of this development.[21] It has offered archaeologists entirely new domains in which to study material traces, and has given historians, art historians, and anthropologists a whole new portfolio of questions with which to reapproach their own realms. For Michael Shanks, this trajectory continues beyond the borders of even this irredentist archaeology. Positing archaeology "as the study of what remains" makes it a key tool for probing the contemporary environment. In particular, he wants us to see how archaeology offers the foundation for a design history capable of making sense of a world thoroughly dominated by things. Perhaps inevitably this leads him to revalue the role of historical archaeology. If all this seems very different from Meskell's archaeology, it is. Shanks, perhaps only partly tongue-in-cheek, has redefined his practice, and perhaps that of "his" archaeology, as well: "Actually, I'm a neo-antiquarian."[22]

John Pocock in his multivolume study of Gibbon has emphasized the challenge he faced in finding a literary form in which to write an evidence-rich narrative. The problem faced by the antiquaries in this new world had as much to do with writing as with thinking.[23] Our question here then becomes: what is the heuristic style of the *neo*-antiquarian? Bernard Herman presents it as dialectic, using his example of the puffer fish, or toad, which is made into food "through a violent act of translation"—an editing that takes what was extraneous and separates it from the commodity. (The puffer fish is rendered edible by cutting off the head and pulling the skin so as to turn the fish inside out and make the flesh accessible.) Herman continues: "All encounters with things proceed in this fashion—we are committed to the deadening of things as a means to rendering them tractable—and then quickening them through description and interpretation." Herman puts the emphasis squarely on the imaginative ability to use, see, and talk as the only way out of an impasse which is otherwise entirely negative. He seems to imply that even if this ends up being a reduced reality, it can be vivid, full with information, and provocative.

Herman began as a folklorist and art historian and the sensibility of oral culture shapes his approach to material culture. Ruth Phillips is an anthropologist, and she, too, focuses on experience and embodiment. Both remind us that just as the antiquaries of old read, they also traveled, handled, smelled, and tasted. But her focus here is on the slippages between the visual and the material, where assumptions filter through undetected and unexamined. Translation, she writes, following Peter Burke, involves both decontextualization and recontextualization. The ambiguities of material forms—what do they really mean to different people? never being exactly the same—greatly facilitates that process. Thus, looking at material translation enables her to shed light on cultural encounters. Phillips concludes that we will need language, performance, and also visual and material dimensions if we are to understand as best as we can the complexity of the historical reality.

This brings us back to the model for studies of the material world: the "original," early modern antiquaries who lived through the Age of Contact, both with past and present worlds, and collected, described, and compared objects, as well as texts, rituals, and naturalia. Alain Schnapp's contribution to this volume is then all the more essential. He shows that in antiquity our issues—what is materiality? what is culture?—were present and were bound up with the biggest of questions: mortality. In the realm of the material, this means that ruins and discarded objects are useful because they are material, and at the same time are separated from the commodity cycle.

Objects functioned already in antiquity as ways to re-enchant the world. Schnapp figures the surviving presentations of this in both literary texts and inscriptions as *Stein und Zeit*—the relationship between material memory and the problem of time. The Egyptians gave us the genre of poetic reflection; the Mesopotamians that of archaeology, since burying fragile mud bricks bearing inscriptions in the foundations of temples presupposes that digging up such materials is what people of the future will do. Robert Harrist turns to another example, perhaps the most extreme one, of the application of antiquarian techniques to ostensibly alien materials: writing on mountains. Going to China, back to the Tang period, we find mountains turned into material: nature made into a backdrop for the conveying of presence to posterity. In the process, however, this act—which might have had political meaning when done by or for an emperor, such as Xuanzong (712–756), or a personal one when the act of an otherwise anonymous traveler or scholar—also transformed space. Nature became an object through the human intervention of writing.

Jaś Elsner notes that this complex of issues has always been problematic for the discipline of art history. He reminds us how few objects appear, for instance, in Gibbon's *Decline and Fall of the Roman Empire*, and how what does, such as the Arch of Constantine, functions purely as a cipher, not only for Gibbon, but for Raphael earlier, and Berenson later. Elsner wants us to acknowledge the strangeness of material culture within the study of art. In part, he suggests it is a technical problem: how to talk about things in words. But there is more. What Schnapp points to as essentially human—the conflation of materiality with mortality— Elsner sees as overdetermined. In this process, objects become emblems, sometimes even losing all their historical specificity. In the hands of professional art historians, Elsner writes, this tends always to treat the material as materiality, and thereby reduce the uncomfortableness of the object world to the familiarity of the symbolic. But since words and things communicate meaning differently, what is really needed is a language that is true to the varieties of materiality, but also makes sense to other people. As difficult as this might be to conceive of, taking material seriously, Elsner implies, offers the possibility of freeing scholars from a vantage point anchored either in cultural apologetics or ideological denial—absolutely essential for the modernization of art history as a discipline.

Ittai Weinryb's meditation on Marbod of Rennes (1035–1123) takes up Elsner's challenge. Marbod's reflection on the meaning of the crack he discovered in his "golden bowl"—a vase he purchased as a tourist in Rome—reveals to us a medieval reflection on materiality that is not about visual representation. But since Marbod was also the author of the first medieval lapidary, we see that he was also able to appreciate the purely material dimension of materiality, and to participate, in this context, in the contemporary tendency to impute symbolism to matter. That Marbod was capable of relating to the object world on these all these distinct registers suggests that there is much to rethink in the historiography of the Middle Ages, and much, potentially, to learn from it.

Addressing the current situation, Bill Brown argues that the time is right for tackling the place of the material in the cultural sciences. He notes the steady drumbeat of new publications including the *Handbook of Material Culture* (2006), *The Object Reader* (2009), and the special issue of

Critical Inquiry on "things" which he edited (2001)—to which we could add the *Oxford Handbook of Material Culture* (2010) and the *Cambridge Companion to Historical Archaeology* (2009). The expected big audiences for these books reflect, he argues, a current materialist longing unsatisfied by Marx's historical materialism, and the craving of scholars from elsewhere in the cultural sciences looking for help with "things." Brown calls this, rightly, I think, the "post-postprocessual moment."

Following the arguments of Robert Friedel and Steven Lubar in their pathbreaking *History from Things* (1993), Brown, like Elsner, suggests the need to go back to the stuff itself, the Aristotelian "first cause" that is so often skipped over by scholars en route to what they view as the more interesting explanations. This is precisely where Juliet Fleming comes in, strongly arguing for a new history of the book. The work of Adrian Johns, Ann Blair, and William Sherman over the past decade has brought reading into the world of writing, and both into the making of books. What Fleming proposes is the possibility that writing is not formed by an external material world pressing down upon us, but from our own material reality extruded on to paper. From the premise that materiality is inside us, Fleming reinterprets Derrida's grammatology as a new science of cultural graphology, in which questions of being were encountered and addressed as material. The horizon of analytical bibliography—the "science of the transmission of literary documents"—does indeed open fascinating material possibilities. But Nancy Troy, reviewing the fate of her books at the hands of the Library of Congress's cataloguers, shows us how precarious that transmission is. The gap between her assessment of her work's *telos,* and theirs—and what theirs is based on—maps a new vision of bibliography as cultural history.

The history of the book is one arena where a material focus has already created new areas of questioning. Another is history of science. Pamela Smith reconfigures it as techno-science, such that treated as a cultural history of the material world: (1) it becomes a deep history of technology, and (2) is based on material and commercial exchange. The first, "deep," part suggests that tools, the discovery of fire, the domestication of plants, and astronomical observation—all these paleo, meso, and Neolithic skills—articulate an engagement with nature not very different from our own higher tech. Exchange, in turn, emerges as one of the principles of history of science practiced as techno-science. Exchange points to the globalism of the early modern, but also to craft—between urban culture and artisans—to the collective practice of science—as in the Royal Society—and to the formalization of an exchange between humans and the natural world (for what are experiments if not organized interventions in the natural world?).

The history of food seems ripe for this kind of treatment, but up until now it has generally been ignored—by cultural historians because too material, and by material historians because too ephemeral a phenomenon: the thing itself vanishes, either by intention or necessity, leaving only representations in word or line. Yet, as Deborah Krohn shows, the position of the culinary in premodern times lay precisely athwart the line separating *theoria* from experience, or from tacit knowledge. The recipe, which is the subject of her essay, is where these two extremes meet. Looking at the development of recipes, then, enables us at a distance to chart the meandering passage of tacit into formal knowledge, and food from the impermanent to the theorized.

Music is even less material than food. Its materiality—leaving aside of course instruments and staging—is "visible" only to the ear. Elaine Sisman takes up this challenge of presenting music as a key contact zone for exploring material issues. Music functions in this book as borderline material—sound, vibration, the instruments, the effects on us. But at the same time there is no there: it all happens in time. Sisman concentrates on the example of Haydn's *Creation*, and the particular moment in time of the creation of light and how Haydn represents it. Others, such as Reinhart Meyer-Kalkus, have written about the culture and material culture of audiality in the twentieth century.[24]

But Sisman also opens up a second front on the question of music and materiality: that of performance. For music is embodied, not just in audiences, but in how composers write it, how actors perform it, and how singers voice it. She gives the example of Don Giovanni singing and strumming—two material processes, sometimes working together, sometimes working against each other. And then there are the words he is directing at Donna Elvira's maid—also, maybe working together or apart. This materiality is incredibly complicated, but, potentially, just as generative. "In emphasizing musical issues that cultural history can entail," Sisman suggests, "musicologists may set new terms for debate in the cultural history they have long inhabited."[25]

Jonathan Bloom offers a model for art history, too, writing reform from the perspective of Islamic art. He and Sheila Blair argue that Islamic art offers a methodological opportunity for those wishing to rethink the theoretical definitions of art history.[26] The singular importance of Islamic art for art history as a discipline is precisely that it stands outside the canon, and was thus spared all the diagnosed ills of disciplinization. For him, the cultural history of the material world puts the emphasis on the things made, where the texts may tell us nothing. For him, the movement is from things to questions: What was it made from? How was it made? Who made it? When was it made? Where was it made? And finally, why was it made?

These may seem obvious questions, but if we look at Renaissance antiquarianism, which often provided the first layer of scholarship on ancient and medieval artifacts, we see that much of what they did was taxonomic in the same way—and this includes not only objects, but also things like genealogies or reigns. These only seem basic questions because we already know the answers to them. Art history, by comparison, is a very young field, and in some parts of it, such as Islamic art, there remains so much still to know.

As examples, Bloom looks closely at two objects: a ceramic bowl from Iran now in Copenhagen, and a minbar made in Cordoba for Morocco. What Brown implies is that we need to draw in conservators and curators to begin to answer these questions properly. Just as historians of techno-science, such as Smith, routinely collaborate now with conservators, Bloom suggests that a consequence of putting the material back in is that historians, curators, and conservators will need to work together. This accurate judgment—and laudable goal—will require a new attitude on the part of institutional administrators toward staff time and goals. Right now, how many curators, even at university museums, are encouraged to work with professors, whether in the classroom or on research projects? How many are actually viewed by professors as intellectual equals? And, looking in the other direction, how many curators and conservators are deeply interested in the questions professors ask about the world their objects come from or move through?

Turning from Bloom's Islamic art—eccentric content, perhaps, to Western art history—back to Bordes's European decorative art—closer to, but still off-center—returns us back to the idea of the art object (*objet d'art*). From this perspective, what Bloom proposes is what Bordes describes: the object as the lodestone around which everything swirls, and no question is to be left behind. The CIHA meeting of 2012 was devoted precisely to this point, though phrased somewhat differently: "the challenge of the object."

Horst Bredekamp also takes an off-center part of art history as his starting point: prehistory. Bredekamps's *jeu d'esprit,* which begins with the real making of art in prehistoric times, has a very serious outcome: effectively rewriting the entire history of art. He focuses on Franz Kugler, who worked on 40,000-year-old sculptures in the Swabian Alps. To go back to this effort now, with Kugler at center, and a host of more recent sculptural finds from the period 25,000–40,000 BCE is a way of relooking at the question of art history's role in the humanities. Kugler's *Handbuch* is about the history of man "as the form-conscious producer of artifacts." Describing it this way turns inside-out the role of Near Eastern and Greco-Roman antiquity in the narrative of the history of art. Getting around this "block," as Bredekamp calls it, leads toward the materials themselves. He outlines the possibility of our constructing a material iconology by exploring the different approaches to stone and ivory—the first alternative material—across the threshold between 40,000 and 30,000 BCE. For Bredekamp, this moment marks the "discovery of the world and of man."

Bredekamp sees in Kugler a way of rethinking the narrative of art history—no small matter since Jacob Burckhardt was his student just then in Berlin. Miller looks at an exact contemporary of Kugler—G. F. Klemm—and an exactly contemporary project, and sees a way of rethinking the *Nachleben*, not of the antique, but the antiquarian. Kugler's history of the Berlin collection (ca. 1838) exactly coincides with Klemm's history of collecting (ca. 1837). In 1842, Kugler published his *Handbuch der Kunstgeschichte;* in 1843, Klemm brought out his *Allgemeine Kulturgeschichte.* His story, too, goes from prehistory to the present, and is global. Where Klemm, however, winds up is not in prehistory, but anthropology.

Klemm ends his career by inventing (or at least giving the most robust first meaning to) the terms "*materiellen Kultur*" and "*Culturwissenschaft.*"[27] He began by citing early modern antiquarian literature in books he called cultural history. Klemm's gambit shows how the study of things in fact provides the crucial armature through which the early modern framework of study—antiquarianism—became the modern, whether called anthropology or archaeology. This ability to see in the early moderns the way to new connections in modern times would not recur in Germany again until Warburg—who, after all—called himself a "contemplative antiquary" (*beschauerlich Antiquar*), and did not register at all in France nor in England.

The question now, is that if we find material culture being studied continually between the Renaissance and the twentieth-first century—whether Klemm is the missing link or no—then what does this say about the taken-for-granted assumption that study of materiality has been marginal to the historical and cultural sciences? This suggests the possibility of articulating an entirely new history of historical research, in which the culture of the hand is much more essential than has been realized.[28]

To explore the implications of this de- and re-centering, I propose to return to Rilke. So far as I know, no student of material culture or its history has recognized in his oeuvre the absolutely compelling source it is. For his was no "*Neue Sachlichkeit*," as was that of Williams, Ponge, or the "Concrete" poets, which reacted dialectically *against*.[29] Rilke came to materiality not against, but from, metaphysics. For us, here, interested as we are in exploring the ways in which the material world offers opportunities for thinking about the varieties of the human historical experience, Rilke is, therefore, indispensable. So, acknowledging the limitations of space, and recognizing the violence of the experiment, let us embark upon a reading of Rilke as Virgil to our *cultural histories of the material world*.

Rilke, as noted at the beginning of this essay, began his book on Rodin with the sculptor's hands. "Instinctively one looks for the two hands from which this world has come forth. One thinks of the smallness of human hands, of how soon they weary and of how little time is granted to their activity."[30] If we noted that Rilke was not positing a merely metonymic relationship between hands and wholes, we see here, much more clearly, that he was actually thinking in terms of synecdoche. For Rilke was talking about the human when using the word "hand"—much as we might use the word "heart," viz. "she was all heart." A history of the culture of the hand, then, would be a human history in the broad sense, inflected toward the varieties of making.

And, in fact, the lecture on Rodin, which was published as the second part of the Rodin book, begins by reimagining what a historical practice would look like that took this world as its subject. "If my subject were personalities," Rilke began, "I could begin where you have just left off on entering this room; breaking in upon your conversation, I would, without effort, share your thoughts."[31] This is history as it actually was— Ranke's famous *wie es eigentlich gewesen*. But it is not the history Rilke wants to write. "When I attempt to visualize my task," he continues, "it becomes clear to me that it is not people about whom I have to speak, but things."[32]

Saying "things," he explains, can evoke a silence. In part, we surmise, this is because things are, notoriously, mute. And because things have evoked so little attention among historians. But these are obvious. Rilke wants us to think of another reason: for around things "all movement subsides and becomes contour, and out of past and future time something permanent is formed: space, the great calm of objects which know no urge."[33] Things, in short, make space, and this too is part of the historian's field.

But the silence could also be that of unresponsiveness, our dulled human sensibility. To those who felt nothing at the term—"The word 'things' passes you by"—Rilke directed them to reflect on their own earliest pasts. Return, he urges, "to any one of your childhood's possessions, with which you were familiar. Think whether there was ever anything nearer to you, more familiar, more indispensable than such a thing." Threats and fears abounded, but not here. "If, amongst your early experiences, you knew kindness, confidence and the sense of not being alone—do you not owe it to that thing?" Later, older, "a holy joyfulness, a blessed humility, a readiness to be all things," came to you "because some small piece of wood"—the Cross—"had once shown you them all, assuming and illustrating them for you." Moving from youth to old age, and from toy to cross, Rilke then proceeds to generalize from cross to the world. It "made you familiar with thousands of things by filling a thousand roles, by being animal and tree, and king and child." In that object, and thus, later, in all these objects, lay "the whole of human experience, even to death itself."[34]

This relationship is so deeply within our own experience of the world as to be, most of the time, completely invisible to us. But Rilke probes just as deeply. "How does it come about at all that things are related to us? What is their history?"[35] Rilke's answer meets the depth of his challenge. He offers up a conjectural history of the creative soul easily on par with the masterful models of Enlightenment social theorists.

> Things were made very early, with difficulty, after the pattern of natural things already existing; utensils and vessels were made, and it must have been a strange experience to see the made object as a recognized existence, with the same rights and the same reality as the thing already there. Something came into existence blindly, through the fierce throes of work, bearing upon it the marks of exposed and threatened life, still warm with it . . . This experience was so remarkable and so great that we can understand how things soon came to be made solely for its sake. For the earliest images were possibly nothing but practical applications of this experience, attempts to form out of the visible human and animal world something immortal and permanent, belonging to an order immediately above that world: a thing.[36]

Things, then, came into being in the youth of the species, as in the youth of an individual. Things connected both collective and singularity with the breadth of nature and the depth of time. And these things which came from us but belonged "to an order immediately above that world"—and Rilke returns us to this phrase—did they have to be beautiful? "What kind of a thing? A beautiful thing? No." What counted were the things in which we recognized significance. These things, he writes, lurked all about us. "Do you remember such things? Perhaps there is one which for a long time seemed to you simply ridiculous. But one day you were struck by its urgency, the peculiar, almost desperate earnestness which all things possess."[37] Moments such as this, Rilke writes, restore "things to their real life" ("*die Dinge wieder in ihr Leben eintreten*").[38]

By 1907, then, Rilke had developed an ontology that linked humans and things. Upon this, he sketched out a model of what a historical study fit for this approach might look like. And he also hinted at a possible metaphysics, too, in which things explained not only the place of humans in this world, but our relationship to things eternal. This quest is carried to a still more refined level of mindfulness in the *Duino Elegies,* begun in 1912, and then completed, on the other side of the cataclysm that was the First World War, in 1923. Here, the full implications of objects for our fullest human nature is at the center of the exploration. Nothing less than the meaning of life is his inquiry.

Rilke began from the question of whether transcendence was possible in this world without having to deny its very worldliness. This was a question pondered also by his contemporary, Aby Warburg: was there a way that led "from the lowlands of the scholar's study to the view from the mountains of Sils-Maria"?[39] Laying out the question this way put things and materiality—not a word he used, but what he was referring to—at the center of his reflection. It was this physical reality and the psychological processes in us that it fostered over millennia that divided the human from the angelic. But must it always be so?

Indeed, this question burst out in the first words of the first *Elegy:* "Who, if I cried out, would hear me among the angels' hierarchies?" The problem is that "we are not really at home in our interpreted world" (Elegy I). Interpretation, reflection, self-awareness—all these interposed a layer between people and the world. Rilke holds out the hope that a tree, or a street, or a habit, could slip past the border guards of our self-consciousness and establish the missing unmediated connection. He urges reflection on the star or wave or music whose light, form or sound waits for us, if only we would notice them (Elegy I). The way to reach this state, he suggests, is by close looking. Stare at a puppet in a theater long enough "or, rather, gaze at it so intensely that at last, to balance my gaze, an angel has to come and make the stuffed skins startle into life."

It is "our own presence" which had kept the realms of material and transcendent apart; a practice of close observation could make the border between worlds melt away (Elegy IV).

If the first six elegies are devoted to the various obstacles to this connectedness, the final four make it the centerpiece of Rilke's quest for healing. The turn in the tale, as in the Rodin biography, was made via reflection on childhood. "Children, one earthly Thing truly experienced, even once, is enough for a lifetime"(Elegy VII).[40] This reflection leads Rilke to affirm: "Truly being here is glorious" (*"Hiersinn ist herrlich"*). Even with the worst of this world—the garbage dumps, the poor—"your veins flowed with being" (Elegy VII).

From a generalized affirmation of the world, warts and all, Rilke began the process of connecting in the realm of ruin with the antinomies of the antiquarian. "Where once an enduring house was, now a cerebral structure crosses our path, completely belonging to the realm of concepts."[41] The things themselves were gone, but they had been reconstructed and preserved as mental realities. Temples that once existed, he writes, were no longer known. "It is we who secretly save up these extravagances of the heart. Where one of them still survives, a Thing that was formerly prayed to, worshipped, knelt before—just as it is, it passes into the invisible world" (Elegy VII). This is indeed the fate of all material things. But, Rilke argues, the recovery and reconceptualization of these monuments within us, through imagination, is an even greater triumph. "Many no longer perceive it, yet miss the chance to build it *inside* themselves now, with pillars and statues: greater!" (Elegy VII).[42] Objects and monuments once stood in the world, and even in their decayed, ruinous state, were placeholders of materiality. "This *once* stood in the midst of Fate the annihilator, in the midst of Not-Knowing-Whither, it stood as if enduring."[43] Those who have no ability to take the ruin inside he calls "such disinherited ones, to whom neither the past belongs, nor yet what has nearly arrived" (*"solche Entberbte / denen das Fühere nicht und noch nicht das Nächste gehört"*). Moving from inner to outer, from psychology to archaeology, Rilke recapitulates the history of antiquarianism as metaphysical assertion. To the angels, Rilke speaks the monuments of Western culture: "Pillars, plylons, the Sphinx, the striving thrust of the cathedral," Chartres and music (Elegy VII).

In the ninth elegy, it is not so much the grand monuments but the monumentality of the ordinary that is Rilke's clinching proof. "Why then have to be human"? he asks. "Because truly being here is so much," is his answer. Trying to "hold it firmly in our simple hands" was the goal, but what could ever be taken into the realm beyond, of the angels? The answer, he writes, was not something "unsayable" or transcendent to humans—all this would be obvious to the angels. Instead, evoking a Nietzschean descent from the mountaintops, Rilke's envoy brings "some word he has gained, some pure word, the yellow and blue gentian." Unlike Warburg, then, Rilke did believe that there was a connection between the mountaintop and the lowlands. Flowers, simple in their own way, could yet be staked against the eternal. And this, in turn, leads Rilke into an extraordinary sequence of lines in which material culture is pledged in the game of meaningfulness. "Perhaps we are *here*," he writes, "in order to say: house, bridge, fountain, gate, pitcher, fruit-tree, window—at most: column, tower."[44]

Rilke's choices are not random. These are not merely common objects: they each define a point on the map of human existence, and altogether map the significant contours of life itself. The "house" stands for family and human society; "bridge" for what connects people and stories; "fountain" is the life giving power of nature for people; "gate" marks thresholds and regulates crossings; "pitcher" is the man-made instrument for bringing sustenance from nature to bodies; "fruit-tree" is both product of the elements and nourishment for people; "window" is how we and through which we see the world; "column, tower" the monumental scale of memory and association, but still on a continuum with the prior, more domestic, functions.

"Praise this world to the angel," he argues. This human-all-too-human reality. In the "unsayable" realm—that of experience and emotion beyond words—our ability to impress was too limited. Instead, Rilke insists we focus on the here and the now. In some of his most arresting mix of registers and images he writes:

> . . . so show
> him [the angel] something simple which, formed over genera-
>   tions,
> Lives as our own, near our hand and within our gaze.
> Tell him of Things. He will stand astonished; as you stood
> By the rope-maker in Rome or the potter along the Nile.

> [. . . Drum zeig
> Ihm das Einfache, das, von Geschlect zu Geschlechtern gestaltet,

als ein Unsriges lebt, neben der Hand und im Blick.
Sag ihm die Dinge. Er wird stauender stehn; wie du standest
Bei dem Seiler in Rom, oder beim Töpfer am Nil.][45]

In the world made by things, which is of course the human world, our knowledge is perfect. The "astonishment" of the angel is Rilke's way of awakening our astonishment as well, to see things and practices of making as exquisite bearers of identity, not simply as tools or products. It is not an archaeological sensibility that Rilke is seeking to instill, but a metaphysical one located in the object world itself. He proceeds to describe things as "happy," "innocent," and "ours." Rilke imputes a consciousness to things; they "know you are praising them; transient, they look to us for deliverance: us, the most transient of all."[46] So not only do things exist as if a part of us, but they even need us to survive. With this, Rilke takes the old antiquarian trope of *Tempus Edax Rerum,* in which the fate of objects stood as a metaphor for the transience of all things human and turns it around: that objects survive with meaning is because we humans put meaning into them and thus can find meaning in them years, decades, even centuries, later.

A cultural history of the material world, in Rilke's terms, can be no tautology. On the contrary, it opens on to questions of personal identity and meaning that go well beyond the realm marked out by Burckhardt and his followers; even further than Aby Warburg believed possible. In other words, while for Rilke culture and material are deeply intertwined, thinking about the world they make is just as bound up with something immaterial: man's quest for meaning amid his mortality. Moreover, Rilke denies any specific hierarchy of goods; the simple potter or rope-maker has as much to teach the angels as Michelangelo.

The chapters that follow, glimpses only of some of Rilke's possible histories of the hand, are offered in his spirit: "Perhaps we are *here* in order to say: house, bridge, fountain, gate, pitcher, fruit-tree, window—at most: column, tower. . . ."

But Rilke is not the only inspiration for the particular articulation of this project. The other—and how much more unlikely!—is Emmanuel Ringelblum.[47] Trained as a social historian in Warsaw in the 1930s by a Polish satellite of the early *Annales,* but shaped by his relationship to the Vilna-based YIVO (Jewish Scientific Institute) with its commitment to the material culture of everyday life, when forced into the Warsaw ghetto, Ringelblum was ready. The famous research project he organized there, the Oyneg Shabes Archive, was an early, and surely the most amazing attempt ever, at *Alltagsgeschichte*.[48] It aimed to collect artifacts and experiences that would document the contemporary life of the Jews under occupation and, later, death sentence. The tram tickets, restaurant menus, doorbell buzzers, children's theater programs, photographs, field reports, essays, and poems were all collected, and then buried for posterity. This was a vision of material culture as life itself. It also speaks to a vision of eternity very different from that of the pharaohs or Mesopotamian kings—this is not about just one man, nor about old stones that cannot be deciphered, but of people as they lived. No more serious argument for its value can be made.

One document out of this world that survived did not survive in the tin boxes and milk cans that emerged from the ground in 1946 and 1950 like antiquities from an unbelievably distant past. It was a poem entitled "Things" (*Rzeczy*), by Władysław Szlengel. It narrates the successive deportations of Jews into the Warsaw ghetto—into the successively smaller, poorer, and more desperate confines of the always-shrinking ghetto—and then finally to the *Umschlagplatz* and Treblinka. Szlengel writes about Jews by writing about the Jews' things. As they move, the inventory shortens.

> Furniture, tables, and stools,
> Small valises and bundles,
> Bedding pots—yes, indeed!
> But already without rugs,
> No sign of silverware,
> No more cherry wine,
> No suits, no featherbeds,
> No little jars, no portraits,
> All these trifles left on Śliska.

After the next relocation, to a shop block—this would have been after the Great Deportation, in September 1942—there is even less.

> No more furniture, no stools,
> No pots, no bundles.
> Lost are the teapots,
> Books, featherbeds, little jars.
> To the devil went
> The suits and plates;
> Dumped together in a rickshaw

A valise and a coat,
A bottle of tea,
A bite of caramel;
On foot without wagons
The gloomy mob strides.

When the people are gone, though, the things remain, in homes taken over by others, and are used as if owned. Until one day, when all these Jewish things march away along the train tracks and disappear. Szlengel's poem was itself only discovered in 1960, when a Polish peasant was chopping up just such a vagrant table for firewood and came upon the manuscript hidden within.[49]

Rilke to Szlengel by way of the *Annales,* the YIVO, and Ringelblum describes the arc of ambition, possibility, and seriousness on which hang our cultural histories of the material world.

NOTES

1. Rilke, *Rodin and Other Prose Pieces,* trans. C. Craig Houston, intro. by William Tucker (London: Quartet Books, 1986); "The Rodin Book" (First part, 1903; second part, 1907), 18, translation modified. "Es gibt im Werke Rodins Hände, selbständige, kleine Hände, die, ohne zu irgendeinem Körper zu gehören, lebendig sind. Hände, die sich aufrichten, gereizt und böse, Hände, deren fünf gesträubte Finger zu bellen scheinen, wie die fünf Hälse eines Höllenhundes. Hände, die gehen, schlafende Hände, und Hände, welche erwachen; verbrecherische, erblich belastete Hände und solche, die müde sind, die nichts mehr wollen, die sich niedergelegt haben in irgendeinen Winkel, wie kranke Tiere, welche wissen, daß ihnen niemand helfen kann." *Auguste Rodin* (Leipzig: Insel Verlag, n.d.), 32–33.
2. Rilke, *Rodin and Other Prose Pieces,* 19. "Aber Hände sind schon ein komplizierter Organismus, ein Delta, in dem viel fernherkommendes Leben zusammenfließt, um sich in den großen Strom der Tat zu ergießen. Es gibt eine Geschichte der Hände, sie haben tatsächlich ihre eigene Kultur, ihre besondere Schönheit; man gesteht ihnen das Recht zu, eine eigene Entwickelung zu haben, eigene Wünsche, Gefühle, Launen und Liebhabereien." Rilke, *Auguste Rodin,* 33.
3. Bloch taught Lamprecht for long after. See François-Olivier Touati, "Marc Bloch et Mabillon," in *Dom Jean Mabillon, figure majeure de l'Europe des lettres,* ed. Jean Leclant, André Vauchez, and Daniel-Odon Hurel (Paris: Académie des inscriptions et belles-lettres, 2010), 433n74; and Huizinga devoted his inaugural lecture at Groningen in 1905 to the *Lamprechtstreit* in Germany. See Gerhard Oestreich, "Huizinga, Lamprecht und die deutsche Geschichts-

philosophie: Huizingas Groninger Antrittsvorlesung von 1905," *Bijdragen en Mededelingen betreffende de Geschiedenis der Nederlanden* 88 (1973): 143–70.

4. Roger Chickering, *Karl Lamprecht: A German Academic Life (1856–1915)* (Atlantic Heights, NJ, 1993); Gerhard Oestreich, "Die Fachhistorie und die Anfänge der sozialgeschichtlichen Forschung in Deutschland," *Historische Zeitschrift* 208 (1969): 320–63; Luise Schorn-Schutte, *Karl Lamprecht: Kulturgeschichtsschreibung zwischen Wissenschaft und Politik* (Göttingen: Vandenhoeck & Ruprecht, 1984).

5. Ernst Gombrich, *Aby Warburg: An Intellectual Biography* (Chicago: University of Chicago Press, 1975); Maria Michela Sassi, "Dalla scienza delle religioni di Usener ad Aby Warburg," in *Aspetti di Hermann Usener filologo della religione,* eds. G. Arrighetti et al. (Pisa: Giardini, 1982), 65–91; Roland Kany, *Mnemosyne als Programm. Geschichte, Errinerungen und die Andacht zum Unbedeutenden im Werk von Usener, Warburg, und Benjamin* (Tübingen, 1987); Bruce Lyon, "H. Pirenne and the Origins of Annales History," *Annals of Scholarship* 1 (1986) 69–83; Bruce Lyon, *The Birth of Annales History: The Letters of Lucien Febvre and Marc Bloch to Henri Pirenne (1921–1935)* (Brussels: Académie royale de Belgique, 1991).

6. Jürgen Kocka, "Ideological Regression and Methodological Innovation: Historiography and the Social Sciences in the 1930s and 1940s," *History and Memory* 2 (1990): 130–38; on Aubin see Eduard Mühle, *Für Volk und deutschen Osten. Der Historiker Hermann Aubin und die deutsche Ostforschung* (Düsseldorf: Droste Verlag, 2005).

7. Heinrich Dilly and James Ryding, "Kulturgeschichtsschreibung vor und nach der bürgerlichen Revolution von 1848," *Ästhetik und Kommunikation* 6 (1975): 15–32

8. I thank Bernie Herman for suggesting this. It reminded me that Walter Benjamin, in his essay on Eduard Fuchs, had traced the line between Engels and Franz Mehring, and between Mehring and Fuchs. That between Fuchs and Benjamin was, of course, only implied. See "Eduard Fuchs, Collector and Historian," in *Walter Benjamin: Selected Writings, volume 3, 1935–1938* (Cambridge, MA: Harvard University Press, 2002), 260–302.

9. A very brief survey of attempts at terminological overview might include, W. T. J. Mitchell, "Interdisciplinarity and Visual Culture," *Art Bulletin* 77 (1995): 540–44; W. T. J. Mitchell, "What Is Visual Culture?" in *Meaning in the Visual Arts: A Centennial Commemoration of Erwin Panofsky,* ed. Irving Lavin (Princeton, NJ: Princeton University Press, 1995), 207–17; James Elkins, *Visual Studies: A Skeptical Introduction* (London: Routledge, 2002); Whitney Davis, *A General Theory of Visual Culture* (Princeton, NJ: Princeton University Press, 2011). I am grateful to my colleague Jeffrey Collins for a discussion of these references.

10. Rilke, *Rodin and Other Prose Pieces,* 19. "Rodin aber . . . weiß, daß der Körper aus lauter Schauplätzen des Lebens besteht . . . ." (*Auguste Rodin,* 33).

11. Thomas Nipperdey, long ago, in a series of influential articles, for example, "Kulturgeschichte, Sozialgeschichte, historische Anthropologie," *Vierteljahresschrift für Sozial- und Wirtschaftsgeschihte* 25 (1968): 145–64; or "Die

anthropologische Dimension der Geschichtswissenschaft," in *Geschichte heute. Positionen, Tendenzen, Probleme*, ed. Gerhard Schulz (Gottingen: Vandenhoeck & Ruprecht, 1973), 225–55, presented the teleology of cultural history as a form of *Oppositionswissenschaft*, organized to debunk dominant ideologies. "Staging" offers the same possibility of decentering, but escapes from the dialectical trap opened up by Nipperdey's definition.

12. However, outside of art history, this term persisted, from the work of Leroi-Gourhan into the journal *Techniques et Cultures*.

13. For example, the "Roundtable on Globalization," *October* 133 (2010); and especially the interventions of Nagel, Wood, and Flood on 7–8.

14. See for example, Frank Trentmann, "Materiality in the Future of History: Things, Practices, and Politics," *Journal of British Studies* 48 (2009): 283–307.

15. David R. Brauner, ed., *Approaches to Material Culture Research for Historical Archaeologists: A Reader from Historical Archaeology* (California, PA: Society for Historical Archaeology, 1991; 2nd ed. 2000); Arthur Berger, *What Objects Mean: An Introduction to Material Culture* (Walnut Creek, CA: Left Coast Press, 2009); *Handbook of Material Culture* (London: Sage, 2006); Karen Harvey, *History and Material Culture: A Student's Guide to Approaching Alternative Sources* (London and New York: Routledge, 2009); Dan Hicks and Mary C. Beaudry, eds., *The Oxford Handbook of Material Culture Studies*, (Oxford and New York: Oxford University Press, 2010); Victor Buchli, ed., *The Material Culture Reader* (Oxford: Berg, 2002); Christopher Tilley et al., eds., *Handbook of Material Culture* (London: Sage, 2006); W. Kingery, ed., *Learning From Things: Method and Theory of Material Culture Studies* (Washington, D.C.: Smithsonian Institution Press, 1996); S. Lubar and W. Kingery, eds., *History from Things: Essays on Material Culture* (Washington: Smithsonian Institution Press, 1995); Thomas J. Schlereth, ed., *Material Culture: A Research Guide* (Lawrence: University Press of Kansas, 1985); Fiona Candlin and Raiford Guins, eds., *The Object Reader* (Abingdon, UK: Routledge, 2009); Ian Woodward, *Understanding Material Culture* (Los Angeles: Sage Publications, 2007); Ian Hodder, ed., *The Meanings of Things: Material Culture and Symbolic Expression* (London: HarperCollins Academic, 1991).

16. Carlo Ginzburg, "Vetoes and Compatibilities," *Art Bulletin* 77 (1995): 534–37.

17. Thomas Campbell, ed., *Tapestry in the Renaissance: Art and Magnificence* (New Haven, CT: Yale University Press, 2002); Thomas Campbell, ed., *Tapestry in the Baroque: Threads of Splendor* (New Haven, CT: Yale University Press, 2007); Tristan Weddigen, ed., *Metatextile: Identity and History of a Contemporary Art Medium* (Emsdetten/Berlin: Edition Imorde, 2011); Tristan Weddigen, ed., *Unfolding the Textile Medium in Early Modern Art and Literature* (Emsdetten/Berlin: Edition Imorde, 2011).

18. "Tangible Things" was on display in the Special Exhibitions Gallery at Harvard's Science Center during the spring semester 2011. http://www.fas.harvard.edu/~hsdept/chsi-tangible_things.html, and grew out of "United States in the World 30. Tangible Things: Harvard Collections in World History."

19. Edmund de Waal, *The Hare with Amber Eyes: A Family's Century of Art and Loss* (New York: Farrar, Straus and Giroux, 2010).
20. Webb Keane, *Signs of Recognition. Powers and Hazards of Representation in Indonesian Society* (Berkeley and Los Angeles: University of California Press, 1997), 32.
21. For example, Ian Hodder, *Reading the Past. Current Approaches to Interpretation in Archaeology* (Cambridge: Cambridge University Press, 1986; revised editions 1991, 2003); *Archaeological Theory Today* (Cambridge: Polity Press, 2001); and edited collections including *The Archaeology of Contextual Meanings* (Cambridge: Cambridge University Press, 1987); *The Meanings of Things: Material Culture and Symbolic Expression* (London: Unwin Hyman, 1989); Lynn Meskell and R. Preudel, *Contemporary Archaeology in Theory* (London: Routledge, 1991); Lynn Meskell, *Object Worlds in Ancient Egypt: Material Biographies Past and Present* (Oxford: Berg, 2004); Lynn Meskell and Bob Preucel, eds., *Companion to Social Archaeology* (Oxford: Blackwell's, 2004); Lynn Meskell and Rosemary Joyce, *Embodied Lives: Figuring Ancient Maya and Egyptian Experience* (London: Routledge, 2003); Lynn Meskell, *Private Life in New Kingdom Egypt* (Princeton, NJ: Princeton University Press, 2002).
22. http://chorography.stanford.edu/MichaelShanks/Home;   http://www.mshanks.com/2010/06/antiquarians-at-the-getty/. Also, *The Antiquarian Imagination* (Walnut Creek, CA: Left Coast Press, 2012), 42.
23. J. G. A. Pocock, *Barbarism and Religion* (Cambridge: Cambridge University Press, 1999–); Peter N. Miller, "Writing Antiquarianism: Prolegomenon to a History," *Antiquarianism and Intellectual Life in Europe and China, 1500–1800*," ed. Peter N. Miller and François Louis (Ann Arbor: University of Michigan Press, 2012), 27–57.
24. Reinhart Meyer-Kalkus, *Stimme und Sprechkünste im 20. Jahrhundert* (Berlin: Akademie Verlag, 2001).
25. Sisman, in this volume.
26. Sheila S. Blair and Jonathan M. Bloom, "The Mirage of Islamic Art: Reflections on the Study of an Unwieldy Field," *Art Bulletin* 85, no. 1 (2003): 152–80.
27. Klemm's "materiellen Grundlagen der menschlichen Kultur" seems the first use in a title, and is preceded—according to Google's Ngrams—by a single reference to "materiellen Kultur" in Johann G. Müller's *Der mexicanische Nationalgott Huitzilopochtli* (Basel, 1847), 25; and then is followed by another near the beginning of volume 2 of Lamprecht's *Deutsches Wirtschaftsleben im Mittelalter* (1885). Klemm is the first to use "Culturwissenschaft" in the title of a work, though again, according to Google's Ngrams, there is a fairly extensive example of prior use of the term in Moritz von Lavergne-Peguilhen, *Grundzüge der Gesellschaftswissenschaft* (1838), section 8 "Allgemeine Kulturgesetze," (§63), "Kulturwissenschaft."
28. For one attempt to suggest what this "world turned upside down" might look like, taking the history of antiquarianism as the example, see Peter N. Miller *Peiresc's "History of Provence," Antiquarianism, and the Discovery of the Medieval Mediterranean, Transactions of the American Philosophical Society* (Philadelphia, 2011).

29. I later came across N. M. Willard, "A Poetry of Things: Williams, Rilke, Ponge," *Comparative Literature* 17 (1965): 311–24, but its ambitions lie elsewhere.

30. Rilke, *Rodin and Other Prose Pieces*, 3. "Man erinnert sich, wie klein Menschenhände sind, wie bald sie müde werden und wie wenig Zeit ihnen gegeben ist, sich zu regen" (*Auguste Rodin*, 7).

31. Rilke, *Rodin and Other Prose Pieces*, 45. "Hätte ich Ihnen von Menschen zu sprechen, so könnte ich dort anfangen, wo Sie eben aufgehört haben, da Sie hier eintraten; in Ihre Gespräche einfallend, würde ich, wie von selbst, zu allem kommen" (*Auguste Rodin*, 78).

32. Rilke, *Rodin and Other Prose Pieces*, 45–46. "Aber, da ich es versuche, meine Aufgabe zu überschauen, wird mir klar, daß ich Ihnen nicht von Menschen zu reden habe, sondern von Dinge" (*Auguste Rodin*, 78).

33. Rilke, *Rodin and Other Prose Pieces*, 46. "Alle Bewegung legt sich, wird Kontur, und aus vergangener und künftiger Zeit schließt sich ein Dauerndes: der Raum, die große Beruhigung der zu nichts gedrängten Dinge" (*Auguste Rodin*, 78).

34. Rilke, *Rodin and Other Prose Pieces*, 46–47.

35. Rilke, *Rodin and Other Prose Pieces*, 47. "Wodurch sind überhaupt Dinge mit uns verwandt? Welches ist ihre Geschichte?" (*Auguste Rodin*, 80).

36. Rilke, *Rodin and Other Prose Pieces*, 47. "Sehr frühe schon hat man Dinge geformt, mühsam, nach dem Vorbild der vorgefundenen natürlichen Dinge; man hat Werkzeuge gemacht und Gefäße, und es muß eine seltsame Erfahrung gewesen sein, Selbstgemachtes so anerkannt zu sehen, so gleichberechtigt, so wirklich neben dem, was war. Da enstand etwas, blindlings, in wilder Arbeit und trug an sich die Spuren eines bedrohten offenen Lebens, war noch warm davon . . . Dieses Erlebnis war so merkwürdig und so stark, daß man begreift, wenn es auf einmal Dinge gab, die nur um seinetwillen gemacht waren. Denn vielleicht waren die frühesten Götterbilder Anwendungen dieser Erfahrung, Versuche, aus Menschlichem und Tierischem, das man sah, ein Nichtmitsterbendes zu formen, ein Dauerndes, ein Nächsthöheres: ein Ding." (*Auguste Rodin*, 81).

37. Rilke, *Rodin and Other Prose Pieces*, 47. "Erinnern Sie sich solcher Dinge? Da ist vielleicht eines, das Ihnen lange nur lächerlich erschien. Aber eines Tages fiel Ihenn seine Inständigkeit auf, der eigentümliche, fast verzweiflte Ernst, den sie alle haben" (*Auguste Rodin*, 81).

38. Rilke, *Rodin and Other Prose Pieces*, 48.

39. " . . . es schien kein Weg aus der Flachebene der Gelehrtenstube zur Schau auf den Bergen von Sils-Maria zu führen . . . ," quoted in Kurt W. Forster, "Warburgs Versunkenheit," in *Aby M.Warburg. "Ekstatische Nymphe . . . trauernder Flußgott." Portrait eines Gelehrten*, eds. Robert Galitz and Brita Reimers (Hamburg: Dölling und Galitz, 1995), 196.

40. "Ihr Kinder, eine hiesig / einmal ergriffenes Ding gälte für viele" (Rilke, *Ahead of all Parting*, 370–71).

41. "Wo einmal ein dauerndes Haus war,/ schlägt sich erdachtes Gebild vor, quer, zu Erdenklichem völlig gehörig, als ständ es noch ganz im Gehirne" (Rilke, *Ahead of all Parting*, 370–71).

42. "Viele gewahrens nicht mehr, doch ohne den Vorteil,/ daß sie's nun *innerlich* baun, mit Pfeilern und Statuen, größer" (Rilke, *Ahead of all Parting*, 372–73).

43. "Dies *stand* einmal unter Menschen,/ mitten im Schicksal stands, im vernichtenden, mitten im Nichtwissen-Wohen stand es" (Rilke, *Ahead of all Parting*, 372–73).

44. "Sind wir vielleicht *hier*, um zu sagen: Haus,/ Brücke, Brunnen, Tor, Krug, Obstbaum, Fenster,—Höchstens: Säule, Turm" (Rilke, *Ahead of all Parting*, 384–85).

45. Rilke, *Ahead of all Parting*, 384–85.

46. Rilke's imputation of a kind of consciousness to objects, which might have been metaphorical only, has of course been followed up in dead seriousness in recent years by Bruno Latour, Michel Serres, and others.

47. Samuel Kassow's masterpiece will not be surpassed for a long time: *Who Will Write Our History? Emanuel Ringelblum, the Warsaw Ghetto, and the Oyneg Shabes Archive* (Bloomington: University of Indiana Press, 2007; then Random House, 2009).

48. See Peter N. Miller, "What We Know About Murdered Peoples" (Review of Samuel Kassow, *Who Will Write Our History? Emanuel Ringelblum, the Warsaw Ghetto and the Oyneg Shabes Archive*), *New Republic*, April 9, 2008, 34–39.

49. The story is told in Kassow, *Who Will Write Our History?*, 318–19. I take the translation from there, slightly amended.

PART 1

Art's Challenge

ONE

Design History and
the Decorative Arts

Glenn Adamson

I'd like to begin with two premises. The first is that decorative art history, as a way of doing design history, is deeply out of fashion. The second is that it needs to be rehabilitated.

For the last twenty years or so, the general feeling among historians with an interest in objects has been that decorative art is a dream, and that one of our main objectives should be to wake up from that dream. Thus the phrase "decorative art" has been repudiated—both in terms of subject area, and methodology. This is true of material culture studies in America and design history in Britain—which differ because of prevailing currents in those two nations' academic structure, but not in any fundamental methodological sense. Under both of these banners, scholars have insisted on the importance of analyzing the quotidian, the everyday: objects that belonged to the whole range of the population, including the vast majority without access to what might be called "high style" commodities—the artifacts with which museums now are filled to bursting due to their high rates of survival, and enduring aesthetic and market value. Both design history and material culture have rejected the tools that belong to decorative art history, which were initially developed in the late nineteenth century. These tools are often summarized under the catchall word "connoisseurship," but we might substitute for this loaded term a list of seemingly neutral techniques such as formal analysis, the reconstruction of lines of stylistic influence, and the detailed study and classification of processes of making. The general trend has been away from such interpretive tools and toward an emphasis on evidence—often resulting in a focus on "objects considered not individually as works of art but collectively as industrial production," as Richard Goldthwaite memorably puts it. So the shifts in design history toward the study of consumption, toward social and economic history, have been accompanied by a concomitant shift away from the techniques and attitudes of art history.

There are good reasons for this movement, many of which have to do with the positive achievements of a broad, empirical study of artifacts, and many of which have to do with inherent problems in the concept of decorative art. These problems should be acknowledged. First and most obviously, the very phrase seems to designate a subsidiary, even frivolous, category, only one little step away from the even more out-of-fashion term "minor arts." Defining a class of objects as "decorative" tacitly acknowledges the existence of a pendant category of fine art, and it is hard to employ that distinction without implying a hierarchy of historical importance, in which paintings deserve more serious study than pots. Art history itself has undergone a parallel shift, for precisely this reason—it is no coincidence that the trend toward a social history of art and the emergence of design history as a discipline were roughly simultaneous—both were attempts to escape the prejudicial ranking system of the past. So art historians are now looking at such areas as book illustration, portrait and snapshot photography, comic books, once-ignored academic genre paintings, and other formerly debased genres with considerable enthusiasm.

A second problem, which perhaps complicates the one just described, is the implicit elitism of the term "decorative art." This is partly a simple matter of record—decorative art historians and institutions over the course of the nineteenth and twentieth centuries routinely structured their discourse around the celebration of elite objects to the exclusion of more commonplace ones, and even allowed representative objects to be destroyed while exceptional ones were preserved. But even if we were willing to overlook this history, we would have to acknowledge that elitism is written into the very DNA of the idea of decorative art. While the material culture of the wealthy is no more—and no less— material than that of the poor, in most historical circumstances their decorative art was certainly more decorative. Highly ornamented objects were so for a reason—to mark them out as being more important, and better than other objects. This relates directly to a final problem for the construct of decorative art, which is the extension of this hierarchy into the present day through the powerful forces of the marketplace. Auction houses, private collectors, and dealers have no trouble seeing themselves as involved in something called decorative art. In fact, the turn away from decorative art in design history has led to an equally emphatic departure from the salesroom by many scholars in the field. The result is that well-informed marketplace professionals often have connoisseurial knowledge about canonical decorative art objects that is superior to most academically trained curators, and vastly superior to that of nearly all academic design historians. It has gotten to the point that many design historians imply, perhaps somewhat defensively, that even to work on canonical decorative art, something like Sèvres porcelain, is regressive. And when, as members of the design history field, we do study such material, we have a tendency to pointedly avoid getting into anything that smacks of connoisseurship. We do not enter willingly into discussion of fine details of construction, matters of provenance and, above all, questions of style.

All of this is to say that decorative art probably seems to most of us, as object historians, to be a limiting category—more a way of shutting out vast tracts of the past than returning us to some kind of comprehensive historical understanding. But there are reasons to return to the idea of decorative art, not as a competing discipline for design history, but rather as an aspect of its practice. The appeal of decorative art at this point is perhaps partly due to the fact that it has been methodologically dormant for some time, and is therefore ready to be refreshed.

We might begin by breaking the term decorative art into its constituent parts, "decorative" and "art." If we abstract the first of these into "the decorative" it immediately becomes much more interesting: it suggests a fundamental way of thinking about form which has invited comment from many quarters, not only in design discourse, but in also in fields as diverse as architecture, art, rhetoric, and philosophy. Ornament's many guises—as supplement, didactic sign, instance of base materiality, zone of animism, and so forth—make it an outstandingly flexible term for analysis, but we do not read much about it in design history publications. This is odd, given that the founders of design history were very much historians of decoration—people like Gottfried Semper, Owen Jones, and Alois Riegl. But today it is art and architectural historians, rather than design historians, who have claimed these figures as their own intellectual forebears—and here I am thinking of scholars like Margaret Olin, Michael Ann Holly, or Kenneth Frampton. Similarly, it is noteworthy that we hear so much about the traditions of Marxist thought, or about a socially engaged theorist like Foucault, but comparatively little about a text of art theory like Derrida's *The Truth in Painting*, which deconstructs aesthetics through the metaphor of the decorative frame. If ever there was a book about art which should belong to design history more than art history, *The Truth in Painting* would be it, yet while it is a staple of art history courses it does not seem to be a foundation stone for our discipline.

Broader and more contentious by far is the second word in decorative art—a term that some design historians are uncomfortable using in any context, and most try to keep at a distance. This is partly a matter of disciplinary boundaries, or the lack thereof—design history's great strength, institutionally speaking, is its interdisciplinarity, and so embracing the questions of art history again might seem a retrograde or limiting maneuver. I admit to partiality here, as I was myself trained as an art historian and once had trouble stepping outside of that self-identification. Yet without the concepts and tools of art history, it is hard to see how we can account for what my colleague Marta Ajmar at the Victoria and Albert Museum recently called "the individuality of objects." It is all too easy to underestimate art history, and assume that as a field, it is still addicted to a narrative of geniuses whose achievements demand decoding. But as I have already mentioned, the remit of art history has expanded rapidly in recent years. The discipline has also devoted itself to a thorough and fundamental theoretical engagement with the question of artistic autonomy, and the way that this autonomy is maintained through the power of institutions. Once artistic presence is established as a troubled (and troubling) phenomenon, art history offers the great advantage of a unique theoretical framework regarding its objects of inquiry, which hangs upon the endless interpretability of objects.

Of course, this is the near opposite of design history's presumptions about its own objects of study. In the most extreme cases, designed things—such as textiles or shoes—become data points which help to plot economic and social networks. More usually, as in Jules Prown's influential metaphorical readings of objects, there is a single moment of interpretation which unlocks the meaning of a given artifact. Without completely invalidating either of these approaches, it seems like there should be room within the field to put the object in charge—to grant its power at the outset, and assume that it can never be fully accounted for. This, I would suggest, is to think like a decorative art historian. It does indeed involve a danger of creeping elitism because it implicitly, but inevitably, raises the specter of quality. If we grant that objects may be too complex to tabulate as historical matter, then we might next wish to argue that more complex and densely wrought artifacts (which often, though not always, were elite artifacts when they were first made and used) will better sustain our attempts at analysis. Thinking in terms of decorative art might, in the end, even involve a grudging admission that paintings are, in fact, better able to sustain extended analysis than pots, and indeed that some pots have more to say than others.

I find it remarkable that most design historians are not willing to give this commonsense notion the time of day. My suspicion is that we practice a kind of bad faith when claiming that all historical artifacts are equally worthy of study. From a decorative art perspective, some artifacts (like some paintings) capture the irretrievable webs of meaning that attended the moment of their production better than others, and that qualitative difference must be respected. Such distinctions worry design historians; they feel like ideological prejudice. But if they are real, and pervasive within historical mentalities, then they cannot simply be wished away, and I would suggest that decorative art might, after all, be a good, even a necessary, framework to engage with them.

A last and perhaps even more controversial point I would make is that decorative art history is, more than anything else, the history of style. I mean this in a very conventional sense—which includes such terms as baroque, rococo, neoclassicism, and so forth. Again, few words could be less fashionable among design historians than style. The overwhelming trend is to ignore such monolithic categorizations as both ahistorical and overly general. Only when style becomes a tool of conscious political and ideological reform, as in the use of classical architecture by the Fascists for example, does it become an acceptable subject for study. But this is no solution to the notoriously difficult question of a period style—it just sets the problem to one side. It is worth recalling that one of material culture's founding essays was Jules Prown's "Style as Evidence"—a phrase that captures all the optimism of design history as an empirical field of study, but also its pessimism regarding style as a self-standing achievement. If style is (just) evidence, then it is a more-or-less mechanical reflection of the social conditions that gave it birth, not something to be dissected and analyzed in its own right. With this in mind, we might ask how a term like "rococo" could be rehabilitated as a term of analysis for the eighteenth century. Presumably this could only happen if it is taken seriously, as a phenomenon whose alienness demands a circumspect series of analytic procedures, taking into account coterminous intellectual history, as well as social history.

To conclude, then, I argue that the tools and terms of decorative art—ornament, style, and connoisseurship among them—deserve a new airing in our field. As head of research at the Victoria and Albert Museum, which was founded on the basis of those values and therefore has a very socially elite collection, I can see that this is more than an academic matter. There is a great need, institutionally, not just to worry about the skewed sample that this museum's artifacts represent, but to exploit its quality, if I may use that loaded word, in a progressive way. We need to look at elite artifacts in a nonelitist way, while taking seriously the possibility that they have something to say to us that less exalted objects just may not. The builders of the V&A's collection in the nineteenth century thought they were assembling objects that would teach us. Though we view these artifacts very differently today, it may be that we do not need to dismiss this conviction entirely. We no longer believe in objective principles of good design, and we certainly abjure the notion that some people are intrinsically better than others, and that their possessions reflect that difference. But we might well want to believe that some designed objects, conceived as decorative art, could be held up as remarkable—as things that should incite wonder, as well as analysis. Most of us began our careers as design historians because we felt the power of objects when confronted with them, and we felt we needed to do justice to that feeling. There is an essential truth there—one that we may have lost sight of. Through the unlikely and outmoded framework of decorative art, we might just find a way back to that beginning.

TWO

The Materiality of Art

Philippe Bordes

Works of art are enrolled by historians for their capacity to evoke the material world of the past in two ways: as illustrations that offer a filtered reconstruction of a fragment of that lost world, and as objects counting among the most precious remains left to behold and study. Increasingly, they are marshaled both as articulate images of that objectified world and as an integral part it. Predicated on iconographical interpretation, the former approach has been particularly favored by cultural, social, and economic historians. At best, such studies of artistic strategies of representation confront the surviving images with other sources of information and elaborate not only a history of such imagery—the proper task of the art historian—but also recover the reality of usages and practices alluded to by the representation. The interpretative difficulty, of course, is the hiatus between representation and reality that artists have spanned with the help of visual codes, conventions, traditions, and innovations, while under the spell of a creative impulse and the duress specific circumstances that historical investigation can rarely retrieve. Historical fascination is stimulated by a fundamental paradox of artistic representation: although it deprives objects of their actual materiality, it can simultaneously underscore this quality. A number of contemporary works of art have played with this paradox—either with reference to traditional modes of illusionism, or recently as redefined by the immateriality of digital imagery. Artistic agendas continue to be inspired by the potential of the modernist notion of truth to material, perhaps most radically formulated by Diderot when, in wonder, he claimed that the paint of a still life by Chardin had become one with the matter of the object represented.

The second approach is related to this position since it envisions the work of art as a material object in itself. More often than not, nearly everything concerning its history is lacking, and there is very little hope of understanding how it came to exist and survive. Whatever information is available—authorship, date of execution, technique, provenance, ownership, state of conservation—rarely reveals how the object was employed over time. Unfortunately, when considering the work of art in this way, even art historians who should know better have been led to downplay its artistic specificity. Studies in the history of collecting and the art trade—driven by the belief in the spiritually uplifting dimension of the taste for art, and mostly concerned with elite social practices—have surprisingly much in common with the strain of Marxism that reduces the artistic experience to the social appropriation of a commodity.

Both of these approaches fail to grapple directly with the artistic nature of the work of art. Ignored in the first instance is the craft by which it manages to deploy its mimetic iconography, and in the second instance, the means by which it elicits a socially conditioned experience distinct from the consumption of objects that are not art. The first approach reduces the work to an image; the second, to a signifier. The key fault in both of these approaches appears to be a lack of concern for the material nature of the art object that determines the experience. Formulated from within the particular conditions of art historical practice in France, the critique aims to help reinvigorate the low-key modernist empiricism that plagues the institutional and intellectual mainstream. Greater intellectual investment in the materiality of art also entails reconsidering relatively unfashionable theorists such as Gottfried Semper and Adrian Stokes. Though reference to their metaphysical materialism might seem retrograde, and though many of the progressive issues of visual studies and material culture studies are here set aside, hopefully these suggestions will not be read simply as conservative and bygone to those who have chosen to move on in these directions and let the discipline that flourished in the nineteenth and twentieth centuries die its natural death. By foregrounding its materiality, the point is not to restrict, but to strengthen, available modes of interpretation of the work of art.

The concept of art predicated on individual creation and invention, elaborated during the Renaissance and so crucial to the development of the institutions of art history in the nineteenth and twentieth centuries is founded on the value attributed to the immateriality of art. Around

1500, the most advanced princely patrons competed openly with each other to acquire works drawn on paper, or painted on plain woven fabric by famed artists. They were eager to have in their possession just about anything produced by a big name. The precious metals, gems, rare textiles, and labor-intensive workmanship continued to be an integral component of the value of their most treasured possessions, but the materials used to fabricate the paintings and drawings they now also coveted could, in themselves, be negligible. As has often been stressed, the value of the latter lay rather in the expression of divine artistic genius. The modesty and fragility of the material resources engaged in the creative process in fact reinforced the seemingly miraculous nature and high prestige of the work of art. The traditional sense of materiality was further undermined in all media by the systemic development of diverse modes of illusionism that distracted the viewer from the complex and often highly creative procedures of crafting. Part of the attraction of art was to see sky instead of blue paint; flesh instead of marble; shiny hammered armor instead of cast bronze. Some artists even sought to create the illusion that their creation was without weight and form, freed from the natural laws of gravity and chiaroscuro. Over time, as techniques evolved and as older crafting processes became increasingly less familiar, the performance of artists and artisans came to appear near magical. The quality of many of the most hallowed and cherished works of art in museum collections and scholarly publications is still today sanctified on these terms.

Along with this historical invention of art as we know it, since the Renaissance, great care and cost has been allotted to preserve, present, and enshrine works of art, with ornamented frames and finely crafted protective cases and pedestals, part and parcel of an elaborate mise-en-scène in homes, churches, and museums. All of these adjuncts are characterized by an insistent materiality that brings the work of art back down to earth, so to speak. They activate visually what is basically an objectifying and socializing process: framed or placed under glass, the painting or drawing becomes a piece of furniture and part of the interior, the altar, or the collection. The work of art trades its immediate vulnerability to tear and wear for the burden of an efficient carapace that conventionally is said to serve its visibility. But it can also be argued that such material adjuncts as the frame and pedestal also transform, and even denature, the work of art. One of the lessons of material-culture studies is that the resulting complex of associated objects—painting and frame, sculpture and pedestal, engraving and album—is both more and less than the untampered state of the work of art. A visit to conservation laboratories, where one sees unframed pictures, disassembled sculptures, and upturned objects, is always a jarring visual experience: the feeling can be compared to being in a morgue, confronted with dead matter, or to dining in a three-star restaurant, when the full force of a familiar taste is revealed. The process of framing and staging locks the work of art into a social environment and temporality external, and even at times alien, to it. However successful, it seems to indicate a lack of confidence in its capacity to sustain itself on its own. It makes clear that the self-sufficiency of the work of art and its pure visibility, much like individual authorship, are fictions of art history. The most extreme transformative operation of framing occurs when the varnished surface of a painting hung on a wall, seen from a certain angle, shoots back a blank reflective surface: as a piece of furniture, it is experienced only as a material object.

Thought through, still more radically, this cautionary stance helps to understand a common practice of art history and its significance for the discipline: the illustration of works of art cropped of their surroundings, freely floating shapes on the surface of the page or screen. Indeed, works of art are never experienced thus isolated from their immediate and extended visual contexts. The critical concerns of material culture have put on the agenda of art history the need to dispel this conventional idealism, which has justified the now widespread and mutilating practice of interpreting on the basis of reproductions. As certain crude constructions of visual studies have proven, the dissolution of the work of art is here at risk. That art historians are willing to take corrective steps is suggested by a recent evolution in scholarly illustrations: paintings are on occasion now reproduced with their frame or hanging in the home of their owners, while in the graphic arts, the irregular contours of sheets of paper are respected. Both of these trends mark a new concern for the work of art as material object. In architectural and sculptural studies, one can witness a recent impetus to research the geographical and technical extraction of the stones and marbles employed. Enmeshed aesthetic, economic, and symbolic factors are invoked to historicize the new material information collected.

As mentioned earlier, the emergence of the category of art during the Renaissance did not prevent princes and patrons from continuing to value what is currently referred to as *objets d'art*—finely crafted and costly objects that might have no greater function or use other than to attest to the magnificence of the owner. One need only to think of the late medieval practice of showing off to guests rows of plates and vessels in silver and gold, along with sets of tapestries resplendent with threads entwined with filaments of these same costly metals. Nonetheless, the artistic design of these objects, whether through iconographical or ornamental embellishment, was increasingly perceived as a factor of the value of the object. Although the applied arts were never quite admitted into the realm of the fine arts during the reign of the academic and Beaux-Arts systems, roughly from the mid-sixteenth to the mid-nineteenth century, there were continuous points of contact and exchange through individual and collective initiative, and in response, to the fluctuations of taste and fashion. Art history, with its focus on specific histories for each medium, has not given such interactions and exchanges fully their due. One promising perspective might be to overturn the traditional primacy of the academic *arts du dessin* that art historians have internalized. It can be argued that the *objet d'art* is the most consolidated category of the work of art, insofar as it appears to reconcile more conclusively than any other form or medium its defining material and immaterial qualities.

This perspective has been largely encouraged by developments in twentieth-century art. The material nature of the work was newly foregrounded and often considered to be its primary content. Although most explicit in sculpture, with the vogue for direct carving in the early part of the century, and the recourse to large-scale industrial fabrication toward the end, the materiality of art has replaced the traditional mimetic functions established during the Renaissance. This evolution has led to a displacement of art historical focus, from the realm of interpretation to that of meaning, from analysis based on external factors to one founded on internal evidence. The material qualities of the work have been the essential modes of entry to exercise this critical reevaluation. The intense development of conservation studies in recent decades is the most explicit and dynamic proof of this. It can also be troubling for the historian, since it often seems a resurgence of late-nineteenth-century scientism. Based on epistemological illusions, the discourse is too often one of mystery solving. In many exhibitions and publications highlighting restored works that are especially popular in countries with a rich artistic heritage, the material diagnosis of the object could not be more alien to the critical prospects of a cultural history of the material world. When a historical perspective is invoked, it is more likely to be that of the restoration practice than of the object.

Evolving approaches to twentieth-century art are another positive sign, as the works are perceived more and more clearly as belonging to their time. In other words, it becomes easier to see them historically and culturally. As the social functions of their forms and materials become more explicit, their affirmed materiality produces a noticeable shift in art historical inquiry. In the course of the twentieth century, art historians were much preoccupied by the migration of symbols and motifs, and once modernist formalism triumphed, by the migration of forms. Formalists must be credited with having undermined the iconological paradigm that dominated the discipline of art history after World War II, and the consequent severe restrictions it placed on what might be admitted as art. The twentieth-century rapprochement between form and material, along with greater awareness of the primary role of the medium in the creative process, have anchored formalism in the reality of experience and reinforced its authority. Still missing, however, is consideration of the social life and impact of forms—an elusive effectuation that can only be recovered through focused efforts of historical reconstruction. The many failed attempts to extract meaning from a stylistic rapprochement among objects produced across centuries—a regrettably common practice in exhibitions and museum presentations in France—are eloquent testimony of to the price of this neglect. Perhaps most promising from a contemporary context is the renewed attention given to those supplementary formal elements—in particular, ornament—that now are made to carry the weight of an aesthetic surplus that ultimately qualifies the object as art. This suggests a mode of revisiting the past, in which sociological concerns—the object as acquisition and possession, as successively or concurrently private and public—are no longer dissociated from the artistic dimension. When historically reconstructing the process of production and reception, such a separation tends to mystify the former and reduce the latter to a peremptory correspondence between style and taste. Given this situation, the questions raised by material-culture studies are stimulating indeed for the art historian. They can, and should, be harnessed to respond to the strongly felt need to define more clearly the objects of art history and the terms by which they can be brought out of a dead past and back to life.

PART 2

The Place of the Material

THREE

Mutually Contextual: Materials, Bodies, and Objects

Brigitte Miriam Bedos-Rezak

For some time now, scholarship in the humanities and the social sciences has seemed to be traversing a mountainside, zigzagging, one turn after the other. We are, at the moment, well engaged in the material turn, and it is tempting, in the sequential logic of such a road, to consider that taking this particular turn puts us some distance from its predecessor, the linguistic turn—immediate or not, depending if one is inclined to count the visual turn, the cultural turn, the mediatic turn, the digital turn, the posthuman turn, and so forth. Should this temptation to see the current interest in the material world as a reaction to, a liberation from, the antecedent textualization of human experience be resisted? I say yes. Firstly, chronological sequence does not imply consequence, and has little, if any, explanatory power. Then, to oppose the material to the linguistic would perpetuate those trapping dichotomies, which, despite their conceptual force, are really limited to the predictable oscillation of a pendulum that prevents the opening of new theoretical horizons. Finally, to situate textuality and materiality as opposites is to disregard the fact, as problematic as polarization, that the two have substantially merged in the scholarship currently devoted to material culture. A cultural history of the material world appears, therefore, fraught with the hazards of paradox.

On one hand, such a history may reinscribe and perpetuate the dichotomies inherent in scholarly epistemologies such as: culture and nature, mind and matter, real and ideal, matter and form, senses and intellect, body and soul, abstract and concrete, subject and object, person and thing, material and social, material and cognitive. Indeed, the notion of a material world has already contributed—particularly in the fields of anthropology and history—its own polarization, between material and materiality.

On the other hand, a cultural history of the material world has had the effect of subsuming the material world within hegemonic antimaterial and social constructivist theories.[1] Thus, despite blogospheres and scholarly literature, the material turn may not yet have occurred. Yet, if a cultural perspective has focused on social and symbolic meanings to the detriment of material relations, how might an alternate perspective avoid yielding the precise opposite?

The underlying question lurking behind the conundrum of polarization is the ontological and epistemological status of a material world that is external to culture, outside society. To address this issue, I offer a rapid survey of contemporary debates before sketching an agenda of some relevant issues pertaining to the Middle Ages—my area of specialization. I conclude by suggesting some ways in which I believe that the project of this series might advance our understanding of the material world in history.

Poststructuralist positions are challenging to studies of the material world. They are loath to acknowledge nondiscursive realms of reality and experience. In promoting the primacy of language as a model for understanding culture, they endow the human sciences with a "textual analogy" in terms of which material culture should be conceived of and read as text.[2] The difference between things and texts is thus erased.

Although material things are transposed and represented in other media, this is not to say that they are experienced solely as signs—linguistic or other. A growing amount of newer scholarship on the material world, while recognizing textualism as a vital source of inspiration, nevertheless posits that things are present in the world differently from words, by having a material dimension that is more than a matter of mind, cognition, and communication.[3] Such an appreciation of the material *qua* material might be expected to require that it be granted full participation in the human action visited upon it. An example of this may be found in the case of basket making. Here, no material surface is available as *tabula rasa* mutely to receive the force of an antecedent mental blueprint. The surface of the basket emerges from the practice of weaving reeds; its form develops from the mutual engagement of the weaver's bodily skills with the material.[4]

This approach emphasizes the process of making things, whereby

things comprehend objects and persons. It insists that artists and craftsmen work within the world, knitting things together rather than acting
upon a material from outside.[5] It submits that both persons and objects
are being formed in the very moments of their entanglement while
making something.[6] Such an approach, with its phenomenological and
Heideggerian slant, challenges the still operative metaphysical separation of mind from matter on several levels. This dualism is still operative because histories of the material world tend to promote a mode
of enquiry focused primarily on a specific type of physical evidence,
artifacts—that is, objects that exist as already made.[7] Locking the material into its manufactured identity privileges conceptual, perceptual,
and intentional dimensions; the materiality of things comes to be assigned to their conceptualization, use, and agency as manufactured objects, and not in the stuff and physical processes of which they consist.
Thus, the place of the object in relation to its stuff remains unaddressed,
and materiality is turned into an abstraction, referring to the cultural
aspects of objects. By contrast, the "phenomenological" approach, in
its insistence that both stuff and its human users are material, limits the
experience and agency of materials to organic qualities—their capacity
to flex, bend, adhere, and color. Material properties, however, are not
fixed attributes, but emerge from the situation of materials: a feather
in a person's hair is an ornament; a feather on parchment is a pen. In
such cases, the object materializes with a practical activity, within a series of contacts between materials, hands, head, eyes, skin; creation was
not imported. Even if a craftsman has a mental image of the object he
or she wishes to produce, the object will actually emerge from contact
between material, tool, hands, and eyes. This kind of attention to the
relation between materials—an attention that takes into consideration
that humans are material—permits two anti-dualist remarks. First, that
the material is not an indifferent receptacle of culture—that artifacts
do not proceed uniquely from mental conception. Second, that objects
survive as such beyond specific use or interpretation, while they are vulnerable to all that can happen to things: wearing, tarnishing, eroding,
aging, and rotting. The occurrence of such events is not a matter of
socialization, although we tend to ascribe material degradation to use,
rather than to organic processes.[8] These latter, however, should further
the understanding that their materials enable objects to resist being fully
social signs. True, they are at the mercy of codes and systems, but their
physical materiality has its own landscape of contingencies, which affects
both the objects' destinations and meanings.[9]

Neither the processual materialization of objects, nor their ecological destiny, seems of much interest to scholars in the humanities and the social sciences. Hence the thrust of the analytical shift away from the textual focuses on things' symbolic communicative and representational aspects, privileging a concern for the deeds of things in the world: the ways in which physical objects interact with humans, shaping their lives and experiences. Where the linguistic turn had dematerialized things, the postlinguistic approach embodies and objectifies abstract social phenomena, considering that artifacts, through representation, consumption, and circulation, are active constituents of selfhood, values, social categories, understanding of self and others. It is through the medium of things that social and cognitive formations are enabled, reproduced, or destabilized. In such epistemology, the attention is not to material, but to material form. It is, once again, the formed material—the temple, the statue, the book, the pot, the ax—that encompasses objectification of cultural meanings, and embodiment, if not extension of personhood. This in turn means that—when clothing, tapestries, relics, chests, and/ or enameled boxes are considered—they stand for the social relations to which they provided, and continue to provide, a canvas of inscription. Interpretation of things is thus situated within an unlimited hermeneutics of meaning since the capacity of objects to work for given users is not an inherent property, but must continuously be sustained by social interaction. However participatory in the process of social being, the material becomes an outcome of cultural processes that are not themselves material, thus leaving the participation of material itself with little agentive or explanatory power for these processes. Analysts looking at objects created in the past see them as sources by which to access past people's culture—a world beyond the material itself. The very fact of the ongoing presence of the object as material stuff is rarely, if ever, taken into consideration.[10] Yet, where does the evidentiary nature of a twelfth-century object that survives into the twenty-first century reside if its relevance today emerges through our own interaction with it? How retrievable are the earlier waves of social acts embodied by the object? Where are they located? Conversely, how are we to deal with the disappearance of things known to have existed? Such questions point to the difficulties inherent in researching objects so as to uncover the ways in which they mattered beyond their concrete existence, when the particularity of materials and of their specific travail has been cancelled by the uniformity of social operation. In the same way that culture organizes human beings beyond their individual existence as physical organisms, materiality comprehends objects beyond their material properties. If materiality incorporates culture, a cultural history of the material world seems a tautology.

How then might we practice a cultural history of the material world in which "the materials of which the objects are made are not swallowed by the objects made from them?"[11] This question has a philosophical dimension—one that concerns the definition of reality in general, and particularly the ontological and epistemological status of a material world conceivable as external to processes of valorization. In early twenty-first-century culture, relativism advances the notion that there are only discursive claims about physical reality, and that such claims are only valid in relation to a particular subjective way of perceiving that reality. Whatever one's position about relativism and its ferocious anthropocentric position, there is no doubt that claims about physical reality are multiple and historically situated. That the contingency of these claims resides within discourse still begs the question of the relationship of language to reality. Claims, however, are made on the basis of observed physical evidence. In the controversy about geocentrism versus heliocentrism, Robert Bellarmine (d. 1621) examined a book—the Bible—while Galileo Galilei (d. 1642) observed the sky through a telescope.[12] We can safely say that Bellarmine, Galileo, the Bible, and the telescope existed, as still do the sky, the sun, and the earth. The differentiated clustering of coexisting material things—eye-bible, eye-telescope—however, yielded differing results. His dogmatic Catholic views may have directed Bellarmine to a Bible, but a similar system of beliefs did not stop Galileo from improving and using the telescope. In this case, the relationship between cultural beliefs and the material world was unsystematic at the personal level. However, the Bible was at that point more available and more familiar than a telescope, with the result that the seventeenth-century majority experience of looking at the sky was principally mediated by bookish, rather than by telescopic, evidence. In another domain—medieval medicine—physical observation also involved books rather than the patients' bodies. The things described by physicians, by Bellarmine, and by Galileo were commensurate with the physical evidence they observed; the reasons for their diverging claims reside in the things observed, not in the factuality of that which they report. In my reading of these examples, I consider material nexuses, in which physical, environmental, sensorial, and intellectual elements are in play, not as independent interacting agents, but associated in particular clusters of practical operations. Thus anchored in pragmatic experience, all elements are mutually tested, constrained, or enabled by their own work in such experience. Of importance, therefore, is the identification of these materials and their various clustering in the flow of practice. There is the possibility of matching materials to claims made about them, which is not to say that the world of materials either dictates, or can be confused with, claims about them. From my research on inscribed matter and imprinted material—medieval seals in particular—I developed the notion that materials and objects have an existence that is independent of human experience; that materials gather in unpredictable as well as in intended fashions; that objects index modalities of causation and situation that are not necessarily culturally informed;[13] that the properties in a given object will obtain various qualitative relevance given its particular contextualization with other materials, as well as with practice and interpretation; and finally, that since, by virtue of this ongoing material clustering, the material properties of an object will always be in excess of those that have obtained relevance in a given gathering, material things remain unpredictable.[14]

Two examples may help substantiate these claims. A chirograph issued in 1177 recorded in duplicate an exchange of goods between two members of the French elite: Count Matthew of Beaumont, and the Abbot of Saint-Denis, Geoffrey (fig. 1).[15] The original document was cut in half, so that each party to the exchange would keep a record of the transaction. On this particular chirograph, the two texts were divided by a full, artistically rendered image of Christ on the cross (fig. 2).

It was through that image that the deliberate cut was made, splitting the representation of the divine incarnate corpus. The very appearance of a body on parchment draws attention to the fact that the parchment is skin, implying material continuity between Christic and animal skin. From this nexus, a paradigm of eternity emerges: the skin has become everlasting parchment when separated from the animal's too mortal flesh, even as the pierced body of Christ—itself a translation of eternity into temporality—offered a triumph over death, an abrogation of the temporal limits of human life. Skin, thus, clothed the contingency of social interaction as acts inscribed in eternity. The medium central to this operation is the act of cutting, rendered possible and significant by the medial quality of the parchment, while the cut itself reveals the material innerness of mediality (fig. 3). The interaction between operation and material substance not so much resembled as reenacted the Word made flesh and crucified, as was also ritually performed in the sacrament of the Eucharist. The rending of the chirograph, by literally penetrating flesh, recapitulated the crucified Christ's sacrifice in a way that guaranteed the inscribed textual commitment even as Christ had guaranteed divine commitment.[16]

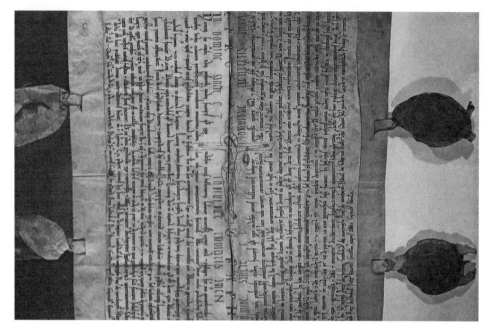

Fig. 1. Reconstructed chirograph. The document records in duplicate
an exchange of goods between Matthew, Count of Beaumont, and
Geoffrey, abbot of Saint-Denis (1177). Each part of the chirograph
had been kept by the relevant party, and are now housed in different
archival repositories. The comital portion is in the French Archives
nationales, Paris, J 168 no 2 (AE/II/181); the abbatial portion, in the
French Archives départementales du Val-d'Oise, Pontoise, 9 H 81.
(Photo by the author, with kind permission of the Archives nationales,
and of the Archives départementales du Val-d'Oise.)

A second example links the considerable body of seal metaphors deployed by intellectuals of the central Middle Ages to the sealing practice
which they and their contemporaries employed.[17] The basis of the seal's
utility as both a sign of authorization and a conceptual tool was its actual process of imprinting, which established and confirmed a regime
of causality (fig. 4). Such a process implied two things. Firstly, it generated the seal impression as an image of origin. Secondly, it involved
contact between tangible things—hands, seal-die, and wax—producing
a mode of reference that was organized around these very things and
their properties. The wax, for instance, was at once malleable, able to receive the form of the die and of the sealer's fingerprints, or alternatively,
was hard and unreceptive, or even unstable, apt to melt and thus to

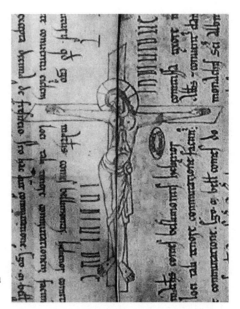

Fig. 2. Detail of the division separating the two parts of the chirography. (Photo by the author, with kind permission of the Archives nationales, and of the Archives départementales du Val-d'Oise.)

lose its image. Anselm of Bec (d. 1109), Hugh of Saint-Victor (d. 1141), Alain de Lille (d. 1202), and Peter of Blois (d. 1203)—to name just a few commentators—remarked on this ability of the wax to move from resemblance to dissemblance without any change in its own ontological status. They made analogy between the wax image (*imago*) and man who, though originally imprinted in God's image, lost his likeness to the divine—but not necessarily his humanity. In both seal practice and seal metaphor, there was acknowledgment that the image that was impressed would alter the appearance of the wax, but also consideration that the material and medial qualities of the wax informed and conditioned the image received. Form and matter act reciprocally, although the appearance of wax impressions, from unintended marks (fingerprints), deformity (accident), to intentional resemblance (the goal of a proper stamping of the die), derives from the wax's intrinsic characteristics, not from the idea or design of an image maker.[18]

In testing the heuristic of my earlier theoretical formulations, I have directed attention to the clustering and mutual contextualizing of materials in twelfth-century image making, investigating the ways in which, in their association, humans, gods, animals, and particular types of images swapped properties and formed specific collectives.

Fig. 3. Abbational portion of the chirography, Archives départementales du Val-d'Oise, Pontoise, 9 H 81. (Photo by the author, with kind permission of the Archives départementales du Val-d'Oise.)

In conclusion, I would like to share my sense of the shifts in discourse that *Cultural Histories of the Material World* might enable. The series is jumping into a fundamental and longstanding debate—that of the nature of reality. The moment may be ripe to promote studies in which difference is not conceived according to the prevailing ontological regimes of dualities and negativities. Thus culture, history, and the material world would retain their difference, one that is non-oppositional and relative, facilitating collaboration, delegation, and exchange both among scholars, and in the treatment of the topics at hand. In the current academic climate, as discussed in this essay, the practice of material-culture studies has not yet fully addressed the materiality of objects.

As a medieval historian, I have a choice to engage objects or manuscript texts about objects. What is the status of these texts in a cultural history of the material world? One answer is easy. Books and documents are themselves objects, so a material approach to them may index layers of being that a mere reading would have left behind. More difficult, is to access and assess the cluster "text," the multiple trails of material encounters (hand, feather, the oak gall of the ink, skin) that have converged on the manuscript page.[19] Perhaps most difficult of all is to consider whether one may assume some sort of mutuality between the textual argument and its materiality. Augustine (d. 430) specified that true knowledge was beyond sensorial perception, and accessible only via the

Fig. 4. Seal Matrix and detached seal impression of the Collegial Chapter of Saint-Quiriace of Provins (early fourteenth century). Archives nationales, Service des sceaux, Collection de matrices, no 18. (Photo by the author, with kind permission of the Archives nationales.)

mental image immanent to the soul and imperfectly remembered by man.[20] The idea was that the material world existed, but was not real, and that signification did not refer to actual things, nor did it need to refer to them in order to have meaning. Such a view was broadly accepted in the early Middle Ages and somewhat constrained the role of the material world in informing practice and experience. When this perspective changed, at the turn of the second millennium, the cultural landscape of the epoch (1050–1225) soon was filled with texts, images, and artifacts in unprecedented numbers. When Mabillon drew materials and meaning together in the 1680s, he was synthesizing in the spirit and age of Descartes and Newton. We are now living through an equally unprecedented revolution, and should expect an equally significant shift in epistemologies of knowledge and exposition.

NOTES

1. Bjørnar Olsen, "Material Culture after Text: Re-Membering Things," *Norwegian Archaeological Review* 36, no. 2 (2003): 87–104, at 88.
2. See the literary analogies in many titles: Hodder, *Reading the Past* (1986); Tilley, *Reading Material Culture* (1990); Tilley, *Material Culture as Text* (1991). Régis Debray, *Vie et mort de l'image* (Paris: Gallimard, 1992), 53–60.
3. Christopher Tilley, "Theoretical Perspectives. Introduction," in *Handbook of Material Culture*, ed. Christopher Tilley et al. (London: Sage, 2006), 1–11, at 8; B. Olsen, "Scenes from a troubled Engagement. Post-Structuralism and Material Cultural Studies," in *Handbook of Material Culture*, 85–103, reprinted in Olsen, *In Defense of Things* (Blue Ridge Summit, PA: Rowman and Littlefield Publishing Group, 2010), 39–62.
4. Tim Ingold, *The Perception of the Environment: Essays in Livelihood, Dwelling, and Skill* (London: Routledge, 2000), 339–48.
5. Julian Thomas, "Phenomenology and Material Culture," in *Handbook of Material Culture*, 43–59, at 54, 57.
6. Tim Ingold, "Writing Texts, Reading Materials. A Response to my Critics," *Archaeological Dialogues* 14 (2007): 31–38, at 35.
7. Tim Ingold , "Materials Against Materiality," *Archaeological Dialogues* 14 (2007): 1–16, at 1, 11. This article prompted a very interesting debate about the epistemological meaning of materiality.
8. If I drop a plastic glass, it will not break, but a china cup will.
9. Webb Keane, *Signs of Recognition. Powers and Hazards of Representation in Indonesian Society* (Berkeley and Los Angeles: University of California Press, 1997), 32.
10. It is significant that the otherwise comprehensive *Handbook of Material Culture* has an index with no entry to Carbon 14, DNA, pollens, etc.
11. Tim Ingold, "Writing Texts, Reading Materials," 33.
12. I am inspired to use these examples by John R. Searle, "Why Should you Believe it," *New York Review of Books*, September 24, 2009, 88–92. In this essay, Searle reviews the book by Paul A. Boghossian, *Fear of Knowledge: Against Relativism and Constructivism* (Oxford: Oxford University Press, 2007). I wish to thank my husband, Ira Rezak, for bringing this essay to my attention.
13. On this and the Perceian concept of abduction, see Alfred Gell, *Art and Agency* (Oxford: Oxford University Press, 1998). Think, for example, of the ability of the clay to dry, of some metals to soften, of textiles to move in the wind.
14. Webb Keane, *Signs of Recognition*, 1–28.
15. Each part of the chirograph had been kept by the relevant party, and are now housed in different archival repositories. The comital portion is in the French Archives nationales, Paris, J 168 no 2 (AE/II/181); the abbatial portion, in the French Archives départementales du Val-d'Oise, Pontoise, 9 H 81.
16. A full analysis of this chirograph can be found in Brigitte Miriam Bedos-Rezak, "Cutting Edge. The Economy of Mediality in Twelfth-century Writing," *Das Mittelalter* 15 (2010): 134–61.

17. Brigitte Miriam Bedos-Rezak, *When Ego was Imago. Signs of Identity in the Middle Ages* (Leiden: Brill, 2010).

18. Georges Didi-Huberman, "The Order of Material: Plasticities, Malaises, Survivals," in *Sculpture and Psychoanalysis,* ed. Brandon Taylor (London: Ashgate, 2007), 195–211, at 199–200.

19. Tim Ingold, "Writing Texts, Reading Materials," 13–14.

20. Stephane Dorothée, "Signum et le métalexique: la notion de signe linguistique chez saint Augustin," in *Latin et langues techniques* (Paris: Presses de l'Université Paris–Sorbonne, 2006), 155–69, at 166–68.

FOUR

Museum Display, an Algonquian Bow, and the Ship of Theseus

Ivan Gaskell

In 2008, a new long-term exhibit opened in the Arthur M. Sackler Museum at Harvard University.[1] Named *Re-View*, it draws on all parts of the museum's collection. This highly selective presentation of the museum's holdings is to be on view in successive versions while the neighboring Quincy Street building that had housed the Fogg Art Museum since 1927 is closed for renovation and expansion. The first version of *Re-View* closed in 2010.

One floor of the 2008–10 version of *Re-View* was devoted to the Western tradition from classical antiquity until 1900. With only six galleries available, the curators responsible had to compress the story they sought to tell both chronologically and geographically. I was one of two scholars responsible for planning the display of European and American art between 1600 and 1900 in three adjacent galleries, my collaborator being Theodore Stebbins Jr. Rather than follow the common practice of dividing the works by continent and tracing formal and stylistic developments within each, we decided to treat the material as belonging to a single extended moment in a single cultural area. We arranged the works we selected thematically—showing, for instance, history paintings together (a Poussin beside a Winslow Homer), and landscapes together (a Ruisdael next to a Sargent). Two constant themes were the persistence of motifs and modes of representation from classical antiquity, and the increase in cultural encounter during this period, eventually encompassing the world.

To exemplify cultural encounter, we included objects that are not normally considered part of the Western tradition. We showed a sixteenth-century bronze staff finial representing a bird of prophecy from the Benin Kingdom in what is now Nigeria beside a Giambologna bronze falcon from sixteenth-century Florence. We presented a bow, said to have been taken from an Indian by an English colonist in 1660, among European and European-American history paintings. I shall use the bow to explore aspects of what I take the production of cultural histories of the material world to involve within an art museum.

The bow is delicately fashioned from a single piece of hickory wood. It is over five-and-a-half-feet long, subtly asymmetrical longitudinally about the handgrip. A faded inscription in ink states, "The bow was taken from an Indian in Sudbury, Massts AD 1660 by William Goodenough who shot the Indian while he was ransacking his house for plunder." This information has long been accepted literally, causing the object to be known as the Sudbury Bow.[2] Successive members of the family of the man who had captured it are said to have preserved it until Reverend Charles C. H. Crosby donated it to the American Antiquarian Society in Worcester, Massachusetts, in or before 1826.[3] In 1895, the society presented it to the Peabody Museum of Archaeology and Ethnology at Harvard University, which generously lent it to the Arthur M. Sackler Museum for the new exhibit in 2008.[4] If the inscription, which is in what appears to be an eighteenth- or early nineteenth-century italic hand, indeed preserves information that had previously been handed down orally, the bow must be counted a very rare survival of an indigenous North American artifact from the seventeenth century.

Before examining this possibility in a little more detail, let us pause to offer an initial assessment of what such a thing might ideally provide to historians. All material things available to us are traces of the past. Many material things embody human making or intervention. When Westerners consider material things—things available to the human senses or their extensions—they classify them, whether as things made, adopted, or modified by humans on the one hand, or as things purely in nature on the other. Human-made things—artifacts—are the result of the purposeful modification of materials. The bow we are considering is an artifact. Adopted things are not modified by humans, but are imbued by them with particular qualities. They can be small and portable—like a shell carried as an amulet—or vast like a river or mountain invested with socially acknowledged properties. Modified things include living beings in whose reproductive cycles humans have intervened, such as selectively bred crops and domesticated animals. These definitions imply an anthropocentric viewpoint, for they suggest that human making, adoption, and modification are unavoidable wherever humans might be found, or to whatever their reach extends perceptually, including the most distant detectable heavenly bodies. It can be objected that histories of the material world might be conceived in which humans play but a marginal role, if any: a history of ocean currents, for instance, or of insects, or of the formation of igneous rocks. This is incontrovertible. Humanity is but a recent and vulnerable arrival on this planet. Yet the particular care of history, as distinct from, say, oceanography, entomology or geology, is the activity of human beings, even though this can usually best be understood in conjunction with other constituents of the material world.

Cultural historians of the material world are often, though far from exclusively, concerned with artifacts. However, opinion as to what constitutes the human-made varies from society to society. In the Christian tradition, for instance, some devotees hold certain miraculous images that might appear painted to be acheiropoietic—not the products of human hands.[5] Intimately connected with notions of divine making is variation among societies regarding what is living and what is not, the animate and the inanimate. Our bow may have been human made, but it does not follow that those who made and first used it subscribed to a Western understanding of its material—hickory wood—as once living, but subsequently dead. To them, the bow, made of a once-living tree, may well have retained its living status. As historians, we are obliged to bear in mind that conceptions of materiality vary considerably among societies, and that any given material object can be conceived of in more than one way—whether simultaneously by different groups with different beliefs, or consecutively within any given social group as uses and beliefs change. As a historian, my aim is not ontological definition; rather it is to acquire an understanding of any given thing that ideally takes as many socially viable conceptions of it into account as possible, and to describe differences and—when appropriate—changes among them.

If non-Western conceptions of material objects can be peculiar, confusing—or even nonsensical—to Westerners, the bases in Greek philosophy of Western notions of materiality are also generally unfamiliar, other than in colloquial derivations. Even before considering the binary distinction between the term *material* and its antonym, *immaterial*, puzzles arise over identity, persistence, and the consequences of change over time. In what sense is the bow that concerns us the same material thing when displayed in the Sackler Museum as the bow previously displayed in the Peabody Museum, or again as the bow belonging to the American Antiquarian Society, or to the putative William Goodenough, or, before him, to the unidentified indigenous person who used it, who may or may not have been its maker? Museum scholars generally subscribe to the persistence of identity of the objects with which they work. This is no small issue, given the perceived need to intervene in their physical states through conservation treatment. Material things constantly change, whether as a result of direct or indirect human action, or other processes, both gradual and sudden. Curators and conservators usually seek to arrest change, at the very least. The historian using a material thing as a trace or source should ideally be well informed of the nature and sequence of the physical changes it has undergone. This can often only be attempted with the collaboration of conservators and analytical scientists. Underlying any such analysis, though, is generally an assumption of the persistence of the identity of the object concerned. At what point, though, if ever, does a material thing change to such an extent that its original identity is compromised or even lost? This is but one puzzle among those that philosophers have long discussed under the rubric, the Problem of Material Constitution (PMC).[6]

Identity presents a particular puzzle within the PMC.[7] It found prototypical articulation in the account of the Greek historian and philosopher Plutarch (AD 46–ca. 122) of the Ship of Theseus, the legendary founder-king of Athens. "The ship wherein Theseus and the youth of Athens returned has thirty oars, and was preserved by the Athenians down even to the time of Demetrius Phalereus [ca. 350–ca. 280 BC], for they took away the old planks as they decayed, putting new and stronger timber in their place, insomuch that this ship became a standing example among philosophers, for the logical question of things that grow; one side holding that the ship remained the same, and the other contending that it was not the same."[8] Plutarch presents us with a paradox: a thing that incrementally changes physically in its entirety, and yet retains its original identity—or does it?

In his discussion of the individuation of material things, the seventeenth-century philosopher Thomas Hobbes introduced a further complication to the Ship of Theseus paradox. He illustrates what he counts as the absurdity of the idea that "two Bodies existing both at once, would be one and the same Numerical Body" by supposing that the planks removed for replacement from the Ship of Theseus could themselves be reconstituted to form an identical vessel, so that there would be not one but two vessels with claims to be the Ship of Theseus.[9] Hobbes contends that identity is a matter of naming, a claim taken up with respect to artworks (among other things) by later philosophers including Nelson Goodman and Arthur Danto.[10] Whether or not this provides a satisfactory solution to the Ship of Theseus paradox (and not all agree that it does), Hobbes's analysis of individuation reminds us of the role played by immaterial constituents (such as names) in the definition of what we take to be material things.

In the case of the bow, we can be confident that, but for the effects of aging on the wood and the loss of certain original appurtenances (including the bow string), the item is materially substantially the same as when it was made: physically, it is constitutionally simple, in that the greater part of it, which survives, is not made of replaceable parts, but is a single stave. Yet it now carries a name: the Sudbury Bow. Its identity as such is culturally contingent. Its name is an element of its immaterial transformation from whatever it might have been in the minds of its maker and first user into a trophy commemorating heritable family pride in the subjugation of an enemy, and subsequently, into an anthropological specimen. The latest immaterial transformation of the bow is from a specimen displayed in the Peabody Museum to illustrate the material lifeways of Eastern Woodlands Indians into an artwork displayed in the *Re-View* exhibit in the Sackler Museum.

The two successive museum identities of the bow—as specimen and as artwork—are the result of cultural appropriation. This is understandably a distrusted phenomenon, but one that is not invariably offensive or harmful.[11] However, the power relationship between originating and appropriating groups can be asymmetrical and persistently unjust, leading to demands by originating groups or their successors for the appropriate treatment of things by appropriators or their successors, including museums, even to the extent of their return. Just as important as an acknowledgement of the fact of appropriation must be an appreciation of differences in dominant modes of perception of appropriated things fostered by originating groups on the one hand, and by museums on the other. The engagement of first users with tangible things was often multisensory, involving actions such as touching, lifting, sounding, kissing, and carrying. As Elizabeth Edwards, Chris Gosden, and Ruth Phillips have pointed out, far from being excluded in museums "multisensory engagement with objects remained fundamental to the investigation of material culture, but ... [as] part of the privileged access accorded to a new priesthood of curators and museum professionals."[12] Curators, conservators, and analytical scientists handle, heft, manipulate, smell, and occasionally disassemble museum objects, whereas the experience of ordinary visitors is confined to no more than visual inspection—viewing objects, either at a distance or through a protective barrier of plexiglass. As Edwards and her colleagues point out, this limitation is a necessary consequence of mass access, a matter of security in its widest sense, preventing incremental damage, as well as accidents and theft. That this should be the reason does not lessen the privilege these conditions confer on vision over the other senses, exacerbating the differences between the engagement of Western museum visitors with a wide range of tangible things, and that of originating or successor groups, whose members likely value other forms of sensory engagement. The same can hold true even within Western culture: to what extent can we claim to understand the qualities of, say, a particular kind of chair on display without being able to sit on it? Some kinds of artifacts, including bows, are found in a variety of societies; so, to what extent can we claim to understand the qualities of the bow recently on display in the Sackler Museum without being able to assess its balance in the hand, let alone to string it and feel its draw weight? In a study room, a curator might be able to experience at least some of the bow's tactile qualities, but, when presenting it in a gallery, the focus must inevitably be on its visual characteristics. However constraining, this is a condition imposed by the medium of museum gallery display, and it undoubtedly has epistemological consequences. While it can illuminate certain qualities of an object, display cannot exhaust it.[13]

Even with in the visual realm of display, there is, of course, more than one way of exploiting the visual characteristics of a thing. In the Peabody Museum, where the bow was displayed until its loan to the Sackler Museum, it was set vertically against a backboard in a large vitrine containing many other tangible things representative of the material culture of Eastern Woodlands Indians. It was part of an ensemble—one of a number of varied things treated equally—rather than a focus of attention. It took up as little space within the vitrine as possible, and its vertical position implied that it was at rest. This display very effectively served its curator's purpose of illustrating material lifeways shared by related cultural groups. The display of the bow in the Sackler Museum was radically different, serving quite another purpose. In its temporary change of location from an anthropology to an art museum, it is almost inevitable that its character should have changed from that of a representative specimen of a particular way of life to a thing with unique qualities presented for aesthetic contemplation. Different circumstances promote attention to different aspects of a complex thing. No tangible thing reveals all of itself in any one set of circumstances. Curators have a responsibility to contrive specific circumstances in which particular characteristics of specific things can become apparent. As the presentation of the bow in the Sackler Museum exhibit was my initiative, I shall try to account for it.

First, I wished to encourage focused attention on the bow by presenting it on its own, in the round, so that visitors might see it from as many viewpoints as possible. In the context of an art museum, this means presenting it on the same terms as a sculpture, implying cultural value. Further, I aimed to present the bow not as a thing at rest (as it was in the Peabody Museum display), but as a dynamic object, implying use. I had a mount contrived for it so that it was inconspicuously supported diagonally in space, at a commanding height, suggesting a drawn bow in action. Although this presentation accentuated the dynamic, sculptural aspects of the bow, and permitted viewers to see it in the round, as a thing apart, there are problematic consequences.

The elongated curvilinearity of the bow brings to mind sculptures by Constantin Brâncuși (1876–1957), notably *Bird in Space* (first version, 1922–1923), an icon of European modernism prized for its balance and refinement. Troubling questions follow. Did the presentation in the Sackler Museum amount to an unambiguous invitation to view a seventeenth-century American Indian bow in terms of a twentieth-century modern European sculpture? If so, did it compound any offense caused by the appropriation of the bow? Did this presentation amount to cultural misrepresentation? This is a delicate matter.

It might be helpful if we consider in a little more detail aspects of what occurs in consequence of the cultural appropriation of material things, such as this bow.[14] When a thing moves from one society to another, one or more of three attitudes is in play: (1) the new users employ and interpret it solely on their own terms without regard to the uses and interpretations of its earlier users, either oblivious to those earlier uses, or purposefully to expunge them; (2) the new users discern familiar characteristics that they value, and that they assume earlier users also discerned and valued; (3) the new users attempt to learn the terms of use, interpretation and value of the earlier users by means of cultural acquisition and translation, acknowledging that these may differ from their own wholly or in part, but in the belief that their acquisition will bring them advantages.

I term these three attitudes, respectively, *supersession, assumption,* and *translation*. Translation is especially complex, because in some instances new users wish to understand a thing purely intellectually, and in others with emotional engagement. All three attitudes are legitimate, but this does not exempt their application from ethical scrutiny in individual cases, nor from acknowledgment of their shortcomings. Ethically flawed practices include depriving or withholding from subordinated social groups artifacts that are properly their own, mistreating or unwarrantably exposing artifacts that have sacred significance, and using artifacts to promote or uncritically perpetuate asymmetrical power relationships. Furthermore, the application of each of these attitudes varies depending on the terms in which a thing is considered. Westerners are more likely to accept and incorporate subaltern aesthetic terms into their own belief systems than they are to accept subaltern magical or religious terms. Therefore, translation by Westerners in the case of the magical, sacred, and divine is likely to be more reserved and cautious than in cases of aesthetic values. Furthermore, there is likely to be greater scope for assumption—recognizing or ascribing characteristics valued in common—in aesthetic than in sacred terms.

In their examinations of artifacts in both aesthetic and sacred terms, Western scholars generally favor translation. They expect that through translation they can retrieve the original, supposedly paramount, meaning of a thing, thereby enhancing intellectual and aesthetic understanding. This is often a worthy aim, but, even if this were possible—if translation were not itself a species of new use—translation ignores both vital characteristics of things, and enduring human practice acknowledged by supersession and assumption. Supersession and assumption recognize that artifacts perdure and are physically and cognitively adaptable, and that human beings put artifacts to various uses over time. Furthermore, translation is as open to abuse as are supersession and assumption. Western (and some other) anthropologists have persistently used translation to promote colonialism and other forms of asymmetrical power relationship between hegemonic and subaltern peoples. Some of the drawbacks of supersession and assumption are more readily recognizable. Supersession—the uncompromising cognitive adaptation of an artifact regardless of its earlier use—can unjustly promote the suppression of the cultural identity of earlier users. Assumption can bolster hegemony by fostering panculturalism—a belief that works from all cultures exhibit common aesthetic characteristics. The error of panculturalism is not that societies can produce, recognize, and value identical aesthetic characteristics, but that such common characteristics count for more than those that might be peculiar to a given society. Each attitude, therefore, has its drawbacks, as well as its advantages.

Returning to the bow with these distinctions in mind, we should acknowledge that humans view things comparatively, drawing on memories of a wide range of items. For Westerners (and others) to view the bow in implicit comparison with *Bird in Space* is one effective way of focusing on certain of its characteristics (curvilinearity, balance, refinement). This might be helpful, but only so long as it does not encourage the error of panculturalism. As long as viewers do not make any comparison with a Western item at the expense of the cultural peculiarity of the bow, they are likely to respect its origin. Its display in *Re-View* did not explicitly encourage viewing the bow in terms of European modernism through directly available comparisons.[15] Instead, it invited consideration of the mythology of hunting, for the bow was juxtaposed with representations of the hunt in the form of a fourth-century BC Greek red-figure nestoris (attributed to the Choephoroi Painter) with a scene of the death of Actaeon, and a monumental painting, *Diana on a Chase* (1805), by Washington Allston. The bow was on display because it is an Indian artifact, presented as of value owing to its indigenous status. The juxtapositions invited attention to its potential use as a hunting implement rather than as a weapon of war, so as not to reinforce a Western stereotype of Indian belligerence.[16] As such, it was a reminder that the spread of European settlement to North America—specifically New England—was not a historical starting point, but that human presence—with all the cultural complexity that this implies—long predates the arrival of newcomers from beyond the ocean.

Let us consider the bow itself in more detail. The inscription informs readers (implicitly understood to be European as opposed to indigenous) that it allegedly changed hands in violent circumstances during the early years of the English colonization of what became New England. What attraction might a bow have had for an English settler, presuming that he actually took it from an Indian antagonist?

For the English, bows were characteristic of Indians, particularly Indians of high status. The Algonquian "weroan or great Lorde of Virginia" represented from both the front and the back in an engraving by Theodor de Bry in the 1590 edition of Thomas Harriot's *A Briefe and True Report of the New Found Land of Virginia,* after a watercolor by John White, holds a strung bow. Harriot, a careful first-hand observer who learned an Algonquian language, observed of the "princes of Virginia" that "They carye a quiver made of small rushes holding their bowe readie bent in on hand, and an arrow in the other, radie to defend themselves. In this manner they goe to warr, or tho their solemne feasts and banquetts. They take much pleasure in huntinge of deer where of there is great store in the contrye . . ."[17] Harriot acknowledges three distinct uses of bows by the Indians he had noticed: warfare, hunting, and ceremony. A bow-bearing Indian even became the emblem of colonial endeavor. The first seal of the Massachusetts Bay Colony, chartered in 1629, represents an Indian holding an arrow pointing downward in his right hand— signifying peace—and a bow in his left, with the words "Come over and help us" in a phylactery.[18] This seal was in use until 1686, and again from 1689 to 1692.

Bows were more than signifiers of Indianness for English colonizers. As Joyce Chaplin has pointed out, they had a special place in the colonizers' own self-image.[19] Proficiency in archery was a value shared by Indians and colonists, though in culturally distinct ways. Until the end of the sixteenth century, the bow and arrow had remained the principal English missile weapon; enrollment of archers for military training ended in 1595. Nonetheless, many English persons continued to view prowess in archery as a measure of manliness—both individually, and communally. Not until the lighter and more reliable wheel-lock arquebus superseded the ungainly matchlock did firearms make significant inroads in North America.[20] The Frenchman Samuel de Champlain and his Indian allies' defeat of the Iroquois Mohawks beside Lake Champlain in 1609 demonstrates that the wheel-lock arquebus, especially when multiply charged, was immensely effective against lightly armored Indian archers used to fighting in close order.[21] Indian battle tactics changed swiftly in response to diminish warriors' exposure. They abandoned both massed formations and wooden armor—and Indians rapidly acquired firearms. Although gunpowder weapons began to replace bows, their use continued in North America during at least the first third of the seventeenth century, owing to supply problems (especially of gunpowder), cost, the relative efficiency of the respective weapons (reliability, rate of fire, range, and accuracy), and cultural resistance. English colonists continued to use bows regularly until about 1640. Thereafter, they long retained a nostalgic respect for archery bolstered by similar sentiments expressed in the metropole by writers such as William Wood, whose *Bow-mans Glory; or Archery Revived* was published in 1682.[22] Nostalgia was compounded by identification. In the Indians who practiced the fine crafting of bows, and their use in hunting, military exercises, warfare, and ceremony, English settlers saw earlier, virtuous versions of themselves. Nourished by studies of the works of Julius Caesar and Tacitus, their dominant historical mythology led to a belief that just as the Romans had civilized the valiant, virtuous ancient Britons—forebears of the English—so their descendants—the modern English—would, in turn, lead the Indians from savagery to civility. Confronting an Indian, an English colonist saw a contemporary equivalent of his own ancestor: savage, but uncorrupted. As Chaplin has pointed out, this measure of identification was a condition of mutually intelligible conflict as well as of peaceful coexistence. The bow acted as what she terms "a historical marker" in this relationship.[23]

These circumstances may help to explain the continuing significance of the particular bow we are considering to its first white possessor— William Goodenough of Sudbury, Massachusetts, we are told—and to his successors, to whom it likely served as a signifier of their forebear's martial settler skills. What, though, of the specific conditions of acquisition by that first Englishman? A search of online genealogical databases and Alfred Sereno Hudson's monumental *History of Sudbury* (1889) reveals the presence in Sudbury, following its division from Watertown and its incorporation in 1639, of five siblings—three brothers and two sisters— named Goodnow. All had come from Wiltshire in England. The oldest was John (1595/96–1654). The middle brother, Edmund (1611–1688), was successively ensign, lieutenant, and captain of militia, and builder of the fortified house known as the Goodnow Garrison.[24] Thomas (1617– 1666), the youngest brother, was one of the Sudbury inhabitants who moved to Marlboro—a new plantation to the immediate southwest of Sudbury, incorporated in 1660.[25] There is no record of a William Goodenough, Goodnough, Goodenow, or Goodnow in such Sudbury records as I have been able to consult. Although tensions certainly existed, neither is there any record of any violence between colonists and Indians in either Sudbury or Marlboro in or around 1660. However, William Hubbard, one of the earliest to give an account of the later conflict known as King Philip's War (1675–1676), noted in 1677 that "Further also where it is said, p. 7. that the Indians had lived peaceably with the English here near forty years, ever since the Pequod Warr; it is to be understood with reference to publick acts of Hostility; for particular mischiefs have been committed by several Indians in some parts of the Country but the actors not abetted therein by any of their Country-men."[26] There may have been an isolated incident in or near Sudbury that led to the death of an Indian at the hands of a settler—one of the Goodnows—in or around 1660. In 1675–1676, things were very different. The New England colonies came under the most severe military threat they were ever to experience. The assault on Sudbury by at least 500 Nipmuc warriors in April 1676 led to great loss of life. In addition to the Indian dead, over thirty colonists, many of them members of a column sent from Boston, were killed. Might this have been the occasion of the capture of the bow? While not impossible, this is improbable, for by then most, if not all, belligerents had firearms. Indicative of a wider symbolic shift from bow to gun among Indians is the captive Mary Rowlandson's eyewitness account of a ritual that preceded the departure of a Nipmuc war party for Marlboro and Sudbury in which the participants used guns, not bows.[27] As we have seen, the inscription on the Peabody Museum bow is likely to express an orally transmitted tradition. Oral tradition often preserves true or plausible accounts, though in this case there is no corroborative evidence. Furthermore, there is much circumstantial evidence that casts doubt on the account given by the inscription. Consequently, the inscription is best taken as evidence of an enduring white, local—likely family—tradition exemplifying one aspect of the New England mythology of colonization.

Where does this leave the bow itself, independent of the inscription? We should not dismiss the logical possibility that it is not what it purports to be, whether as result of honest error or pious fraud. Relics—and this is a secular relic—are notoriously subject to fakery.[28] However, its status as a bow of New England Indian manufacture has never been doubted (to my knowledge), and there is no specific reason to do so now. I used it in the Sackler Museum to proclaim an uncompromising Algonquian presence, challenging the implicit claims to hegemony of the Western tradition. The bow was not present to suggest inclusiveness—it was present to remind viewers of the habitual want of acknowledgment of indigenous peoples and their values in American society.[29] It was, however, a complex presence, and was irreducible to a single meaning. In any given display of any given thing, a curator can only gesture toward a limited range of its characteristics, and the display of the bow is no exception. Cultural historians can, and should, make use of curatorial manipulations of material things to explore their contingencies and interrogate their immaterial, as well as their material, aspects. In doing so, they might take note of the consequences of the Ship of Theseus paradox: while things may perdure, they never stop changing.

NOTES

I should like to thank Peter N. Miller and the participants in the workshop, "Cultural Histories of the Material World," at the Bard Graduate Center, New York, in

January 2010. I also benefited from presenting a version of this paper at the colloquium "Materiality and Cultural Translation," at the Weatherhead Center for International Affairs, Harvard University, in May 2010. I should particularly like to thank the organizer, Ruth Phillips. I gave a joint presentation on the Sudbury bow at the Arthur M. Sackler Museum in December 2009 with Laurel Thatcher Ulrich, who, as always, generously supplied me with invaluable insights and information.

1. The Arthur M. Sackler Museum is a constituent, with the Fogg Art Museum and the Busch-Reisinger Museum, of what for many years was called the Harvard University Art Museums, renamed the Harvard Art Museum and renamed yet again in July 2010 the Harvard Art Museums.

2. Describing and discussing the bow in 1923, Saxton T. Pope referred to it as "King Philips's Bow" (alluding to the Wampanoag sachem also known as Metacom who led an Indian war of resistance to colonial settlers in 1675–1676), despite transcribing part of the attached label, including the date (1660) of its reputed capture: *Bows and Arrows* (Berkeley and Los Angeles: University of California Press, 1962), 34. Originally published as *A Study of Bows and Arrows* (University of California Publications in American Archaeology and Ethnology 13, 9, 1923).

3. Note in the Accessions Ledger, Peabody Museum of Archaeology and Ethnology, Harvard University, 95-20-10/49340.

4. I should like to acknowledge the generosity of the staff of the Peabody Museum, notably its then director, William Fash, who not only loaned one of the most celebrated objects in its collection, but removed it from display in the Hall of the American Indian.

5. Hans Belting, *Likeness and Presence: A History of the Image before the Era of Art*, trans. Edmund Jephcott (Chicago: University of Chicago Press, 1994), 55.

6. A useful recent discussion of the Problem of Material Constitution is offered by Christopher M. Brown, *Aquinas and the Ship of Theseus: Solving Puzzles about Material Objects* (London and New York: Continuum, 2005).

7. Particularly useful discussions include David Wiggins, *Sameness and Substance* (Cambridge, MA: Harvard University Press, 1980); and Randall R. Dipert, *Artifacts, Art Works, and Agency* (Philadelphia: Temple University Press, 1993), especially chapter 7, "Toward a Metaphysics of Artifacts: Individuation, Identity through Time, and Group Agency."

8. Arthur Hugh Clough, trans., *Plutarch's Lives* (New York: Dutton, 1910), I, 15.

9. Thomas Hobbes, *Elements of Philosophy, the First Section, Concerning Body* (London: Andrew Crocke, 1656), 99–101 (1st Latin edition, *De Corpore*, 1655, II, 11, 7).

10. See, in particular, Nelson Goodman, *Languages of Art: an Approach to a Theory of Symbols* (Indianapolis: Hackett, 1976); Arthur C. Danto, *The Transfiguration of the Commonplace: a Philosophy of Art* (Cambridge, MA: Harvard University Press, 1981).

11. See A. W. Eaton and Ivan Gaskell, "Do Subaltern Artifacts Belong in Art Museums?" in *The Ethics of Cultural Appropriation*, ed. James O. Young and Conrad Brunk (Oxford and Malden, MA: Wiley-Blackwell, 2009), 235–

67; also Ivan Gaskell, "Ethical Judgments in Museums," in *Art and Ethical Criticism*, ed. Garry L. Hagberg (Oxford and Malden, MA: Wiley-Blackwell, 2008), 229–42. Useful contributions to the discussion of cultural appropriation include Michael F. Brown, *Who Owns Native Culture?* (Cambridge, MA: Harvard University Press, 2003); and James O. Young, *Cultural Appropriation and the Arts* (Oxford and Malden, MA: Wiley-Blackwell, 2008).

12. Elizabeth Edwards, Chris Gosden, and Ruth Phillips, "Introduction," in *Sensible Objects: Colonialism, Museums and Material Culture*, ed. Elizabeth Edwards et al. (Oxford and New York: Berg, 2006), 19.

13. Saxton T. Pope went to the trouble of making a replica of the bow so as to be able to assess its functional characteristics. He reported a draw weight of 46 pounds, and a range with a flighted arrow of 173 yards, describing it as "soft and pleasant to shoot" (Pope, *Bows and Arrows*, 34).

14. This discussion is adapted from Ivan Gaskell "Encountering Pacific Art," *Journal of Museum Ethnography* 21 (2009): 202–10.

15. Unlike, for example, the Sainsbury Centre for the Visual Arts, University of East Anglia, Norwich, England, where sub-Saharan African, Oceanic, and other subaltern artworks are presented for formal comparison with works of European modernism (see A. W. Eaton and Ivan Gaskell, "Do Subaltern Artifacts Belong in Art Museums?").

16. Presenting a cultural artifact from a society other than one's own ideally entails consulting with representatives of any successor community with a direct interest in the artifact concerned, about its status and appropriate uses. My decision to emphasize hunting resulted from my discussions with Tobias Vanderhoop, tribal administrator of the Aquinnah Wampanoag Tribe, to whom I am grateful for insights and advice.

17. Thomas Harriot, *A briefe and true report of the new found land of Virginia* (Frankfurt, 1590), pl. III. For the John White drawing, see Kim Sloan, *A New World: England's First View of America* (London: British Museum Press, 2007), 120–21, cat. 13.

18. "The History of the Arms and Great Seal of the Commonwealth of Massachusetts." http://www.sec.state.ma.us/pre/presea/sealhis.htm.

19. Joyce Chaplin, *Subject Matter: Technology, the Body, and Science on the Anglo-American Frontier, 1500–1676* (Cambridge, MA: Harvard University Press, 2001), 80–115.

20. Patrick M. Malone, *The Skulking Way of War: Technology and Tactics among the New England Indians* (Lanham, New York, Oxford: Madison Books in cooperation with Plimoth Plantation, 1991), 32–36.

21. David Hackett Fischer, *Champlain's Dream* (New York: Simon & Schuster, 2008), 1–3, 268–70.

22. See Tony Kench, "Sir William Wood (1609–1691) and the Society of Finsbury Archers." Posted at the Web site of the Worshipful Company of Bowyers: http://www.bowyers.com/longbow/williamWood.html.

23. Joyce Chaplin, *Subject Matter*, 83, 101.

24. Alfred Sereno Hudson, *The History of Sudbury, Massachusetts, 1638–1889* (Boston: Town of Sudbury, 1889), 34.

25. Alfred Sereno Hudson, *The History of Sudbury, Massachusetts, 1638–1889*, 37.

26. William Hubbard, *A Narrative of the Troubles with the Indians in New-England, from the first planting thereof in the year 1607. to this present year 1677. But chiefly of the late Troubles in the last two years, 1675. and 1676.* (Boston: Published by Authority, 1677), "To the Reader."

27. Mary Rowlandson, *The Soveraignty & Goodness of God, Together, With the Faithfulness of His Promises Displayed; Being a Narrative of the Captivity and Restauration of Mrs. Mary Rowlandson* (Cambridge, MA: Printed by Samuel Green, 1682), 51–52; discussed by Jill Lepore, *The Name of War: King Philip's War and the Origins of American Identity* (New York: Knopf, 1998), 97–98.

28. Compare the so-called Penobscot War Bow in the Canadian Museum of Civilization (catalogue number III-K-84), Gatineau, Quebec, Canada, discussed by Gordon M. Day, "The Penobscot War Bow," *In Search of New England's Native Past: Selected Essays*, ed. Gordon M. Day, Michael K. Foster, and William Cowan (Amherst: University of Massachusetts Press, 1998), 14–159.

29. Regrettably, a comparison between the Arthur M. Sackler Museum display of the bow and other art museum displays that include North American indigenous works in conjunction with those of the colonizers, such as in the National Gallery of Canada, Ottawa, is beyond the scope of this chapter.

FIVE

Cultural Histories of the Material World: Whose Material World?

Sabine MacCormack

Let me begin with a story about my friend Inés. She was born in the Andean *puna*[1] high above the tree line, in an adobe house with a thatched roof. Her first language is Quechua, which she now teaches at the University of Notre Dame. Her second language is Spanish, learnt at secondary school. The school was three-days' walk away from where Inés was born. She walked there accompanied by her grandfather and by the llama that carried the food she would eat during the coming month or so—quinoa, freeze-dried potatoes, and dried maize. When periodically she returned home for holidays and to pick up more food, her grandfather asked her to write what she had learned on a rock with a charred, wooden twig. Quinoa and potatoes grow at high altitudes. After being harvested, potatoes are left exposed to frost over night, and during the day they unfreeze in the intense sunlight of the *puna*. Once unfrozen, family members dance on them to squeeze out the moisture, leave them outside for another night, dance on them again during the day, and repeat until they are completely dry. Now they are no longer called *papa*, (potatoes), but *chuñu*. Weighing little, *chuñu* is easily transported, and keeps for a long time—and you have to boil it for a long time too, to render it edible. To keep Inés in school, her family provided her food, sold some llamas to pay the school's fees, and in due course she earned a degree at the University of Cuzco.

Not long after Inés arrived at Notre Dame, she had an appointment on the thirteenth floor of a campus building. Entering the building, she could not find the stairs. In the vestibule, people kept emerging from a double door that opened all of a sudden, and other people entered that same double door which then closed behind them. Nothing else appeared to be happening. Rather than trying to ask in her beginner's English what was going on, Inés took her heart in her hands and followed someone into those doors. After the elevator had gone up and down a couple of times, with people leaving and entering, Inés, having observed that almost everyone pressed one of a row of buttons with a number on it decided to try that too, in due course arrived on the thirteenth floor and also returned to ground level, all without climbing the elusive stairs. Her sense of triumph telling the story was great. Inés knows how to pasture llamas and sheep, how to shear them and clean their fleeces, how to spin yarn and weave the intricate reversible patterns of traditional Andean cloth. She can raise quinoa, potatoes, maize, and other crops of the high Andes, and she used to watch the moon and the sun to see when these crops should be planted and harvested. Even in the United States, she has an uncanny ability to predict the weather.

How are we to contextualize and understand such divergent experiences of life in the material world, and do so historically? It would seem—at least at first sight—that current interest in identity, gender, class, status, and ideology all too often gets in the way. In a recent conference on the much discussed topic of Andeanness—"lo andino"—held in Cuzco, this elusive quality was examined as a myth, an identity, a possible obstacle to economic and political progress, as a marker of race or class, and more. The historical and ongoing cultural achievements of Andean people, among which their agricultural expertise must rank high,[2] were hardly mentioned in three days of conversations among some dozen participants, but the photograph of a pair of Andean women appears on the cover of the resulting publication titled *Vigencia de lo andino,* ("Norms of Andean life").[3] The book is representative of a considerable body of literature about Andean people in which agriculture and herding only figure on rare occasions. The same can be said of the principal Andean art forms, music, poetry, and weaving. There are, of course, reasons for this state of affairs. If there is such a quality as "lo andino," then we must allow for a great deal of regional variation that has profound historical roots, as any student of Andean textiles will know.[4] Besides, even remote rural communities like the one where Inés was born are not islands, hermetically sealed from the rest of the country. Schools, roads, electricity, water and sewerage and—above all—migration to the city, especially to Lima, have brought rapid and bewildering change. For migrants and their children, traditional agricultural, artisanal and artistic skills tend to become distant, if not irrelevant: they will not earn you a living in Lima,[5] just as the skills Inés acquired as a child will not—at least on the surface—help her to live in the material world we take for granted in the United States. This is not to say that a person cannot live—whether simultaneously or sequentially—in disconnected material, and even disconnected cognitive, worlds.

But what might be the cross-cultural understanding and epistemology that we can address to the skills, the skilled work that is involved in creating different material worlds, and also the skills and work of maintaining these worlds? For without skill and understanding the material worlds in which human beings live would never have come into existence. The search for such understanding is not new—it goes back at least as far as Greek and Roman didactic poems and manuals on nature in all its aspects, and on human work and artifacts,[6] among them the agricultural manuals by Cato the Elder, Varro, Columella, and Palladius and their medieval, early modern and modern descendants and successors— where we might even include the contemporary *Farmer's Almanac* as a distant heir. A concern expressed in several of these didactic works is that the knowledge and skill communicated in them is a *techne* or *ars*—a specialized expertise with its own rules and, above all, its own dignity.[7] This is why at the beginning of the *Ten Books on Architecture,* Vitruvius outlined for his patron, Emperor Augustus, the branches of knowledge thanks to which architecture was an autonomous art,[8] about which he himself was writing not as an observer, but with both practical and theoretical expertise, with what he described as his understanding of *fabrica,* practice or *opus,* work on the one hand, and *ratiocinatio,* the grounds of this understanding, on the other.[9] *Ratiocinatio* has been translated as "reasoning," and in Vitruvius's usage, it can also mean a mathematical calculation, and on occasion, it can also be translated as "epistemology."[10]

Like Vitruvius, so the Roman agricultural writers distinguished theory from practice, the theoretical understanding of astronomy, climate, seasons, soils, and the properties of plants and trees from the practical expertise of working a particular piece of land. For Cato the Elder, there was, in addition, a religious *ratiocinatio*—although he did not use this term—and for a religious practice, as he states several times, the farmer must maintain correct relationships with the divine presences of the countryside.[11] Even so, Cato's main purpose was not religious, but economic. He advocated farming because it was profitable and less risky than trying to become rich by trade; besides, farming made for good soldiers.[12] Profit also interested Varro and Columella, even though Columella was at pains to urge that agriculture be recognized as an art, and in pursuit of its elevated status as he perceived it, quoted regularly from Virgil's didactic poem, the *Georgics*. Despite their different aspirations, Cato, Varro, and Columella shared a general purpose: they addressed their treatises not to individuals who were working the land themselves, but to owners, and to some degree, also to managers of estates. Romans valued agriculture as an honorable profession, distinct from commerce and the artisanal trades, but this did not mean that one should labor on the land or raise livestock with one's own hands.[13] Notwithstanding Vitruvius's explicit interest not only in *ratiocinatio*, but also in *opus*, the same can perhaps be said of architecture—at least if we attend to the message of folio 13r of the late antique *Vergilius Vaticanus*, depicting the building of Dido's Carthage, where we see one architect and two over-seers supervising five workers.[14] The image invites us to conclude that Vitruvius wrote primarily for the architect and overseers—masters of *ratiocinatio*—and not so much for those who possessed the skills of stone masons and construction workers.

Perhaps, however, Palladius—who wrote his three treatises on ag-riculture, veterinary medicine, and grafting in the later fourth or fifth century—was thinking of a rather different relationship between skill and knowledge. For even if Palladius did not directly address those who worked on an estate, he did write for an owner who personally partici-pated in the running of his landed property. This, at any rate, is sug-gested by the arrangement of the agricultural treatise. Palladius had read Varro and Columella, and he used the latter extensively. But where the earlier writers arranged their treatises by the different crops that were to be grown, and different livestock to be raised, Palladius described the labors to be performed each month, beginning with January and end-ing with December. Less consistently, this approach had already been employed by Pliny the Elder, and of course, by Virgil in the *Georgics*. As for Palladius, he viewed the country estate from the inside, with the eyes of someone living there month by month and season by season. In addi-tion, like Vitruvius, he highlighted that he was not writing in an elevated style because his text had a vital practical dimension: people working the land, he observed, are not accustomed to making sense of difficult Latin.[15] This may help to explain the relatively sparse manuscript tradi-tion for Cato, Varro and Columella, while Palladius generated over 100 extant manuscripts, and several late medieval and early modern vernac-ular translations—including one into Spanish in 1385, which is at the same time the earliest agricultural treatise in that language.[16]

Popular though Palladius was, one writer who did not read him was the Andean historian Guaman Poma de Ayala, who in 1613 finished a long illustrated history of the Incas, and of Peru under the Spanish—the *Nueva Crónica y Buen Gobierno*. Nonetheless, as I try to show, Palladius and Guaman Poma are akin in outlook in that we do not find in their texts the distinction between *opus, fabrica,* and skill on the one hand, and *ratiocinatio,* epistemology on the other.

The *Nueva Crónica* contains two agricultural calendars—one Inca, and the other Spanish and Christian.[17] Guaman Poma derived the format of his agricultural calendars, both extending from January to December, from the ecclesiastical calendars that were published in his day as prefatory material in missals and breviaries. He appears also to have seen published ecclesiastical calendars with illustrations that in turn were derived from books of hours depicting the labors of the months. But his understanding of work and skill, and of the grounds for his own knowledge of organizing agricultural and pastoral work in the Andean environment is indigenous. Multiple reasons led Guaman Poma to include these calendars in his *Corónica,* including his desire to explain to his addressee—Philip III of Spain—that Inca had been preferable to Spanish governance, and more broadly, to explain Andean history and culture. Throughout his two calendars, Guaman Poma described what or ought to be, or was being, done as inseparably linked to how it was to be understood.[18] Like Palladius, he wrote from within the cognitive system and the concurrent conglomerate of skills that were his subject, accepting the inner coherence and validity of the conglomerate without question.

Put differently, the skills and knowledge—*opus* and *ratiocinatio,* as it were—of Andean people required no defense or explanation. Guaman Poma took the value of both for granted without seeing any need to distinguish between them. This is where his vantage point, his gaze, differs fundamentally from that of the contributors to *Vigencia de lo andino,* and from similar publications. Perhaps more important, Guaman Poma's gaze differed from that of most of his Spanish and Creole contemporaries, in whose estimation Andean people required instruction and supervision, just as centuries earlier, Cato, Varro, and Columella had believed that the workers—who, for the most part, were slaves—laboring on an estate had to be supervised by a manager. Skill, and the ability to perform the work, were separated from understanding the work in its wider context. Whether those who possessed the skill to do the work also possessed the *ratiocinatio,* the epistemology to contextualize the work did not matter.[19]

In such a perspective, it is possible to separate the activity of the body—that is, *fabricatio* or *opus,* from that of the mind and the soul, the locus of *ratiocinatio.* One might then say that Inés—the Quechua-speaking child of the *puna,* mistress of many skills—might not possess the *ratiocinatio* to put those skills in perspective. The falsity of such a view is demonstrated in a small way by Inés' experience of the elevator, and in a larger sense it is demonstrated by the ability of thousands of Andean migrants to live and survive in the city. That their experience would be more positive in an epistemological regime that does not separate skill and knowledge, *opus* and *ratiocinatio,* goes without saying.

Why is all this relevant to *Cultural Histories of the Material World?* As I indicated earlier, the diverse material worlds in which we live are unthinkable without the work, skill, and knowledge that perennially create, maintain, change, and also destroy them. I think our chances of conceptualizing and describing these material worlds would be greatly enhanced by joining *opus* and *ratiocinatio* into a continuous whole. How this can be accomplished will of course vary, depending on the culture or cultures in question, and on their time and space. But without the historical perspective to see the question we will certainly be unable to answer it.

NOTES

1. *Puna:* Quechua word for the highland plateaus of Peru and Bolivia.
2. This has been a perennial concern of John Murra: see, in particular, his *Formaciones económicas y políticas del mundo andino* (Lima: Instituto de Estudios Peruanos, 1975); and his *The Economic Organization of the Inca State* (Greenwich: JAI Press, 1980). See also, more recently, Peter Gose, *Deathly Waters and Hungry Mountains. Agrarian Ritual and Class Formation in an Andean Town* (Toronto: University of Toronto Press, 1994); Julia Meyerson, *'Tambo. Life in an Andean Village* (Austin: University of Texas Press, 1990); Paul Trawick, "The Moral Economy of Water: Equity and Antiquity in the Andean Commons," *American Anthropologist* 103, no. 2 (2001): 361–79.
3. Xavier Ricard Lanata, ed., *Vigencia de lo Andino en los albores del siglo XXI* (Cusco: Centro de Estudios Regionales Andinos Bartolomé de las Casas, 2005).
4. Elena Phipps, Johanna Hecht, and Cristina Esteras Martín, *The Colonial Andes. Tapestries and Silverwork 1530–1830* (New York: Metropolitan Museum of Art, 2004); Kevin Healy, *Llamas, Weavings and Organic Chocolate. Multicultural Grassroots Development in the Andes and Amazon of Bolivia* (Notre Dame: University of Notre Dame Press, 2001), 267–89, on ASUR, the weaving cooperative organized by Verónica Cereceda and Gabriel Martínez.

5. Karsteon Paerregaard, *Linking Separate Worlds. Urban Migrants and Rural Lives in Peru* (Oxford and New York: Berg, 1997).

6. Marco Formisano, *Tecnica e scrittura: Le letterature tecnico-scientifiche nello spazio letterario tardolatino* (Rome, 2001); Manfred Fuhrmann, *Das systematische Lehrbuch; ein Beitrag zur Geschichte der Wissenschaften in der Antike* (Göttingen: Vandenhoeck & Ruprecht, 1960).

7. The question as to whether household management is a *techne* or not is the first to be addressed by Xenophon in the *Oeconomicus.*

8. Vitruvius, *On Architecture*, 2 vols, trans. and ed. Frank Granger (Cambridge MA: Loeb Classical Library, 1955), I:1,18 de artis vero potestate.

9. Vitruvius *On Architecture* I:1,1 15.

10. For "reasoning" see the translation by Ingrid Rowland in Vitruvius, *Ten Books on Architecture*, ed. Ingrid D. Rowland and Thomas Noble Howe (Cambridge, Cambridge University Press 1999), I:1, 15; see also *Oxford Latin Dictionary* s.v. "ratiocinatio."

11. Georg Wissowa, *Religion und Kultus der Römer* (München: Beck, 1971 [1912], 37–38.

12. Marcus Porcius Cato, "Preface," in *On Agriculture*, ed. and trans. William Davis Hooper (Cambridge, MA: Loeb Classical Library, 1967).

13. See Silke Diederich, *Römische Argrarhandbücher zwischen Fachwissenschaft, Literatur und Ideologie* (Berlin: De Gruyter, 2007).

14. David H. Wright, *The Vatican Vergil. A Masterpiece of Late Antique Art* (Berkeley and Los Angeles: University of California Press, 1993), 21.

15. Palladius, *Opus Agriculturae. De veterinaria medicina. De Insitione*, ed. R. H. Rodgers (Teubner 1975), I:1 neque enim formator agricolaque debert artibus et eloquentiae rhetoris aemulari, quod a plerisque factum est, qui dum diserte locuntur rusticis, adsecuti sunt ut eorum doctrina nec a dissertissimis possit intellegi.

16. Palladius Rutilius Taurus Aemilianus, *Obra de Agricultura. Traducida y comentada en 1385 por Ferrer Sayol*, ed. Thomas M. Capuano (Madison, WI: Hispanic Seminary of Medieval Studies, 1990).

17. Felipe Guaman Poma de Ayala, *Nueva Crónica y buen gobierno*, 3 vols., ed. J. V. Murra, Rolena Adorno, and J. Urioste (Madrid Historia 16, 1987), I:235–59; III:1130–1167 (of Guaman Poma's numeration).

18. Sabine MacCormack, "Time, Space and Ritual Action: The Inka and Christian Calendars in Early Colonial Peru," in *Native Traditions in the Postconquest World*, ed. Elizabeth Hill Boone and Tom Cummins (Dumbarton Oaks 1998), 295–343.

19. See Laura Lee Downs, "Toward an Epistemology of Skill," in *Manufacturing Inequality. Gender Division in the French and British Metalworking Industries, 1914–1939* (Ithaca, NY: Cornell University Press, 1995), 79–118.

SIX

The History of Facebook

Daniel Miller

In the introduction to this volume, Peter N. Miller eloquently argues for three things: a respect for the culture of the hand, a respect for material culture, and a respect for cultural history. To contribute a chapter about a woman using Facebook in Trinidad[1] looks, at first, like some absurd misunderstanding that has gone topsy-turvy into the diametric opposite direction. In fact, however, the intention of this chapter is to be entirely supportive of the larger project. Because it seems of considerable importance to argue that these points are as important today with regard to contemporary culture as they ever were, and there are few things more emblematic of contemporary culture than Facebook.

In order to make that point, I would have to suggest that, contrary to what seems intuitively obvious—to regard Facebook as anything but the culture of the hand, or something that is material or historical—actually, Facebook is an entirely appropriate example of all three. Furthermore, there is a good deal at stake in this insistence. Recently, I contributed an essay to accompany a new exhibition cosponsored by the Victoria and Albert Museum and the British Craft Council called *The Power of Making*. It was a celebration of the material culture of the hand, but the objects that displayed were quite eclectic. They included ancient crafts such as stonewalling and leather working, as well as highly contemporary objects such as 3D printers, sculpture made from coat hangers, and dresses fabricated from cassette tape.

In my essay "The Power of Making," I argue that this exhibition lies in the core trajectory of the foundation of the V&A, which was originally called the Museum of Manufactures.[2] The intention was always to find a route between art and industry that avoided reduction to either. This also meant that the V&A would embrace the popular worlds of fashion, house ornaments, and hairdressing. One reason for retaining this path is that it celebrates the power of making as something in which everyone can participate; it resists the restriction of craft to elites or those designated as artists.

On what grounds can we defend the inclusion of Facebook as exemplary of these more hallowed traditions? Several of the objects in *The Power of Making,* including the aforementioned 3D printer, have been made with the aid of digital technologies. Given the rise of computer-aided design, it would actually be absurd to try and separate out design that was mediated by digital forms from all others. The digital is an integral part of the design world. Furthermore, it is widely accepted that this has led to an extraordinary democratization of creative work. Where previously the general public had been a relatively passive audience with regard to media, today almost everyone is involved in crafting websites, or YouTube videos, or iPod playlists. I use the word "craft" deliberately. These are things that are done well or done badly as attested to by our peers, and can command considerable skill and aesthetic imagination developed over years. In practice, the work of the hand always meant the work of the mind realized by the hand, and this remains true of digitally mediated communication.

We have got it equally wrong with the question of materiality. Most people take it for granted that the rise of digital technologies represents the demise materiality itself. Instead of physical books and CDs, we have a merely ephemeral or vestigial culture. But in a recent introduction to a book on digital anthropology, I have argued along with Heather Horst that an insistence on the materiality of the digital should be one of the six foundational principles of this subdiscipline.[3] Christopher Kelty's detailed account of the development of open source clearly illustrates how the ideal of freely creating new forms of code was constantly stymied by the materiality of code itself, since one line of development quickly becomes incompatible with another.[4] Matthew Kirschenbaum points out the huge gulf between metatheorists—who think of the digital as a new kind of ephemerality—and practitioners of computer forensics, whose job it is to extract data from old or broken hard discs, and who rely on the fact that it is actually quite difficult to physically erase digital information. As he notes, "computers are unique in the history of writing technologies in that they present a premeditated material environment built and engineered to propagate an illusion of immateriality."[5]

The study of cultural history generally implies a notion of depth in time—either events or processes unfolding over some substantial period. In this piece, I want to speculate about a different kind of cultural history—where something that is more-or-less contemporary, existing for a mere six years, can be considered an historical artifact. Given this shallow depth of time, the temptation is to concentrate only on this object as a new invention. The highly successful film *The Social Network* played to this assumption by focusing upon the personality of Mark Zuckerberg. By contrast, the kind of material culture fostered within anthropology would recognize that Facebook was just one of many such social-networking sites—including MySpace, Orkut, and Friendster—that might have become dominant, and were developed in quite different circumstances, and that to understand the site in terms of cultural history we need to turn from its inventor to its users. The success of these sites connects to much bigger forces concerned with the reemergence of forms of social relation that have been threatened by other aspects of modernity. I argue elsewhere that it is conservatism, rather than anything unprecedented, that accounts for Facebook's success.[6] But in our particular context, thinking about Facebook forces us to reexamine our sense of the possible relationship between time and the historical artifact.

For this reason, I am presenting Facebook from an entirely different perspective, in which Mark Zuckerberg does not appear except as a peripheral figure. Instead, I consider Facebook as an historical artifact from the perspective of a single user—a young woman named Nicole, who lives in Trinidad, and who is featured in my book *Tales from Facebook.* I have called her "The History Woman of Facebook," to reveal how a cultural artifact that is merely six years old may, nevertheless, be seen as historically and culturally significant.

It seems crazy to think of Facebook as some dusty archive, yet for Nicole, the Facebook she knew is already history. She talks wistfully, in a spirit of pure nostalgia, about someone named "Mark." Of course the "Mark" she refers to with such familiarity is Mark Zuckerberg, the founder of Facebook. Nicole has never met him, but she speaks with heartfelt enthusiasm about their time together. In 2004, Nicole was studying in the United States at one of the first colleges where Facebook became popular after its initial release from Harvard. Rather than being outwardly focused, it initially reinforced Nicole's intimate small college experience where everyone knew one other. Facebook was used to organize parties, meet for dinner, and exchange news. Nicole associated it with the enjoyment of her time as an undergraduate. This created an intense conservatism with respect to Facebook. She desperately hoped that Mark would not release his invention beyond the college environment, and that he would not make changes to the original format. Facebook was something she felt she owned, and that Mark in turn owed something to her and her fellow pioneers. She clearly relishes the time when, in Trinidad, she could look down on the MySpace brigades who simply did not know what she was talking about. She returned as John the Baptist—denounced such false prophets, and gave hints that the social-networking messiah had come down to earth and would eventually be revealed (though only to university students).

She still retains a level of scorn for the newbies of social networking. People today do not use Facebook—they defile it. She cannot bear to hear mention of games such as Mafia Wars. Her original Facebook friends all wanted to fly off when their fledgling swan turned into such an ugly duck. But, as she puts it, by that time, "We were so frigging addicted to Facebook, we were not going to get off it, so that's that." Far from it—she reckons that, until her child was born, she was on Facebook for only half her waking hours. It could have been more. It is still very rare that, on waking up, she reaches for her toothbrush before her keyboard. The problem is that Facebook is just too close to friendship. The more you put up, the more friends will comment. The more they comment, the more you feel you have to comment on them. You cannot withdraw without causing slight and offence. Over the years, they have given you so much comment and concern that you cannot just fold your cards when they are still up for the game.

Recently though, she has started to become uncomfortable with this ratcheting up of Facebook's place in people's lives to the extent that you have not been to a restaurant unless you have posted that you have been there. "The Twitter effect," as she calls it. For example, her friend Nafeisha was over the other day and had pulled some songs from a mutual friend's iTunes over the wireless connection. An hour later, she notes that Nafeisha has posted that she was "cooking up some tunes from the razorshop." And Nicole was thinking, cooking up what tunes? All she did was download some songs from a friend's hard drive. But then, for other people, this was "cooking up some tunes in the razorshop." Today, on Facebook, an individual must present oneself as a kind of cool-sounding, popular person to whom other people will respond. The temptation is to dismiss all this as some kind of mask or artifice that makes us more superficial. But Nicole knows both Facebook and people too well to be dismissive. She knows that Nafeisha would be doing much the same thing with or without Facebook. When did you ever see Nafeisha not doing everything in her power to look cool and sexy? Not only that, but you could spend all day crafting these postings intended to make yourself seductive and powerful, and still end up being seen by your peers as a pretentious fool. Given how easy it is to get things wrong, it was perhaps not such a bad way of being judged—cheaper than a new pair of shoes, and more authentic as a reflection of a person's labor and ability. Nicole sees all this, but still cannot help feeling that these games and performances have diminished Facebook itself. She still stalks her putative boyfriends' ex-girlfriends on Facebook, but even this feels wrong, not because it is stalking, but because in the "old days" people put up really interesting stuff about their likes and dislikes on the information page and now it is as though they cannot be bothered. So when she finally did reduce her commitment to Facebook, it is not certain that the birth of her son was entirely the cause.

Nor is it as if Facebook just had two phases: the pioneer phase, and the present. It continually changes, producing a succession of these betrayals of her commitment. Earlier on, "We clamoured and shook our fists at Mark for cheapening our elitist little circle." More recently, Nicole got into groups. She liked the way these might be scattered across the world: they brought all sorts of people together in a small virtual community. She would check out her groups every day. Her favorite was a group called "I stay up late and I don't do anything productive." She thought much of it was hilarious. But then someone hacked into it, and started posting racist and anti-Semitic material. Then gradually, people seemed to lose their commitment to groups in general, just when she felt they had become more worthwhile, not less. In this case, she could not blame Mark; it was the users who were fickle.

Although she spends so much time complaining about these changes, Nicole can still be an "early adopter" for developments she actually quite likes. She quickly took to window-shopping, if not actual shopping, on Facebook. Her favorite clothing store is a Facebook site that only advertises its stock online. She browses it regularly, and if she had the money she would buy from there. But with an infant to look after, this is out of the question. Still, whenever you see her, she can tell you what items she would buy if she could. Currently, it is a white corset top.

Nicole knew that she could easily become a Facebook history bore. No one was too interested in the old days, in the black-and-white snapshots of Facebook's time as a toddler network way back in 2004. But Nicole's historical relationship to Facebook took a perhaps even less expected turn. She really did turn it into a dusty archive. A couple of years ago, there was a difficult personal issue when she met a guy she had had a "thing" with some time before, and who had come back into her life. If she was going to reenter his orbit, she had to decide for herself what there was to learn from the earlier encounter. How much of it had been his fault, and how much of it hers? She knew that now she was a different person, which is what made it so difficult to determine. So she turned to Facebook. She patiently trawled backwards, turned the pages one by one, retracing every conversation and posting that documented this relationship all those years ago so that she could once reappraise what had been, and determine whether it was sensible to reengage with him in the present. This was a pretty laborious procedure, even when she isolated wall-to-wall postings. On the other hand, there was an unexpected dividend. What she unearthed was extremely funny. She felt she had been hilarious in those days, as was he. In response, she carefully copied all the best bits, "all those insane stupid things," from 2004 onward, and put them into a paper "novelty book" she could keep as a memory of who she had once been, and what she had been capable of in those times.

Nicole found other ways to deepen Facebook's relationship to the past well beyond its own relative youth. She used Facebook to get in touch with friends as far back as primary school—a formative time, full of sharp memories. As it happens, her parents had always been into recording and photographing and making films, so she has many pictures of those years. From these, she had created an album, posted it on Facebook, and tagged pretty much everyone that she remembered from school. There was a huge reaction. Everyone was pleasantly shocked: "they were all 'Oh My God, where did you get those pictures,' blah blah blah." After that, they really started to reestablish contact in a more intimate, serious kind of way. It was essentially a new set of friendships—based not on common experiences in the present, but on a shared past. It has produced a broader range of friendships than her contemporary circle in Trinidad. Nor have these remained solely online. There were invites to weddings she otherwise would definitely not have received.

Facebook transformed itself for her once more, when she fell in love. Indeed, it made her realize just how closely intertwined the very experience of love itself can be with Facebook. Ever since college, Facebook

had played a role in her various relationships. Students had seen it almost instantly as a helpful buffer against awkward or embarrassing situa-
tions. You did not really know whether you wanted to go out for a drink
with this guy, but in those days adding someone to Facebook felt natural,
a noncommittal mutual agreement to check each other out.

> I know someone for a while. So I speak to them. I saw them. I hadn't
> seen them in a while. I saw them at the gym. They said "Oh, add me
> to Facebook." We were talking about this charity thing. "So no prob-
> lem. I will add you" And so "oh your pics are amazing, do you want to
> go out for a drink" and this is on Facebook.

She was not one of those who approved of couples quarrelling publicly online; that was kind of horrible. Instead, she would put up a posting consisting of a song lyric about how she was feeling, but indirectly, so
that no one else would be able to interpret it. For example, she posted
the lyrics from a band called Paramour, "I put my faith in you. So much
faith in you. But you just threw it away." At the time, she was annoyed with
her boyfriend because she wanted him to go to a party, but not drink too
much. But he drank just as much anyway. He recognized the import of
the lyric, but no one else did. Why she needed the public domain of
Facebook to do this was less clear. She concludes that it must have been
cathartic, like writing a poem, but not using her own words. But then cathartic is the term she uses to explain Facebook postings more generally,
none of which prepared her for the role that Facebook would eventually
play in her falling in love.

She had known this guy forever. He was friends with her friends, and
moved on the periphery of her circles. There had been plenty of face-to-
face encounters, but always shallow ones, since she had come to a very
early conclusion that he was pompous. And that was the problem. Once
you decide, even as a teenager, to label a guy, then everything about him
gets sort of filtered through these categories, and you never have a reason to go beyond that. He almost certainly would have just stayed on the
periphery. But when she expanded her Facebook friends, he naturally
became a presence there, and, equally naturally, when she is bored she
tends to maco even the more distant Facebook friends.

> And then I realized this guy had a lot of stuff in common with me.
> So just one day I think I asked him if he went to see *Ironman* and
> we started to talk about comic books and stuff. From there on and

after that we started chatting all the time. [What other things did you find you had in common with him?] Um, taste in movies, um type of music uh, I think that was probably it. The movies and . . . oh and video games.

Typically, in Trinidad, people do not use Facebook as a key medium for more intimate courting. Things tend to migrate to a combination of texting and speaking by phone, as happened in this instance. But that does not mean that once it has shown people how much their tastes and opinions are aligned, and has brought them together, Facebook then fades out of the picture. Facebook has also become one of the most important expressions of her boyfriend's love for her. Nicole had never considered herself pretty, and for that reason tended to hate it when people took photos of her and posted them. But he has now taken some 400 photos of her, and tagged every one of them across Facebook. At first, as someone who almost entirely avoided public photographs, she was horrified. But she recognized this is an act of love; a love that is proud of itself, and proud of this wonderful creature that is its object. An act brimming with confidence that the whole world should see who it is he loves. Nicole also knows that this requires her to believe that he really does think she is pretty. And this confirmation that someone can see such beauty in her has started to change her own idea of what she looks like. Of course, her mother had said things like that, about how pretty she was, but that was just what mothers do. But her boyfriend has done this so systematically, so publicly, through Facebook itself, that she is almost beaten down by his truth which is now starting to become her truth. Perhaps she is, at least, sort of pretty.

While this is, by any standard, rather an extreme case, she has noted something parallel in the way some of her friends have become prominent online. She sort of expected that it would be the extroverts who would colonize Facebook—that the friends who were always in your face would be in your Facebook. But she also has a circle of friends from central Trinidad's East Indian community. Several of them were very shy, completely immersed within conservative family life—traditional and demure. Their parents tended to send them to the Presbyterian or convent schools—even though they were Hindus or Muslims—schools that maintained traditional values with respect to deportment and how women should behave in public. What Nicole finds curious is that, although several of these friends remain shy and retiring when you meet them, not just in front of men, but even with girlfriends such as Nicole, some of these same women have been extremely active on Facebook, constantly putting up material, nothing brazen or shocking, not acts of rebellion, but still extensive personal information, opinions, and commentary that give vastly more insight into what they are thinking (often quite surprising thoughts) than you would have ever encountered otherwise. On Facebook, they are not extroverted in the sense of performing or being silly, but they are easily a more dominant presence in Facebook than the extroverts from their real lives.

If those friends were posting more, then Nicole was posting a whole lot less than had ever been the case since that memorable year when her peer group had played midwife to the newly born Facebook. The problem was her own newly born baby. It wasn't just that she had less time to post; it was that she had less to post about. She knew that others had the diametrically opposite experience. She had friends who had barely posted in their Facebook lives, but, once they had a child, it was as though the entire world needed to know every single thing that baby did. If they could have broadcast the baby burping on Facebook, they probably would have. She had honestly not known whether she would become that kind of Facebook mother, but rather hoped she would not. She knew that this would not be under her control, that you never can tell what kind of mother you will turn out to be. If anything, things had gone in the other direction. At first, she thought she had some version of postnatal depression. As time passed, she rationalized her response to childbirth rather differently. She had always thought that babies were extremely boring. You just put stuff into them and cleared up the stuff that came out of them. It took a year or two before they had much personality. She had always felt this, but assumed that, as a mother, she would inevitably react differently to her own infant—but she had not. The fact that she found this stage pretty tedious did not mean she was less likely to bond fully with the personality this baby would no doubt develop over time. Instead, she was quite happy that being a mother did not leave her bereft of the powers of reason and observation that had always made her a top-notch student. She did not feel she would be any less emotional or less in love with her children in the long term. It was just that she was not particularly attached to changing diapers and being woken up several times a night.

If she was bored by what babies did in their first few months, there seemed no reason to bore the rest of the world with intimate details of babyhood. But there was a wider problem. It was not just that mothering was boring. Life in general was inevitably less interesting. A year earlier, when she was out partying, liming, and going to the beach, she would post constantly because there was much to post about. She had become one of those "I just did this"/"I am home now" people on Facebook, keeping everyone updated on every detail. Life had been fun and worth sharing, so if she was not posting now, it was largely because it no longer was.

But that had complicated consequences she had not really thought through in advance; Facebook was so much part of her previous life, and remained so much part of the life of her friends who did not have babies. What was the impact of Facebook on this divergence between her and her friends? Did it compound the problem? Not only unable to participate in their offline life, she was now unable to participate in the equally vibrant and important online life. Where Facebook might have compensated, was it now just too-evident testimony to what she no longer was? Although she had far fewer postings of her own, she had more time than ever to spend looking at all her friends' postings.

There is a bittersweet tinge to this activity. Facebook keeps her up-to-date with her friends. They remain part of her everyday life, as before. This was a huge part of what Facebook could do for you. On the other hand, it constantly reminded her of what she was not doing, could not be doing, and would have just loved to have been doing with them— the limes she is not taking part in, the parties she cannot go to. This has become a critical test of her relationship to Facebook. While her friends' style of posting has remained the same, these take on a completely new significance for her because of her changed circumstances. She has turned into a mother, and she cannot entirely fathom what is happening. She did not have a child in the pre-Facebook era, so she is unable to compare the two experiences. Overall, she thinks that, for all the pangs of missing out, Facebook has the benign effect of making her feel she has not completely lost touch. When the time comes, it will be much easier to rejoin that world, though that might not be true for others. She recognizes that she is probably more self-conscious about this than her peers. She remains hugely interested in Facebook, and not just in its impact on her life. She also sees her life as a kind of documentary about Facebook—what it is, and what it is constantly becoming.

Nicole is Facebook's history woman. For each phase of her life, she has had a completely different Facebook. There was the original identification with the Mark Zuckerberg enterprise. Then came the Facebook that found her love and changed her image of herself. Later, there were the compromises with Facebook as she became a mother. But if each phase has seen Facebook expressing a different woman with different concerns and needs, then Nicole's experiences have also revealed the degree to which, within a few years of its invention, Facebook itself has a significant history.

I hope that this substantive case fully confirms the assertions made in my introduction to this paper: that Facebook can be regarded as entirely eligible for a consideration of the culture of the hand, of material, and of cultural, history. As in all craft work, we see a constant tension between the creative aspirations of the user and the material constrains imposed by the structure that is dictated by Facebook as a company. But, as I would argue is the case of all true craft, there is a clear sense that the struggle with these constraints and the subsequent retained engagement with this creative process is what crafts the person, as well as their visual expression, on Facebook itself. We have every reason to respect this culture of the hand, the material, and the actually quite deep sense of history that already pertains to this particular craft. Its advantage as an example is that it ensures that the wider points made by this volume are as relevant for our understanding of contemporary material culture as for the past and for the entire population, not merely a fragment.

NOTES

1. The substantive section is taken from Daniel Miller, *Tales from Facebook* (Cambridge: Polity, 2011), 136–44.
2. Daniel Miller, "The Power of Making," in *Power of Making*, ed. Daniel Charny (London: V&A Publishing and the Crafts Council), 14–27.
3. Daniel Miller and Heather Horst, "The Digital and the Human," in *Digital Anthropology*, ed. Heather Horst and Daniel Miller (Oxford: Berg, 2012).
4. Christopher Kelty, *Two Bits: The Cultural Significance of Free Software* (Durham, NC: Duke University Press, 2009).
5. Matthew Kirschenbaum, *Mechanisms: New Media and the Forensic Imagination* (Cambridge, MA: MIT Press, 2008), 135.
6. See Daniel Miller, *Tales from Facebook*.

SEVEN

Dirty, Pretty Things:
On Archaeology and
Prehistoric Materialities

Lynn Meskell

Looking over the exciting new initiatives and publications devoted to objects of late, a central question remains unanswered for me: why has archaeology—the study of the human past through its material remains—been largely omitted from a new canon of materiality studies? In this new wave of writing you are more likely to find literary theorists, geographers, anthropologists, historians, and even classicists discussing the constitution of the object world and our human engagement with things, instead of archaeologists. This situation extends beyond a simple statement on the disciplinary standing of archaeology, the misplaced anxiety that theory in archaeology is derivative or weakly applied, or the now-outdated position that the past is generally irrelevant to contemporary issues. I would suggest that the omission of an archaeological contribution is more revealing about a broader scholarly reticence to engage with the messiness of things, their fundamental embeddedness, and their myriad historical residues and entanglements.

Currently, ruminations on the object are squarely focused on free-standing things—those unencumbered by complicated contexts and other substances. One need only think of some idiosyncratic case studies in *The Object Reader:* a rock, a pixel, a tricycle, a surfboard, a snow shaker, etc.[1] And this selectivity frees us to imagine the multiple meanings that radiate out from the object rather than the materials, subjects, things, and settings that coproduce it. The object in and of itself then is manifest as a salient set of representations and significations: it is the locus of histories, politics, personalities, and so on, that can be read off the artifact.[2] From this centripetal perspective the chosen thing resides at the center—it has primacy and is elevated to a new status, whereas its co-products and the matrices in which it is embedded are rendered secondary and supplemental. One example of this way of thinking is evinced by the popular theme of object biographies or the afterlives of objects beyond their initial crafting.[3] We make things—not just at the moment of creation, but over and over we layer histories of meaning onto objects. These dense genealogies can be traced and unpacked. Another strand of scholarship is that is that things make us—best highlighted by the anthropological concern with the project of self-making through things, explorations of identity, and constitutive material culture.[4] Other productive directions have, following Mauss,[5] successfully reimagined object agency further diluting the subject/object (or maker/made) bifurcation.[6] In some of these domains, archaeological evidence has been convincingly brought into play, however, most often this has been achieved with visually evocative, complex, historical data.

So I return to my opening question: why does archaeology not provide the stuff of materiality for a broader audience? Have we fallen short in our intellectual contribution, or have we actually succeeded in demystifying our objects so completely as to render them mundane? One thought is that archaeology is simply too gritty—that its focus on exposing contexts and spatiotemporal matrices, upon the material networks that surround objects, its literal and metaphorical embeddedness—is overwhelming. Contemporary archaeology has moved away from a purely, or purist, object-oriented approach, and concerns itself with multiple associations, layerings, scalar analyses, and specializations. For example, my own work on Neolithic figurines—once the domain of artistic descriptions and quasi-religious projections—is situated within a diachronic spatial analysis, clay sourcing, and manufacture, and similarly involves ascertaining the volumes of midden deposits, comparisons with the percentages of species in faunal assemblages, considerations of human body shape from isotopic data extracted from human bone, and so on. In archaeology, such chains of evidence and associations build a greater richness and understanding of things, but in doing so perhaps things lose their boundedness, their discrete qualities, and what makes them special or separate.

I see a great romance developing around things of late. Candlin and Guins epitomize the captivation and mystification people experience around all manner of objects such as "gifts, money, gadgets, toys, blankets, string, dildos, bird's nests, baskets," and so on.[7] Emotions and actions encircle these items, binding us to them, and their myriad social meanings are unpacked by a now-familiar set of luminaries including Mauss, Simmel, Barthes, Winnicott, Heidegger, and Latour. The London School of Material Culture has also made enormous strides in taking things seriously—specifically, the abundant stuff of modern life, in its banality and glory.[8] They take materiality as a set of cultural relationships that explore the constitution of the object world and its concomitant shaping of human experience. Significantly, many prominent scholars of material culture were initially trained as archaeologists, but have latterly come to eschew the discipline. Daniel Miller suggests that until now, there was "no academic discipline whose specific area of study would be artefacts, the object world created by humanity."[9] Archaeology seems easily elided from this revisionism. In Miller's recent account, the entire discipline of archaeology is cast as a parody of exoticism, lost civilizations, drunken expeditions coupled with an over-weaning love of pottery. His recent books present microethnographies of individual attachments to things, the centrality of stuff within modern life, and they also exemplify the scholarly turn to the social life of things and our own entanglements.[10] This is the very reason I began my own book on archaeological materiality with the qualification that this was not a book about coffee mugs, madeleines, wedding rings, or art works by Duchamp.[11] Archaeologists can offer different perspectives from the vantage of analyzing materials, contexts and associations—which is not to say better, but simply different, and it is a perspective that has some time depth of its own.[12]

The process of archaeology, both in its methodology and interpretation, reminds us of Hegel's discussion of the associative qualities of thinghood, but perhaps even more like Webb Keane's description of bundling. Archaeologists must necessarily operate within the framework of the assemblage, and we have the techniques to traverse archaeological science, materials analysis, and social theory. Ian Hodder argues that prior materiality studies simply focus on evocative things or object agency rather than probing the actual constitution of things, how people are entrapped by their material surroundings, trapped into maintaining them as they falter, fail, decay, and so on. He argues that most archaeological and anthropological accounts of materiality, material agency, or material cognition remain firmly human centered. From his experience working at Çatalhöyük he inverts this dominant view, suggesting instead that artifacts entrap people in long-term relationships of material investment, care, and maintenance so that, in fact, people became entangled and domesticated by things.[13] The examples he draws from Neolithic Çatalhöyük (ca. 7400–6000 BC) are as diverse as clay sourcing and brick making, early domestication of cereals, the development of pottery for cooking and the types of food that this afforded, and so on. An archaeological sensibility thus offers a certain methodological fetishism, to echo Appadurai.[14] It requires following the things themselves, starting from their constitution, rather than their significations. This is a point emphasized by Bill Brown, when he underlines the dominance of fetishizations of the subject, the image, and the word.[15]

I turn here to Hegel because, despite his lack of scientific grounding, he was one of the earliest thinkers to capture the multiplicity of the object, embedded within relational fields, and for his focus on composition as well as sensuousness. For Hegel, the object was a "thing with many properties," what he termed the mediated universal or thinghood.[16] Firmly situated in the here and now, thinghood constitutes a simple togetherness of a plurality, grounded in a material sensuousness. Hegel's famous example—and one I use often—is that of salt, and he unpacks this substance in a highly archaeological fashion. While salt, as a thing, is very present in material form it is, at the same time, manifold. It is simultaneously white, tart, and it is also cubical in shape: salt has a specific gravity, texture, and so on. Hegel's list of also's builds, and is cumulative, rather than reductive. Indeed, all these qualities or aspects of the thing are copresent: they are here, they interpenetrate, and none has a different "here" or presence than the other quality. Each and everywhere these aspects remain the same, united in the materiality of the thing, rather than being separate. In 1807, Hegel did not recognize that the chemical properties of substances might indeed have effects on a substance's shape, color, or gravity, but I do not believe this detracts from his fundamental ideas about copresence. All those "heres," as Hegel explains, do not affect each other in their interpenetration: whiteness does not affect cubical shape, nor does it affect the tart taste. Diverse attributes are thus held together, or fused, by the medium of thinghood.[17] Keane's notion of bundling also rests on the recognition of copresence, and that the necessary attribute is that embodiment that inescapably binds object qualities.[18] Both these perspectives seem to me very archeological in their approach, and offer us productive ways forward.

Prehistoric Materialities: Unearthing Çatalhöyük

What would a prehistoric materiality look like? If we take materiality to be the underlying philosophy of the material world that is operative in a particular cultural context, how would prehistory be different, if at all, from historic and contemporary settings? Moreover, what might it mean methodologically to examine materiality in deep prehistory? When there is no textuality, no leverage from written evidence, and no informants, might we indeed pay closer attention to the lifeworlds of things? We should not assume that this means less data or more license for imagination, but that we are inclined to be more archaeological in our approach, to reveal the layers, pay attention to the processes, trace the circulation, and discard and the multiple lives of objects within and across assemblages.

But is addressing prehistoric materiality more difficult, or just different? When I decided to work at the archaeological site of Çatalhöyük in central Turkey, several colleagues expressed a certain satisfaction that I would now experience the difficulties of writing social archaeology in a context without the texts, houses, tombs, and the elaborate social system of ancient Egypt.[19] Yet what Çatalhöyük lacks in its written sources, it more than makes up for in the richness of its contextual archaeology, the range and depth of repetitive practices across the settlement, and the complexity of retrieval of its myriad diverse evidentiary sources from the intensely micro to macro scales.[20] Social anthropologists working at the site like Webb Keane admit that they were drawn to this project because of the "fascinating evidentiary problems posed by archaeological work. In Çatalhöyük, the materials seem both rich and recalcitrant. It has been surprising to me." Keane goes on to state that it has been, nonetheless, "surprising to see how sophisticated the new technologies in archaeology have become."[21]

Çatalhöyük was identified by archaeologist James Mellaart in the 1950s, and became famous through his popular and scholarly publications from the 1960s excavations.[22] The site became known for its distinctive architecture, art and symbolism through Mellaart's evocative visual reconstructions and narratives. New excavations at Çatalhöyük directed by Ian Hodder began in 1993, and have challenged many of the sensational claims and associations marshaled previously.[23] However, the site still remains associated with controversial narratives of prehistoric matriarchy and mother-goddess worship.[24] Those ideas were forged around the discovery of clay and stone figurines from the site—specifically, corpulent female forms. Significantly, it is the zoomorphic figurines that predominate in the figurine assemblage rather than the anthropomorphic, and certainly more than any identifiable female examples. Because of that centrality and ubiquity, I want to think more carefully about the materiality of animal figurines.

Fig. 1. The Neolithic site of Çatalhöyük, 4040 Area. (Photo courtesy of the Çatalhöyük Project, Stanford University.)

Consider the six cattle figurines made of unfired clay that fell apart as soon as they are removed from their 9,000-year-old matrix of earth and domestic debris. Their makers intended that each of the figurines would represent wild cattle, yet they were hastily made and roughly shaped—albeit with careful delineation of the tail. At Çatalhöyük, heads and tails were deemed the most salient markers of animality across an array of media—from wall paintings, to figurines, to installations. All the figurines found in this one archaeological unit were broken in some way—some were stabbed or punctured, others malformed. They were ostensibly dumped alongside an assemblage of animal bones, potsherds, chipped stone, organic matter, and other debris to constitute the fill for a raised platform in the southwest corner of Building 49. At Çatalhöyük, platforms are constructed and repeatedly plastered white, and some-times they later become places of interment: they are built, then suc-cessively dug down into to place the dead. Some platforms thus become a site for human remains, but also sites of mixing with other artifacts, animal bones, house sweepings, and debris. Therein lies a window into the cultural history of the Neolithic material world. Its "natural" taxono-mies between people and things, or people and animals were radically

Fig. 2. Animal figurines from Building 49. (Author's photo.)

different to our own, yet were entirely sensible and legible within the Neolithic lifeworld.[25] It was one of embeddedness, connectivity between categories of things, blurring the living and the dead, and gritty, broken-down things.

Building 49 is small, but was lived in for a considerable period of time given the number of successive wall plaster applications and the number of people buried within the house walls. Carrie Nakamura and I have argued that this building seems to have a strong association with animals: not just those of a representational nature like the figurines, but with living animals. Within the building, fill excavators uncovered several cattle-horn cores, some of which were plastered to materially emulate their living or fleshed state, and a high proportion of sheep and goat bones. Wild cattle were immensely significant at Çatalhöyük: they dominated large painted murals, their skulls were plastered and painted, and their horns were installed on benches and pillars and emerged from house walls. The inhabitants of the settlement plastered cattle remains to re-vivify them to their lifelike state as their heads and horns protruded from surfaces, whether walls or floors, materially inserting their presence in human daily affairs.

In the makeup of this particular platform in Building 49, and mixed

Fig. 3. Animal figurines with associated finds. (Author's photo.)

with the six quadruped figurines, was an unusual assemblage of small mammals bones: at least three different species of birds, large amounts of eggshell and fish bone, as well as equid, pig, deer, and dog bones; small quantities of cattle bone, antler, some turtle shell; a hedgehog bone; three juvenile sheep, and at least one perinatal sheep/goat.[26] There were also concentrations of eggshell, and even three tiny caches of whole crushed eggs in the platform fill. Taken together, we might imagine that the occupants of the house were successfully engaged in hunting, herding, and gathering practices, but we might equally imagine that these material remains of animals—faunal and figural—were the stuff of magical manipulation or ritual activities. A powerful concern for material manipulation can be found in the figurines themselves.

Such figurines are not mere vehicles for social practices or significations, thus we cannot dismiss them as conduits or proxies. Following Keane, such things

> can never be reduced only to the status of evidence for something else, such as beliefs or other cognitive phenomena. As material things, they are enmeshed in causality, registered in and induced by their forms. As forms, they remain objects of experience. As objects,

Fig. 4. Building 77, horned pedestals around a platform. (Author's photo.)

they persist across contexts and beyond any particular intentions and projects. To these objects, people may respond in new ways . . . These materializations bear the marks of their temporality.[27]

While these quadrupeds were rather expediently made, their final deposition might indicate a concern for rather greater longevity, sealed within a platform and repeatedly plastered over. Despite their rapid manufacture they are easily recognizable as animal forms, and their makers emphasized the angular, fleshy forms of cattle, focusing on their torsos and distinctive tails, instead of legs or hoofs. The clay that was used to mold these pieces came from within 100 meters from the settlement: it was clean, largely inclusion free, and highly malleable. It has even been suggested that the reason for people settling at the site in the first place was its abundant and rich clay resources.[28] Recent work conducted by Louise Martin and myself suggests that Neolithic figurine makers modeled quadrupeds like deer and cattle primarily on the palm of their left

Fig. 5. Assemblage from Building 49, reassembled. (Photo courtesy of the Çatalhöyük Project, Stanford University.)

hand, evidenced by distinctive shaping marks corresponding to the palm and fingers. Some of these examples were never completed. Others were halted in progress and partly destroyed. Intentional puncture marks and deformation of the figurines were practices carried out while the clay was still plastic, and were left in that state rather than manipulated further or "finished" in a modern sense. Cutting or piercing of figurines might also indicate food sharing, partitioning of meat from the hunt, thus reflecting decision making about animal bodies. Animal figurines, like most of their anthropomorphic counterparts, were expediently made and inevitably discarded, rather than revered in burials, placed in niches, buried in caches, and so on, like other materials such as obsidian, ceramics, or ground stone.[29] Of the hundreds of examples of animal figurines excavated from Çatalhöyük, we can say that, after a complete spatial analysis, they were primarily found in middens and building fills, representing secondary deposition. It was the act of making that was significant, rather than some notion of a final product, since these figural objects were not fired like pottery and may never have been intended to endure.

The activities associated with Building 49 might appear to have been highly ritualized to modern eyes, yet it is important to remember that they form part of a suite of repetitive practices we see across the site for over a millennium, suggesting that figural practices were not radically set apart from everyday life. Given the many of hundreds of animal forms that we have uncovered, it is likely that figurine making was part of quotidian activities and constituted the everyday Neolithic materialities.

Fig. 6. Zoomorphic figurine, cut on the left side (identified by Louise Martin, 2010). (Photo courtesy of the Çatalhöyük Project, Stanford University.)

Representing and engaging with animals occupied a central role in the Çatalhöyük lifeworld and extended to social, economic, historical, and spiritual realms. But we can go further than this by using archaeological techniques to comment upon species specificity in particular arenas of social life. Employing the results of faunal analysis we can determine what type of animals were salient in different contexts, whether representational spheres, or in actual domestic consumption. Our evidence in fact demonstrates that wild cattle, like those represented by our six figurines, make up 54 percent of all faunal remains placed in installations and special deposits at the site. Wild cattle also dominate in the animal wall reliefs (46 percent), but surprisingly only constitute 15 percent of the animal remains that were consumed on site. So while they were highly prized in symbolic materializations, they comprised only a small proportion of the Neolithic diet. Contrast this with domesticated sheep, which make up 56 percent of the site's faunal remains, and thus the bulk of meat consumption for the people of Çatalhöyük. Yet as living animals, domesticated sheep were not considered symbolically salient in

Fig. 7. Plastered horns and bucranium from Building 52. (Author's photo.)

the elaboration of village houses. They only feature in 19 percent of the wall reliefs, and 13 percent of installations and deposits.[30] Tacking back and forth between objects and related data sets allows us some vantage on Neolithic thinking about materializing certain categories of things— wild cattle versus domestic sheep, clay versus plaster and paint.

The materials and properties just described characteristically form clusters with other phenomena, and thus are historical in character.[31] Animal imagery and figurines, the fascination with wild cattle, and the installation of plastered faunal elements, also shares a dense web of connections with anthropomorphic figurines, headless figurines, human skull removal and plastering, and other objects of material culture. These associations continue with considerable resilience over the centuries in domestic buildings, which were themselves repeatedly constructed one upon the other. At Çatalhöyük, I have suggested that the greatest parallels occur between humans and cattle in material traditions, since they occupy the most attention, are both shaped, modeled, painted, in both two- and three-dimensional media.[32] I have previously shown that an

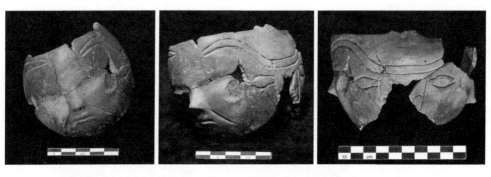

Fig. 8. Face pot combining human and cattle heads. (Photo courtesy of the Çatalhöyük Project, Stanford University.)

evocative materialization of this conceptual assemblage is encapsulated in one remarkable ceramic vessel. Inscribed on the surface, molded, and incised, human and cattle heads mutually constitute each other: the horns of the bull form the eyebrows of the human faces, while the human ears can also form those of the bull when the vessel is turned. In the past, archaeologists would have once typically classified this object as pottery, and considered this distinct from the taxonomies of figurines, plastered bucranium and faunal remains, human representations, and so on. Paying attention to prehistoric materiality, to the constitution of the Neolithic lifeworld, and tracing these material instantiations in fact sutures together objects and philosophies that might otherwise be perceived as separate.

Through this brief contribution I hope to have sketched some potentials inhering in the study of prehistoric materiality. By attending to things, by following them in an archaeological sense, the discipline of archaeology offers a different vantage on material histories and culture. For example, understanding the priorities of figurine makers enables an insight into indigenous taxonomies that transcend those that we moderns consider "natural."[33] While the material groundedness or embeddedness of things is central, so too is the very process of crafting the thing. In terms of figurines, their making and manipulating was an everyday performance that was as salient, if not more so, than the creation of end products. Indeed, it is difficult to trace exactly when the efficacy of some objects ceased for the inhabitants of Çatalhöyük. The group of animal figurines deposited under the platform in Building 49 may be exemplars of an extended object efficacy that continued even after their final deposition or discard. While scholars cannot always determine *a priori* the precise meaning or salience of things for individuals—whether in the deep past, or even in contemporary settings—in the case of Çatalhöyük, we can stitch together some strands of Neolithic practice, preoccupation, and preference. The complexity of archaeological contexts like Çatalhöyük reveals rich potentials for multilayered constitutions of the material world. Uncovering prehistoric materialities may indeed be different from art historical, anthropological, or cultural studies approaches to things, but they are no less theorized or sophisticated. We simply draw upon different bodies of evidence, interpolating a relational approach to things with the acknowledgement that our objects and substances are contextually embedded. That perspective, I would argue, has much to offer our current studies of materiality by seeking to go beyond individual things and more fully understand cultural histories of the material world.

NOTES

1. F. Candlin and R. Guins, eds., *The Object Reader* (New York: Routledge, 2009).

2. J. Baudrillard, *The System of Objects* (London: Verso, 1996).

3. C. Caple, *Objects: Reluctant Witnesses to the Past* (London: Routledge, 2006); C. Gosden and Y. Marshall, "The Cultural Biography of Objects," *World Archaeology: The Cultural Biography of Objects* 31 (1999): 169–78; J. Hoskins, *Biographical Objects: How Things Tell the Stories of People's Lives* (London and New York: Routledge, 1998); N. Thomas, *Entangled Objects: Exchange, Material Culture and Colonialism in the Pacific* (Cambridge, MA: Harvard University Press, 1991); S. Turkle, *Evocative Objects: Things We Think With* (Cambridge, MA: MIT Press, 2007).

4. T. Burke, *Lifebuoy Men, Lux Women: Commodification, Consumption, and Cleanliness in Modern Zimbabwe* (Durham, NC: Duke University Press, 1996); Hoskins, *Biographical Objects;* D. Miller, *A Theory of Shopping* (Ithaca, NY: Cornell University Press, 1998); D. Miller, ed., *Material Cultures: Why Some Things Matter* (Chicago: University of Chicago Press, 1998); D. Miller, *The Dialectics of Shopping* (Chicago: University of Chicago Press, 2001).

5. M. Mauss, *The Gift: The Form and Reason for Exchange in Archaic Societies* (New York: W. W. Norton, 1990); M. Mauss, *A General Theory of Magic* (London: Routledge, 2001).

6. A. Gell, *Art and Agency: An Anthropological Theory* (Oxford: Oxford University Press, 1998); C. Gosden, "What Do Objects Want?" *Journal of Archaeological Method and Theory* 12 (2005): 193–211; L. M. Meskell, *Object Worlds in Ancient Egypt: Material Biographies Past and Present* (London: Berg, 2004); L. M. Meskell, "Objects in the Mirror Appear Closer Than They Are," in *Material-*

ity, ed. D. Miller (Durham, NC: Duke University Press, 2005); D. Miller, ed., *Materiality* (Durham, NC: Duke University Press, 2005); P. Pels, "The Spirit of Matter: On Fetish, Rarity, Fact, and Fancy," in *Border Fetishisms: Material Objects in Unstable Places*, ed. P. Spyer (New York: Routledge, 1998), 91–121.

7. Candlin and Guins, *The Object Reader*, 1.

8. D. Miller, *The Comfort of Things* (Cambridge: Polity, 2008); D. Miller, *Stuff* (Cambridge: Polity, 2010).

9. Miller, *Stuff*, 2.

10. T. Ingold, "Materials against Materiality," *Archaeological Dialogues* 14 (2007): 1–16; T. Ingold, "Writing Texts, Reading Materials: A Response to My Critics," *Archaeological Dialogues* 14 (2007): 31–38.

11. Meskell, *Object Worlds in Ancient Egypt*.

12. Ingold, "Writing Texts, Reading Materials."

13. I. Hodder, "Human-Thing Entanglement: Towards an Integrated Archaeological Perspective," *Journal of the Royal Anthropological Institute* (2010).

14. A. Appadurai, "Introduction: Commodities and the Politics of Value," in *The Social Life of Things: Commodities in Cultural Perspective*, ed. A. Appadurai (Cambridge: Cambridge University Press, 1986), 3–63.

15. B. Brown, "Thing Theory," *Critical Inquiry* 28 (2001): 1–22.

16. G. W. F. Hegel, *Phenomenology of Spirit* (Oxford: Oxford University Press, 1977), 68.

17. Hegel, *Phenomenology of Spirit*, 69.

18. W. Keane, "Semiotics and the Social Analysis of Material Things," *Language and Communication* 23 (2003): 414.

19. L. M. Meskell, *Archaeologies of Social Life: Age, Sex, Class, Etc., in Ancient Egypt* (Oxford: Blackwell, 1999); L. M. Meskell, *Private Life in New Kingdom Egypt* (Princeton, NJ: Princeton University Press, 2002).

20. I. Hodder, ed., *Changing Materialities at Çatalhöyük: Reports from the 1995–99 Seasons* (Cambridge: McDonald Institute for Archaeological Research, 2005); I. Hodder, ed., *Inhabiting Çatalhöyük: Reports from the 1995–1999 Seasons* (Cambridge: McDonald Institute for Archaeological Research, 2005); I. Hodder, *The Leopard's Tale: Revealing the Mysteries of Çatalhöyük* (London: Thames and Hudson, 2006).

21. Quoted in I. Hodder, "Conclusions and Evaluation," in *Religion in the Emergence of Civilization: Çatalhöyük as a Case Study*, ed. I. Hodder (Cambridge: Cambridge University Press, 2010), 350.

22. J. Mellaart, "Excavations at Çatal Hüyük: First Preliminary Report, 1961," *Anatolian Studies* 12 (1962): 41–65; J. Mellaart, "Excavations at Çatal Hüyük: Second Preliminary Report, 1962," *Anatolian Studies* 13 (1963): 43–103; J. Mellaart, "Excavations at Çatal Hüyük: Third Preliminary Report, 1963," *Anatolian Studies* 14 (1964): 39–119; J. Mellaart, *Earliest Civilizations of the Near East* (London: Thames and Hudson, 1965); J. Mellaart, "Excavations at Çatal Hüyük, 1965: Fourth Preliminary Report," *Anatolian Studies* 16 (1966): 165–91; J. Mellaart, *Çatal Hüyük: A Neolithic Town in Anatolia* (London: Thames and Hudson, 1967); J. Mellaart, *The Neolithic of the Near East* (London: Thames and Hudson, 1975).

23. I. Hodder, ed., *On the Surface: Çatalhöyük 1993–1995* (Cambridge: McDonald

Institute, 1996); I. Hodder, ed., *Towards Reflexive Method in Archaeology: The Example at Çatalhöyük* (Cambridge: McDonald Institute for Archaeological Research, 2000); I. Hodder, "Peopling Çatalhöyük and Its Landscape," in *Inhabiting Çatalhöyük: Reports from the 1995–1999 Seasons,* ed. Hodder (Cambridge: McDonald Institute for Archaeological Research, 2005); I. Hodder, ed., *Changing Materialities at Çatalhöyük: Reports from the 1995–99 Seasons* (Cambridge: McDonald Institute for Archaeological Research, 2006); Hodder, *The Leopard's Tale.*

24. See C. Nakamura and L. M. Meskell, "Articulate Bodies: Forms and Figures at Çatalhöyük," *Journal of Archaeological Method and Theory* 16 (2009): 205–30.

25. I. Hodder and L. M. Meskell, "A 'Curious and Sometimes a Trifle Macabre Artistry': Some Aspects of Symbolism in Neolithic Turkey," *Current Anthropology* 52, no. 2 (2011): 235–63.

26. N. Russell, K. Pawlowska, and K. C. Twiss, with a contribution by E. Jenkins and R. Daly, "Animal Bone Report," in *Çatalhöyük 2004 Archive Report* (2004), http://www.catalhoyuk.com/archive_reports/2004/ar04_17.html: www.catalhoyuk.com.

27. W. Keane, "The Evidence of the Senses and the Materiality of Religion," *Journal of the Royal Anthropological Institute* 14 (2008): S124.

28. Hodder, *The Leopard's Tale.*

29. L. M. Meskell, C. Nakamura, R. King, and S. Farid, "Figured Lifeworlds and Depositional Practices at Çatalhöyük," *Cambridge Archaeological Journal* 18 (2008): 139–61.

30. N. Russell and S. Meece, "Animal Representations and Animal Remains at Çatalhöyük," in *Çatalhöyük Perspectives: Reports from the 1995–99 Seasons,* ed. I. Hodder (Cambridge: McDonald Institute for Archaeological Research, 2006), table 14.5.

31. Keane, "The Evidence of the Senses."

32. L. M. Meskell, "The Nature of the Beast: Curating Animals and Ancestors at Çatalhöyük," *World Archaeology* 40 (2008): 373–89.

33. M. Douglas, "Rightness of Categories," in *How Classification Works,* ed. Douglas and D. Hull (Edinburgh: Edinbugh University Press, 1992), 239–71; J. Dupré, *The Disorder of Things: Metaphysical Foundations of the Disunity of Science* (Cambridge, MA: Harvard University Press, 1993).

EIGHT

Archaeology and Design History: A Thesis and Nine Theses

Michael Shanks

Archaeologists research design and design history, but their work is rarely described this way. To understand archaeology's relationship with design, one should first lay aside those identifications of archaeology with methodology and technique, with survey and excavation, with work in the finds lab. Archaeologists do, of course, practice fieldwork and survey—popular representations of archaeology in the media emphasize excavation and discovery, and introductory texts are usually dominated by field and lab techniques—but research agendas in archaeology have always been driven by questions concerning the place of artifacts in history and in human culture. Archaeologists deal in the artifact traces of society, past and present.

In saying this I do not presume a particular notion of artifact, for the distinction between the natural and the artificial, for example, has always been contested in archaeology. Human biology and the environment are by no means self-evidently "natural" in archaeological perspectives on human history; they may be termed artifacts of a sort because they have always been mediated by cognition, perception, and ideology, and a radical distinction between culture and nature is only of local relevance. The classificatory schemes of natural history and principles of evolution and natural selection have also frequently been taken to apply to technology and goods. The human body, as much as domesticated plants and animals, is an artifact as well as biological form, and systems of categories for organizing the perception of the natural world are objects of design. I am also careful to use the term "trace." Ruins and remains are the stuff of archaeological interest, but it is important to recognize that this should not imply the primacy of social relations and cultural forms over some kind of material expression such as an artifact or monument, as implied by the notion of "remains," or what is materially left of society in the wake of historical change.

Archaeological research occurs at the hinge between materiality and immateriality, culture and artifacts, people and things. I argue that archaeology has a unique perspective to offer design history and design studies because of its long-term and comparative perspective on these relationships, with archaeological sources being our sole access to most of the 120,000 years or so history of our species. Specifically, I argue that any resolution of distinction between person and thing, natural and artificial, material and immateriality is local and historically contingent, and none the less real for this. Two slogans capture much of this: we have always been cyborgs, and making things makes people.

Person and thing, materiality and immateriality: the focus on these relationships places archaeology firmly in the context of modernity's relationship with goods and references familiar tensions between cultural values and material forms, the humanities and sciences, between technology and the aesthetic, reason and the emotions. My argument is that archaeology is a recent and particular manifestation of the relationship between people and the life of things. Elsewhere,[1] I have outlined the character of this modern archaeological sensibility that includes a sensitivity to the material passing of self and other, ruin and loss, processes of entropy and decay, the piecing together of traces. The past in the present is the prime component, for example, of the heritage industry, part of the largest economic sector in the global economy today—cultural tourism, as the remains of the past are conserved and offered up for local and global consumption in the politics of personal and local, ethnic and national, identity. My case here is that archaeologists do not discover the past, even as they excavate some "lost" civilization. It is far simpler: archaeologists work on traces of the past. This productive and even creative labor, this poetics connects archaeology with all kinds of memory practice and makes of all of us an archaeologist of sorts. The argument also involves a reflexive symmetry between past and present. Motivated by an interest in the translations between people and things, between material and immaterial goods, archaeologists track and model the dynamics of social and cultural change. In this they study the history of design, but also—in excavation and survey, in making models, forging analyses, offering interpretations, and constructing narratives—archaeologists make the past what it is for us today. Indeed, the main professional sector in archaeology is commonly termed cultural resource management. As much as the study of the history of design, conceived as interactions between people and material goods, archaeologists are in the business of designing contemporary culture. This archaeological sensibility is, I suggest, a conspicuous component of contemporary culture and so of the design of goods and systems, but I will not say much of it in this chapter. I think the broader implications of the theoretical apparatus I present for archaeological understanding of design will suffice to emphasize the indissolubility of history and design practice.

I have started to use the word "design" now in an archaeological context. I am less interested in tightly defining a concept of design than in recognizing that the word has considerable contemporary currency. For me, design is best treated as a diverse and contested field with a ramified genealogy and sometimes contradictory, but cognate, components. This is evident in the debates in archaeology that are outlined in this chapter. It connects with the multidisciplinary, indeed transdisciplinary, application of the term: from God's intelligent design to Giorgio Armani, from architecture to cybernetics, objects to intangible experiences. Nevertheless, let me start by saying that, for me, design refers to processes of originating, conceptualizing, and manufacturing a product or system—material or immaterial. In archaeology, simply because of the character of its material sources—the remains of society, but also for strong analytical reasons regarding the nature of cultural systems, these processes are inseparable from the distribution, consumption, discard, or abandonment of the product or system, and its subsequent decay. Subsumed are matters of individual agency and intentionality—what people want to achieve with the outcomes of their making, and how making things is at the heart of the reproduction of society. As an anthropological field, archaeology has always set design, so conceived, in the context of human ecology and culture, social and cultural change. I draw on a key archaeological concept of assemblage in connecting the understanding of design with a methodology that traces connections through fields of relations, as well as scrutinizes the features and qualities of an artifact.

Nine Archaeological Theses on Design

Let me present nine theses that summarize some key trends in archaeological research into design. This is not a statement of any current orthodoxy in the discipline; it is my personal assessment.

One: The Fallacy of Expression

Does an artifact express its maker's intentions or the context of its origin? I argue it does not, or often does so only minimally. Things are not well explained by referring them to some outside agency or force, such as an artist's will or economic necessity. While there may indeed be strong connections between maker and artifact, artifact and contexts of manufacture and use, these are not well understood as relationships of expression because this subordinates materiality to the will of a maker or the strength of social structure, immediately begging, but leaving unanswered, questions of the nature of raw materiality, of mediation, of the force behind the expression, of what drives the imposition of form upon raw matter, of how things get made. In my work in the design of the ancient Corinthain aryballos (perfume jar), I proposed that it is very reductive to argue that such pots were expressing social structure, or that they were representing Greek myth or an appropriation of Eastern design, even though there are connections with the organization of society, with narrative and Eastern iconography.

Anthropologist Marc Bloch gives an illustration of this point from his fieldwork in Madagascar. Topic: the meaning of architectural decoration. Asked what was the significance of a carving he was cutting into the structural beam of a house, the carpenter replied that it had no meaning; it was just what was proper to carve. A weak thesis here is that the carver was simply not aware of the signification of his work, or could not put it into words (though he did not see the point of trying). In contrast, the work of the anthropologist is sometimes seen as one of establishing what aspects of person and society are expressed in material culture. A strong thesis is that it may not be appropriate to look for this kind of expression, but that the significance of artifacts is better sought in the processes of their making (thesis five).

Two: The Fallacy of Context

To understand an artifact's design it is crucial to look beyond the thing itself. But how is this context to be characterized? If we predefine "context" as involving components such as economic relations, raw material extraction, cultural values, and political ideologies, we invoke two problems. First, we assume the essential character of context, that it involves components such as these listed, and we risk overlooking heterogeneity. Second, this establishes, *a priori*, separation of the artifact from its context— something that interpretation and explanation then have to overcome.

Better, I suggest, is not to begin with a separation of artifact from its life cycle of origination, manufacture, distribution, consumption, conventional conceived as context, but to begin *in medias res*, with a specific artifact in specific practices and processes (thesis five). The context of an artifact is better identified by studying how the artifact worked, how a monument, for example, was built and used, and how it related to other aspects of contemporary experience. I call this an heretical empirics, because it does not assume certain categories that organize society and experience, but looks to define such categories in the process of empirical investigation, and so to generate potentially unorthodox and heterodox characterizations of an artifact (theses six and seven).

Three: The Fallacy of Invention

Many approaches to understanding the design of an artifact give primacy to origin and invention, and seek to understand how and why certain inventions occurred. But it is increasingly clear that invention is by no means an uncommon phenomenon. All the basic components of the farming of managed domesticated species, for example, existed for millennia before the widespread adoption of agriculture in several independent parts of the world. The long-term background of the history of design is one of constant human creativity and innovation. I suggest that invention be distinguished from innovation, and that the key question is not what led to an invention—a question of origin—but rather what prompted the adoption of certain assemblages of artifacts and practices: this is a question of genealogy (thesis eight). A corollary that applies in much of human history is that tradition and cultural stability is an active state of hindering adoption of new designs and solutions. Social structure, values, and norms are the medium, and simultaneously, the outcome of practice. People make their world what it is, but under inherited conditions not of their own choosing. This means that every social act is an iterative and creative one of reconstituting the past in forms that enable future practices.

Four: We Have Always Been Cyborgs

This is rooted in the argument and evidence for the coevolution of culture and biology, that for as long as we have been our human species, and probably before that, (material) culture and biology have been part of the same evolutionary process. Given also the duality of structure, the way an action such as making is distributed through sociocultural structures, past and future, people have always been embroiled in mixtures of material and immaterial forms and systems. With respect, therefore, to both people and things, we should adopt a relational, distributed ontology. Connections, internal relations, make an artifact or person what they are; we find ourselves in others. People have always been prosthetic beings, sharing their agency with others, with things and processes beyond them. We have always been cyborgs—hybrid beings, human-machines.

Five: Making Things Makes People

I propose that understanding the design of an artifact is best done by looking at processes, uses, techniques, and performances, rather than treating the artifact primarily as a discrete bundle of attributes or qualities. Under this distributed ontology, in these networks of connections, these hybrid forms that incorporate both people and things, materialities and immaterialities, values and intangibles, we do well to look at what work is being done. It is useful to think of these assemblages as machines, with the definition of a machine as an interconnected set of resistant parts and functions, of whatever nature, that performs work.

Designing and making is thus much more than simply producing a discrete form. Under the principle of the duality of structure, designing and making are enabled by the preexisting structures, values, forms, expectations, knowledge, and resources available to the maker, and, simultaneously, design and making reconfigure the same into machinic articulations, reweaving the threads of the social fabric. Given also that people are both biological and cultural beings that live in societies, making things makes people what they are.

This is illustrated by a project I ran with DaimlerChrysler, aimed at plotting the future of the use of vehicles, particularly involving media, over the next ten years. The marketing departments of the corporate world are used to understanding products in terms of demographic groups, with particular products appealing to groups defined according to class, income, ethnicity, and region. My lab's research pointed to a different kind of relationship that can be summarized as follows: it is not who you are that makes you want a Dodge pickup truck; using the Dodge makes you who you are.

Six: The Artifact As Scenario

An artifact is so much more than a list of defining attributes. Think less of discrete things, and more of the thing as a gathering, forging heterogeneous connections in its making and use. I call these heterogeneous because all kinds of different things and experiences might be connected: consider again my two examples and how they brought together what appear to us now to be extraordinary associations of know-how and ideologies, past and present. Again, given the duality of structure, we can treat these gatherings as scenarios: models or outlines of contexts, and sequences of possible events. Every act of design and making relates to constraints and possibilities, sketching utopias, and containing the possibility of unimagined and unwanted consequences.

Is Fussell's Lodge a prehistoric earthen long barrow? Yes, but it is also so much more. It acted as a node of articulation—gathering all kinds of practices and experiences, real and imagined, past and future. The monument's attributes are only the beginning of its story.

Seven: The Heterogeneity of Value

Any artifact is an irreducible multiplicity. Some of this is captured in the notion of the total social fact. What an artifact is depends upon how we trace the connections that run through its origination, manufacture, distribution, use, and discard.

Value is a key component of any understanding of design. It is implicit in all choices made in this life cycle: one material or manufacturing process over another, the value of one ancient Greek perfume jar assessed against another by the visitor to a sanctuary. With a perspective of design and artifacts as dispersed and heterogeneous, systems of value or worth are similarly heterogeneous. The value of one aryballos over another intended for gift to divinity depended upon a local assessment of the fit of one aryballos over another.

This is something different from saying that such systems of value are culturally relative and so incomparable. It means we should look to specific contexts of use, technique, performance, and engagement to understand how makers and users assess worth, and how we, as design researchers, may assess the worth of a particular design solution. These may well be comparable across different times and cultures.

Eight: Temporal Topology

Seeking origins and invention in an attempt to understand the design of an artifact implies a linear chronology of discovery and adoption. Viewing design as process and assemblage implies a complementary folded temporality—a topology that can juxtapose old and new with the pros-pect of yet-unrealized futures. An aryballos contained age-old technolo-gies and techniques, forms and iconographies reworked into a radically new assemblage fit to the emerging city states of the Mediterranean. The temporality of an aryballos is thus multiple, including, yes, its date of manufacture and consumption, but also the genealogy of its constituent components. These topological foldings of time can be highly significant in some experiences: for example, in urban planning, where a walk down a street can be a percolating ferment of past traces and remains tied to material embodiments of utopian futures. Landscapes, as built environ-ments, can be similarly rich examples of juxtaposition of ancient features, routes and ways, place-names of forgotten origin, recent plantings that may last only a season, building projects intended to last a millennium.

Understanding the temporality of an artifact can be likened to trac-ing a genealogy in that the present, the state of an artifact, is unthink-able without an ancestral past of multiple lineages. But these relation-ships imply no teleology of necessity, no necessary or unavoidable line of descent from past to present, no necessary coherent narrative, because each generation reworks its past and can, in its historical agency, change direction.

Nine: The Unspoken Life of Things and the Noise of Life

If we look at processes as well as discrete objects, we can be led into a myriad of connections and trajectories. In the heterogeneous network-ing that is the engineering of a thing, there is no end to ramification. An artifact disperses through its scenarios, networks, and genealogies of origination, manufacture, distribution, use, and discard.

Interpretation, as rearticulation, can track certain affiliations or lines of connection, as I sketched with the aryballos. There is always more that remains unsaid, unacknowledged, unseen, because interpretation may not go down a particular track. This is so evident in archaeological fieldwork, or indeed in any scientific research, where there is always a choice to be made of what matters to the research interest. What is left behind, ignored, or discarded is the background noise of history and experience. This is far from inconsequential. First, because something important may have been overlooked: science constantly takes a second look at things and finds something that was missed. Second, because things stand out as significant against this background; without it, there could be no story, no message, no understanding. Third, because this is the noise of the ambient everyday work that makes society what it is—it is the noise of the life of things constantly reweaving our social fabric.

NOTE

1. Michael Shanks, *The Archaeological Imagination* (Walnut Creek, CA: Left Coast Press).

PART 3

Experience and Material

NINE

Swelling Toads, Translation, and the Paradox of the Concrete

Bernard L. Herman

"Toads? We'll have a ton!"

> —Kelli Gaskill, Big's Family Restaurant, Painter vic.,
> Virginia (January 2010)

"since feeling is first
who pays attention
to the syntax of things
will never wholly kiss you . . ."

> —e. e. cummings

The charge that lies at the heart of our enterprise contends, "Historically oriented scholars are finding in the physical embodiments of knowledge new questions and new perspectives from which to address seemingly 'closed,' or at least familiar, issues." Materiality, embodiment, epistemology. Even as we embrace the simultaneity of things as subject and object, as the medium for interrogation and its focus, we curiously tend to accept with little comment the concrete nature of things. And yet it is the graspable substance of things that fascinates us. Things (and by this I intend the grand universe of objects and their evocations) furnish and shape experience even as they are shaped by perception, imagination, and engagement. Writing on how objects operate in the world tends to reductions around design, making, use, and waste. From the outset, then, any exploration into "the physical embodiments of knowledge" is necessarily about writing (a thing in itself), and what happens when things are rendered as words.

Francis Ponge begins his 1941–1944 meditation on the carnation, "Accept the challenge things offer to language." Ponge continues, "Given an object, however ordinary, it seems to me that it invariably presents certain unique qualities which, if clearly and simply expressed, would elicit unanimous and invariable comment . . . What's to be gained from this? To bring to life for the human spirit qualities, which are not beyond its *capacity* and which habit alone prevents it from adopting."[1] Ponge speaks to a poetical instability of things. His prose poem *Soap,* for example, returns again and again to the observation that soap is known finally through water and laving hands—substance and action that leave the object realized and reduced in one sense, and transformative through the physical communication of itself in another.[2]

There is a tendency to embrace the artifact as, well, fact—and to situate the object in tension with or subordinate to an uncontested notion of text. My contribution to this conversation explores first the problem of translation—of how language informs materiality—and second, the paradox of the concrete through a consideration of the ambiguities inherent in things, the questions things enable, of how objects compel us to see beyond the force of habit and convention, and how we might resist the temptation to relegate the materiality of things to the role of illustration. Simply, how we talk about objects all too often constructs the framework that defines and limits how we know them as things. The ownership of the authoritative voice resides at the heart of interpretation. When we actively seek multivocality, however, the object opens itself in ways that invite fresh considerations of what have been described as "object worlds."[3]

Objects are haunted by the paradox of the concrete. Objects possess substance—real and perceived—and substance carries with it the power of certainty. The material qualities of things are somehow reassuring in the ways through which they engage us. The concrete qualities of things speak to embodied experience through sight, sound, touch, smell, and taste. Things possess the aura of heft, of manifesting themselves not as abstractions, but as tangible and real. Their paradox resides in the uncertain relationship between what things are and what things mean. The paradox of the concrete inspired the concrete poetry movement of the 1950s. In concrete poetry (also referred to as visual language), the emphasis falls on the material aspects of writing, drawing attention to the appearance of words and letters (typography) and their positioning on the page, rather than solely on their meaning content. Concrete poetry "abandons the linear arrangement of words for a greater emphasis on design, layout, and organization of space" in which "words point beyond themselves to ideas, to mood/memory experience, extending the way in which language can be used to communicate—to produce an experience" through the viewer's "direct confrontation with the poem."[4] Two fundamental acts define concrete poetry: first, the act of emptying words of their assigned meanings or content and viewing them as objects or images in their own right; second, rendering the word as thing open to reinscription through design, visualization, and viewing. Thus, a concrete poem is "a 'minimal' art of maximal involvement" composed of "compound elements, each clearly articulated & with plenty of room for fill-in" by the reader.[5] The larger implications concrete poetry holds for the material turn are significant. Concrete poetry reminds us that objects—including words—possess an existence independent of their reified meanings, and that periodically the object needs to be emptied of its assigned meanings and read anew for its material presence. In essence, the material certainty of the thing as an object, epitomized by the example of the concrete poem, is offset by the inconstancy and ambiguity of what objects might mean. This paradox of the concrete—the interplay of material certainty and semiotic ambiguity—constitutes what we might think of as the first iteration of a material turn. The second iteration revolves around the question of translation.

Translation is an act of rendering something (word, image, action, thing) accessible in terms that are familiar and comprehensible. To render, like most useful words, is one of many meanings. To render is about giving up and giving in—an act of surrender carrying implications of duress. To render is to cook down to an essence that is at once a reduction and distillation, for instance cooking fat to yield oil. To render is to represent and approximate through expressive means—a modeling that can be literary, visual, performative. To render is to plaster, to cover one surface with another in an action that masks, protects, and unifies. When objects are brought into view, all of these renderings come into play. Translation also entails the belief that what is foreign can be made familiar, and the recognition that the process of translation is always incomplete in its inability to fully communicate nuance and idiom. Thus, the material turn embraces the ambition of translation as the means to render things comprehensible in words. At the same time, the material turn accepts the incompleteness of translation in that endeavor. The problem is not that translation fails in its directive, but rather falls short in accounting for its limitations. At some juncture, the material turn needs to engage the substance of things beyond the words that make things visible. The material turn, quite simply, owes a responsibility to the objects it engages beyond the limitations of words. What that responsibility, inevitably constrained by language, might be remains limited by convention. Thus, the first act of translation in a material turn is not just to make the alien familiar, but also to render the familiar strange.

The material turn I choose is a fish—specifically, the swelling toad or northern puffer [*Spheroides maculates* of the family *Tetraodontidae*] (fig. 1). The voices I engage include the fisherman, the marine biologist, the cook, the gourmand, and the student of things. The choice of swelling toads (known by many names including puffers, blowfish, green-eyes, sea squab, and simply, toads) resides in a critical conversation about what constitutes an artifact and the limits of description. The definition of an artifact is straightforward enough: any thing—real or imagined—that enters human perception and inescapably becomes subject to the necessity of making and communicating sense of and in the world. The limits of description speak directly to the fact that encounters with things engage all the senses, but that our representations of their materiality are mediated and constrained through approaches that privilege sight (image and text) and hearing. Taste, touch, smell, and proprioception are reprised, for example, through synaesthetic acts that let the visual and verbal stand for the tactile or spatial.

In an effort to get at the nature of things and the operations and limits of description in sense making, the Bard Graduate Center organized in 2009 a "materials day" around fish from their acquisition at the New Fulton Fish Market through their preparation and consumption. The concept behind materials day affords "opportunities for students to observe and participate in the making of things in order to experience materiality from a maker's perspective." Our tasks for a materials day based on what we titled "the fish project" were several: to grasp the object in ways that engaged all the senses; to comprehend at the most visceral level the ways in which we transform and make sense of things as creature, commodity, ingredient, food, waste, and memory; to expose the limits and possibilities of representation, particularly in relationship to new media. The goal was to explore strategies for interpretation and representation within a range of epistemological registers, each defined as a "social space characterized by a system of norms, conventions, and procedures." Each register—biological, culinary, ethnographic, artistic, historical—possesses its own expressive conventions of formality, vocabulary, and syntax.[6] Thus, our goal was "to get at the inherent paradox of objects: the concrete qualities of things in full array and their constantly evolving situational and semiotic significances" and to explore categories of how we know things.[7]

Fig. 1. Swelling toads gleaned from crab pots. Bayford Oyster House, Bayford, Virginia, August 2009. (Photograph: Bernard L. Herman.)

Project participants prepared by conducting research on topics that ranged from recipes to the patent histories of objects related to seafood processing. The critical pivot of our endeavor, however, unfolded in a rain-drenched, predawn November visit to the fish market (reportedly the second largest in the world). In a hangar-size anteroom, we received instruction not just on the history of the market in its current location, but also safety warnings about the traffic patterns of speeding forklifts. Crashing, grinding industrial noise levels, the numbing chill of wet concrete and damp air on the tongue, the sweet scent of clear-eyed fish gravel-packed on ice. We interviewed, photographed, filmed, and recorded stall proprietors, inspected and acquired fish. We scaled, gutted, and filleted our fish under the guidance of Molly O'Neill, one of the leading American food writers and author of *One Big Table*.[8] In a simple transformative action, we dipped our hands into the chill silent intimate guts of creatures once living, and grasped for an instant the vast sensorium of things. And then, ingredients (fish no longer) in hand, we left the market, stepping into the warming blue-sky brilliance of an autumn morning.

In the course of our experiential excursion, I unexpectedly found myself in search of toads, a peculiar fish I associate with the foodways of the lower Chesapeake Bay of Virginia and the North Carolina sounds.[9] Swelling toads (toads for short) are awkward-looking fish that range up to a foot or so in length. Taxonomic descriptions by marine ichthyologists paint a dim portrait of the toad's pigmentation.[10] The toad that I know, however, is a far more colorful creature with a prickly hide mottled tan, gray, and brown with yellow highlights on top, and a brilliant bright white abdomen. Reading coloration offers an early clue to the problems of translation that beset the reception of the concrete. A marine scientist views the toad within a palette that categorizes. A different perspective sees the same skin hues in aesthetic terms.

Toads possess an abrasive sandpapery skin, eyes that move independently, and beetled horn-like brows. Their skeletal system is composed of little more than skull and vertebra. The arrangement and musculature of their fins makes them slow and wallowing swimmers. At rest, a toad displays a paunchy physique; threatened, they inflate themselves into taut spheres. Warm-water fish, toads migrate with the seasons, moving into nearshore and estuarine waters in late spring, and returning offshore in late autumn. They appear, for example, in the Chesapeake Bay in May (the females laden with eggs), and depart in early November. The warm months offer an extended period during which toads spawn their young, depositing their sticky eggs in shallow depressions on the bay floor. Unlike some of their distant cousins whose parent (usually the male) tend the eggs until they hatch, the toads of the Chesapeake Bay are left to their own devices.[11] Toads were conspicuous in their absence at the New Fulton Fish Market, but just as a reluctant acceptance of a toadless reality was taking hold, the proprietors of the Blue Ribbon Fish Company remembered a few "in the back," and brought them out for our inspection.

A toad is a complicated object. As our fishmonger hosts were quick to point out, the toad is noteworthy for its capacity to inflate itself into a prickly sphere intended to gag its predators (fig. 2). For fishermen, the swelling toad's defense mechanism out of water was a source of amusement and, occasionally, ribald humor. Virginia waterman Marshall Cox, sitting at W. T. and Tammy Nottingham's kitchen table, gestured to an apple, laughingly pretending that it was a toad inflated with air, "Now pick that toad up. Look it over. Now hold it up next to your ear. Shake

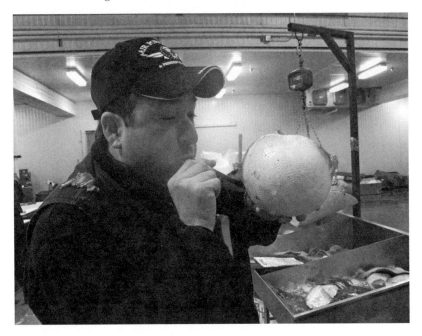

Fig. 2. Inflating a swelling toad. New Fulton Market, New York, November 2010. (Photograph: Bernard L. Herman.)

it. Shake it! Shake it hard. You hear anything? No? Then it must be a female, because if it was a male you'd hear its balls rattling."[12]

The toad tests the boundaries of Leviticus and the dangers of gastronomy. Naturalist chefs, for example, describe toads in contexts that range from their migratory habits to cuisine, noting the existence of well over 100 species, and remarking on the legendary lethal toxicity of Pacific blowfish or *fugu*. Toxicity, a protective mechanism discouraging would-be predators, is limited to the skin, viscera, and reproductive organs. Careless handling during cleaning, however, can taint the meat. The fact that *fugu* improperly prepared can kill the diner led to investigations of the toxicity of Chesapeake Bay and North Carolina toads in the 1960s. Trapping toads in a variety of locations, scientists dissected the animals, liquefied isolated elements of skin, flesh, and viscera, and injected traces into laboratory mice. Two test mice died. The conclusion stated: "The most pressing question, that of whether or not the northern puffer is a safe food, seems to be answered in the affirmative . . . The evidence of toxicity found in certain of the viscera by us and other investigators would hardly lessen the safety factor, since the puffer is eviscerated and skinned before marketing."[13] Still, hesitation tempers gustatory abandon when it comes to toads.

Toads of the Eastern Seaboard possess hard, beak-like mouths that enable them to crunch through hard-shell blue crabs. The preference for crabs leads toads into crab pots where they can corner and consume the trapped crustaceans. Although toads are not considered a fish that schools, they often exhibit group behavior—a fact remarked upon by fishermen, but not elaborated in the scientific and natural-history literature.

Once considered a "trash fish" consumed largely by the poor, Atlantic toads eventually garnered the culinary devotion of a certain class of connoisseurs. In Southern fishing communities, discernment takes on an enthusiastic cast that is as much about identity couched in terms of *terroir* and nostalgia as it is about gastronomy. A November 2009 Facebook entry trumpeted: "Exmore Diner. Today we have Swelling Toads $10.95 . . . served with 2 vegetables and rolls," to which a local gourmand joyously proclaimed, "Swelling toads for $10.95! This is why I love the Eastern Shore!"[14] Evonia Hogan, who grew up in nearby Cheriton, just behind the tomato cannery, recalled her first encounter with toads, touching on themes of delicacy, danger, souvenir, pleasure, and the local.

The toad's capacity to inspire culinary rapture is a comparatively recent phenomenon, and one that increasingly anchors local identity. When the Gaskill family first served toads in their restaurant, they labeled the entrée "chicken of the sea." Subsequently, they changed their marketing strategy to advertising the availability of "toads" (fig. 3). Eastern-shore people knew exactly what the word entailed and came to dine on their "local" histories. A display at the door, complete with photographs, educated diners from "away," and whetted the appetites of those with a taste for the exotic and the local. In either instance, the toad entered the privileged sphere of Eastern Shore of Virginia *terroir*. Part of that process inspired the Gaskills to create specialties including toads stuffed with crab meat (fig. 4).

Toads, once reviled as bycatch, are now the focus of a small, but dedicated fishery. Fishermen catch toads in special crab-pot-like traps baited with crab waste collected from local picking houses, or haul them up in pound nets. Edward Smith of Tangier Island pots: "They used to use the hard crab pot with the bigger mesh for the bigger toads. Now they've fished a few of them out and gone to peeler pots now. Bait them up with crab scrap . . . October is usually the best month for them up in the

Fig. 3. Swelling toads on the menu. Big's Family Restaurant, Painter, Virginia, May 2010. (Photograph: Bernard L. Herman.)

shallows up off of Onancock. Down this way, I'm not sure. Follow the seasons—work their way right on out the [Chesapeake] Bay . . . Grand-pop used to eat quite a few of them. That was the 60s then—the early 70s. Been around for a while—eating them."[15]

The reality of cleaning a toad, as Danny Doughty testified, is rough business—an act of translation from nature/animal to ingredient/commodity (figs. 5, 6, 7). The skill and speed involved in cleaning a large catch, as Eddie Watts of Hungars Creek remarked, was a point of pride with some watermen. Instructions for cooking toads attend to the cleaning process with concision:

Wear gloves when cleaning it. The first step is to cut off the head. Then peel back the skin like a glove, from neck to tail. The innards will drop out, leaving in your hands the backbone with all the meat on it. This can be fried or baked whole, rather like a chicken's leg or a frog's leg.[16]

Fig. 4. Swelling toads served at Big's Family Restaurant, Painter, Virginia, November 2011. Fried toads stuffed with crabmeat (right), and pan-fried toads (left). (Photograph: Bernard L. Herman.)

A flap of skin connecting the severed head to the body provides sufficient purchase to turn the fish inside out leaving head, skin, and entrails in one hand, and the meat of the fish in the other: "You skin him. The guts come with it, and the roe . . . In the fall, of course, he doesn't have any roe—so you're just skinning fish."[17] Theodore Peed, an Eastern Shore of Virginia home cook renowned for his annual game dinner featuring snapping turtle and gravy, emphasized the abrasive skin and hand strength at the center of the translation of fish into ingredient: "It takes a man to skin a toad!" W. T. Nottingham and Marshall Cox, pound fishermen, described cleaning toads shipboard: "You take your knife, cut him right behind the head, peel him like that. Flip him over, put the knife

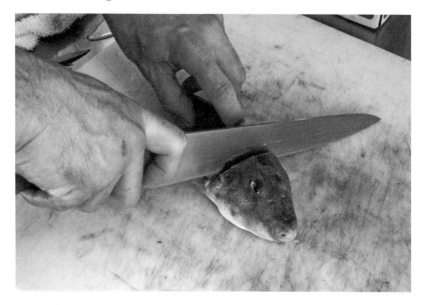

Fig. 5. Cleaning a swelling toad. First cut behind the head. Eastville, Virginia, May 2010. (Photograph: Bernard L. Herman.)

on his head and pull back." What captures my attention is Cox's vivid description of the deft gesture that turns the swelling toad inside out.

The toad is rendered a delicacy through a violent translation that relies on two actions resulting in an array of binary relations: flesh and waste, delicacy and poison, creature and commodity. Skinning a toad is a visceral wrenching editing that separates the animate (everything that defined the toad as a living thing) from the ingredient (the residue that we consume). All encounters with things proceed in this fashion—we are committed to the deadening of things as a means to rendering them tractable—and then quickening them through description and interpretation. Second, turning the toad inside out approximates our desire to discover the hidden and intimate nature of objects through critical acts that are in some measure always violations of the autonomy of things. What the toad in its translation teaches us is an awareness of the critical violence we inflict on things, and how that violence animates the meanings that we cultivate. Thus, a swelling toad plucked from the sea, made the object of jokes, skinned and gutted, cooked and consumed, remembered and narrated, speaks to the unnatural life of the material

Fig. 6. Cleaning a swelling toad. Removing head, skin, and viscera from meat. New Fulton Market, New York, November 2010. (Photograph: Bernard L. Herman.)

turn. Every accounting of a materiality is a rendering: giving up, melting down, parging over. Thus, objects remind us at every turn—at every material turn, at every turning inside out—of how we know the world.

Toads teach us as well about the analogical operations of critical translation. Watermen describe how toads approach the baited pot in the fashion of minnows. Food writers note that the edible relic of the swelling toad yields an alternative to shellfish and frog's legs. A recipe for Toad Provençal notes, "I love frog's legs, but they're hard to find, and often very expensive. The blowfish fillets are every bit as satisfying, but inexpensive."[18] Simply and sadly, as most gastronomes opine, it is "like chicken"—a quality that elevates its status on the basis of a lack of distinction. The toad succeeds as a delicacy through the perception that it is like something else. Something of a gustatory chameleon, the toad bends to the dominion of other flavors—an act of translation in itself. For folks, who grew up with toads on the seasonal table, they taste like home; for diners unfamiliar with the fish, it tastes like authenticity— especially when well seasoned with narrative. An object, distinctive in its found condition, the toad is translated and consumed through analogy. The toad as artifact, as Susan Stewart might describe it, is a creature that is haunted by all its histories.[19]

What has the natural and culinary history of the toad taught us? In

Fig. 7. Swelling toad meat and roe ready for cooking. Eastville, Virginia, May 2010. (Photograph: Bernard L. Herman.)

its rendering, the swelling toad entails surrender, representation, and masking—a forcible intervention into what is naturally hidden and always present—a conversion of the animate into the material and its re-animation as a thing that is culturally revealed and still, flesh divided into delicacy and waste. Ponge offers a way of reaching into the material turn written as a series of resolves on the fraught relationships between materiality and writing. Conjured in a meditation on the Loire, Ponge offers a series of declarations: (1) "Never sacrifice the object of my study in order to enhance some verbal turn discovered on the subject, nor piece together any such discoveries in a poem"; (2) "Always go back to the object itself, to its raw quality, its *difference*, particularly its difference from what I've just then written about it"; (3) "Recognize the greater right of the object, its inalienable right, in relation to any poem"; (4) "The object is always more important, more interesting, more capable (full of rights): it has no duty whatsoever toward me, it is I who am obliged to it"; (5) "The reciprocal clash of words, the verbal analogies are *one* of the means for studying the object in depth"; (6) "Never try to *arrange things*. Objects and poems are irreconcilable." Ponge concludes:

The point is knowing whether you wish to make a poem or comprehend an object (in the hope that mind wins out, comes up with something new on the subject). It is the second phase of this alternative that my taste (a violent taste for things, and for advances of the mind) leads me to choose without hesitation. [1947][20]

The swelling toad leads us finally to the paradox and perils of translation and the concrete.

The toad exists in nature as a native fish, but it relies on culture for its natural histories—narratives that are, in fact, wholly unnatural. In every iteration, the toad metaphorically comments on the material turn—as a process that translates the world into narratives of sense. The preparation of the toad, as ingredient, also speaks to the many ways in which we turn all things inside out, separating what is delectable from what is waste. But, waste possesses its own importance, and the material turn would do well to focus an auguring eye on the entrails and the critical futures they portend. In all of its manifest identities (organism, pest, delicacy, waste, commodity, ingredient), the swelling toad possesses the tangible certainty of its materiality. It is the very nature of its concreteness that enables the toad to accrue and shed meaning over time. Like all things, it satisfies needs that are situational, circumstantial, and semiotic. Individual and collective acts of perception make and remake the artifact: the toad is fish that swells defensively in the gorge of its enemies; it is a chicken-of-the-sea substitute for frog's legs, shrimp, and scallops. In its materiality, the toad (and, as Ponge reminds us, all things) abducted by language renders all readings possible, and in the end, tentative, changing, revelatory.

NOTES

1. Francis Ponge, "The Carnation," in *Mute Objects of Expression*, trans. Lee Fahnestock (New York: Archipelago Books, 1976 and 2008), 37.
2. Francis Ponge, *Soap* (London: Jonathan Cape, 1969).
3. Lynn Meskell, *Object Worlds in Ancient Egypt: Material Biographies Past and Present* (London: Berg, 2004).
4. Michael Joseph Phillips, ed., "Afterword," *4 Major Visual Poets* (Indianapolis: Free University Press, 1980).
5. Jerome Rothenberg, "Pre-Face" in *Esthetics Contemporary*, ed. Richard Kostelanetz (Buffalo, NY: Prometheus Books, 1989), 384.
6. Francesco Panese, "The Accursed Part of Scientific Iconography," in *Visual Cultures of Science: Rethinking Representational Practices in Knowledge Building and science Communication,* ed. Luc Pauwels (Hanover, NH: Dartmouth College Press, 2006), 63–89.

7. Catherine Whalen, personal communication, October 13, 2010.

8. Molly O'Neill, *One Big Table: 600 Recipes from the Nation's Best Home Cooks, Farmers, Fishermen, Pit-Masters, and Chefs* (New York: Simon & Schuster, 2010).

9. J. Lyczkowski-Shultz, "Tetraodontidae: Puffers," in *Early Stages of Atlantic Fishes: An Identification Guide for the Western Central North Atlantic*, 2 vols., ed. William J. Richards (Boca Raton, FL: CRC Press, 2006) 2439–48.

10. Robert L. Shipp and Ralph W. Yerger, "Status, Characters, and Distribution of the Northern and Southern Puffers of the Genus Sphoeroides," *Copeia*, August 29, 1969), 425–33.

11. J. Lyczkowski-Shultz, "Tetraodontidae: Puffers," 2446.

12. Marshall Cox and W. T. Nottingham, interview with Bernard L. Herman, December 31, 2009, Townsend, Virginia.

13. Paul F. Robinson and Frank J. Schwartz, "Toxicity of the Northern Puffer, Sphaeroides maculatus, in the Chesapeake Bay and Its Environs," *Chesapeake Science* 9, no. 2 (June 1968): 136–37.

14. http://www.facebook.com/pages/ExmoreDiner/101742584979?v=feed&story_fbid=202420827776.

15. Edward Smith, interview with Bernard L. Herman and P. G. Ross, March 8, 2010, Westerhouse Creek, Machipongo, Virginia.

16. Davidson (1979), 163.

17. H. M. Arnold, interview with Bernard L. Herman, December 23, 2009, Bayford, Virginia.

18. Peterson, *Fish and Shellfish*, 83.

19. Susan Stewart, "Lyric Possession," *Critical Inquiry* 22 (Autumn 1995): 39.

20. Francis Ponge, "Banks of the Loire," in *Mute Objects of Expression*, 3–4.

TEN

Materiality and Cultural Translation: Indigenous Arts, Colonial Exchange, and Postcolonial Perspectives

Ruth B. Phillips

In 1992, an eighty-four-year-old Anishinaabe (Ojibwe) woman named Madeleine Katt Theriault published her autobiography, *From Moose to Moosehide.* She narrated a life whose first three decades were lived according to a centuries-old pattern of movement across the lands of northern Ontario. Most things people needed came from the lakes and forests, the fruits of cooperative labor organized through the extended family group. She used the example of a successful moose hunt to demonstrate the social relations generated by the hunting life: "While people gathered together, the men made birch bark canoes. Women would set fish nets and pick blueberries, while the children joined in the picking. Everyone was happy and had lots to eat. Women helped one another to tan moose hide and make moccasins for all. My great-grandmother often mentioned how wonderful it was to see Indians help one another and share everything with one another."[1]

When Mrs. Theriault's children were born, her father crafted a cradleboard in which to carry them, and her mother created a fine outer wrapper or "moss bag" embellished with glass bead embroidery in floral designs (fig. 1). "When I had babies," Mrs. Theriault wrote:

> I kept them in a papoose cradle. The cradles have three different sizes: small, medium and large. You would change the back board as the baby grew out of it. We used moss in place of diapers. Using moss on a baby is most healthy.
>
> The baby always smelled sweet and was always warm. We would

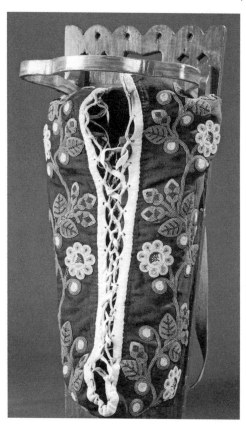

Fig. 1. Michel Katt Jr. and Elizabeth Katt Petrant, moss bag and cradleboard, 1919–38. Wood, metal, cotton, printed cotton and woolen cloth, flannel, hide, seed beads and cotton thread. 65 × 27.5 cm. (Royal Ontario Museum 998.134.1. With permission of the Royal Ontario Museum © ROM.)

change them every so often by discarding the damp moss and replacing it with some clean and fresh smelling. No washing to do, how nice! We kept our babies in a papoose cradle for ten to fourteen months. Some might be walking and still in a papoose board. The board was made of cedar wood, because it is the lightest wood. The front bar is made out of maple wood as it won't break when bent. It also had a board at the feet for standing and a cloth or leather for lacing up the baby inside it. The babies seemed to like to be in a papoose cradle for they would cry to get in it. It was always very hard to break away from this cradle, but they can become too heavy to carry around.[2]

At the end of her life, Mrs. Theriault gave her cradleboard to the Royal Ontario Museum, where it has come to be interpreted by people like myself as a quintessentially hybrid object. In structure and design it is the product of inventions made long before European contact. En-

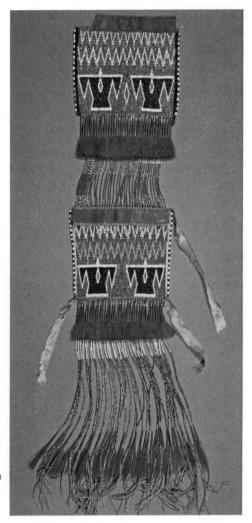

Fig. 2. Anishinaabe artist, cradleboard ornament, late 18th or early 19th century. Hide, porcupine quills, metal, glass beads, animal hair. (Canadian Museum of Civilization III-G-848. Photo © Canadian Museum of Civilization.)

closed by its protective wooden frame, swaddled and padded with moss, rocked by the movements of its mother's travel by foot, snowshoe, and canoe, the cradleboard would have provided Mrs. Theriault's children with embodied and sensory experiences very similar to those of Anishinaabe babies in 1400 or 1700. The visual imagery displayed by the moss bag, however, departs radically from precontact traditions, and reflects the impact of four centuries of European trade and Christian missionization. A century earlier, an Anishinaabe cradleboard would have been ornamented not with floral motifs embroidered with thread and glass beads, but with ochre paints and decorations of dyed porcupine quills woven into images that invoked the protective powers of the great Thunderbirds who dominate the upper cosmic zone of the Anishinaabe universe (fig. 2).

The way of life Mrs. Theriault described came to an abrupt end in the late 1920s, when a new law deprived the Ontario Anishinaabeg of the right to hunt and fish off-reserve. Other laws removed her young children to distant residential schools, and tuberculosis raged through Anishinaabe communities during the first half of the twentieth century, killing Mrs. Theriault's husband while he was still in his thirties. As her life story eloquently demonstrates, Mrs. Theriault experienced these traumatic changes as severe deprivations that were material and sensory and as a radical alteration of the sociality of a communal way of life that could no longer be sustained. Thrust suddenly into modernity, she supported herself through many new kinds of activities—some of which enabled her to continue to wear and make traditional Anishinaabe things, and others requiring new kinds of making and dressing. She reenacted earlier Anishinaabe ways of life for summer tourists at fishing resorts, sewed Indian costumes for a Hollywood movie, worked at menial jobs in a town, and hooked hundreds of rag rugs.

As this snapshot of a twentieth-century Anishinaabe world suggests, for the historian of Native North American art, a cultural history of the material world must be framed by an intercultural perspective. I also argue that intercultural art histories can usefully be investigated as processes of cultural translation whose dynamics inevitably entail losses, but are also productive of new inventions. The example of Mrs. Theriault's cradleboard, finally, also suggests a need to distinguish the ways that cultural translation occurs in relation to visual, material, and discursive components of expressive processes. A kind of splitting appears to occur in the space between the continuities of material forms and the imagery they support—and between the embodied experience provided by material forms and the visual apprehension of their outer appearance. In seeking to understand how translation operates at the nexus of the linguistic, the visual, and the material, it will be useful to look briefly at the succession of "turns" in academic research during the past few decades that have led to our contemporary focus on materiality.[3]

I briefly map the shifts of emphasis in art history, anthropology, and history during the past four decades in order to urge the need for a more integrated approach to the investigation of cultural histories. Through such an approach, the disjointed and disrupted ways in which the material and visual forms of Anishinaabe life and thought have survived into the present can more easily be understood as parts of a unified project of cultural translation.

Genealogies: The Linguistic, the Visual, and the Material Turns

As Peter N. Miller has suggested, the material turn that marks recent scholarship in the humanities and social sciences can be understood as a reaction against the limitations of the "linguistic turn" that ran through art history, anthropology, and history during the 1970s and 1980s. I would also propose, however, that the current focus on materiality in all of these disciplines both emerges from, and overlaps two intervening developments. During the late 1980s and early 1990s, literary and art historical scholars like W. J. T. Mitchell, James Elkins, Nicholas Mirzoeff, and Michael Ann Holly generated a "visual turn," which led to the formation of a new interdisciplinary field of visual studies that has primarily taken root in a number of American universities.[4]

Visual studies draws heavily on theories of the gaze and the spectacle developed within poststructuralist literary and psychoanalytic work, and it insists on the formative psychic and social importance of visual experience as manifested through a broad range of media comprehending art, film, television, new media, advertising, and scientific imaging. The second development was the renewal of interest in material culture and the anthropology of art that began around the same time among a small, but influential, group of primarily British anthropologists. The work of scholars such as Alfred Gell, Howard Morphy, Nicholas Thomas, Marilyn Strathern, Daniel Miller, Christopher Pinney, and Tim Ingold draws on phenomenology, Marxist understandings of production and consumption, and Actor Network Theory. They theorize the ways in which a similarly broad range of material phenomena inclusive of landscape, the built environment, tools, technology, and works of art interacts with humans in processes of social reproduction.

Visual studies, the new material anthropology, and material history share a democratizing and leveling impulse that manifests itself through comprehensive definitions of the phenomena to which they attend. This inclusivity resonates with the broadened range of visual and material expressions addressed within the social history of art, a subfield of art history that has grown steadily in prominence since the advent of the "new art history" in the early 1980s. In all three disciplines, the new concerns have introduced novel sources of evidence for the investigation of histories and cultures. For historians, the material turn has placed new emphasis on the technological, the embodied, and the experiential. For art historians—for whom visual images have, of course, always been central—the visual and material turns have disrupted long-standing hierarchies of fine and applied arts and brought renewed attention to artistic media, techniques, and connoisseurial methods. For anthropologists, the return to material culture studies has fostered renewed critical attention to the colonial accumulations of museums, produced new theorizations of the anthropology of art, and encouraged a focus on consumption in contemporary societies. For all three groups, unaccustomed methods of study have been needed, causing abandoned practices to be dusted off, and new ones to be developed. As already noted, the various avenues leading back to the study of material forms promote interdisciplinarity and convergence. Particularly notable—especially for art historians—has been the intersection that occurs at the site of art works, which have become a subset within the broader compass of visual and material phenomena.

This brief genealogy suggests that the current emphasis on materiality reacts against the reductive tendency of the visual turn, just as that movement had reacted against the tendency of semiotic and other linguistic theories to reduce all images to texts. It also points, however, to slippages that have occurred as emphasis has shifted from textuality, to visuality, to materiality. I would argue that visual anthropology, the anthropology of art, and visual studies all tend to elide important distinctions between images and objects, and the different ways they operate in society. In visual studies, this can result in the treatment of material items as disembodied visual images; conversely, a focus on the material properties of objects through which images are manifested and circulated can disenfranchise the power of the image, whether the object of study is a carte de visite or a computer.

These slippages are particularly problematic in the context of colonial art histories where, given the asymmetries of power, the disappearance of particular visual images does not necessarily indicate permanent loss, since images can continue to be expressed and transmitted through forms of verbal discourse. From the perspective of indigenous art studies, furthermore, the visual turn is problematic because it perpetuates a hegemonic Western ocularcentric tradition that privileges visuality over other senses, impeding understandings of the synaesthetic and holistic nature of much non-Western aesthetic and expressive culture.[5]

Postcolonial Art History and Translation

Overall, visual studies, the social history of art, the new anthropology of art, and material history have helped to break the hold of primitivist canons long dominant within modernism, and have proved hospitable to a postcolonial study of indigenous arts and cultures. Since the 1970s, a central project of art historians and anthropologists who study indigenous arts has been the development of "emic" understandings that more accurately reflect the intentions and meanings of indigenous producers and consumers—a goal that has obvious connections to postcolonial critiques of colonial power relations. In this context, the material turn holds particular promise because it is friendly to the critical analysis of alternative sensory regimes. It is not accidental that a concern with materiality has accompanied the rise of global consciousness and the reframing of curricula and research in "world" terms—e.g. "world" history, art history, and literatures. We return to such global frameworks of study, however, with a very different politics than those that pertained a century ago, when the hierarchical orderings of world cultures rationalized by social evolutionary theories were dominant.

How, then, might cultural translation function at the site of materiality? There is an obvious connection between the notion of translation and the issue of hybridity that has been at the heart of postcolonial studies, as theorized by Homi Bhabha, Mary Louise Pratt, James Clifford, Robert Young, and others. Translation, I would argue, is the active voice of hybridity. The shift from noun to verb urges attention to processes rather than products, and implies outcomes that are inexact, unfinished, and open to revision. Material culture functions differently in intercultural contexts from language, providing both an extralinguistic channel of communication and also a greater latitude for the attribution of divergent meanings to a common sign.

On one level, material translations can involve the identification of coincident or intersecting beliefs, practices, and images. It seems reasonable to believe that when Jesuit missionaries to New France displayed the radiating forms of silver monstrances to their congregants, these men and women recognized this instrument of the mass as an image of the (personified) sun—the most powerful spiritual power in their own cosmos. On another level, translation processes can establish systems of analogues through which equations are proposed between indigenous and exotic valuables. As George Hamell has shown, for example, in the early years of contact in northeastern North America, luminous and light-reflective materials such as glass beads and trade silver became analogues for indigenous valuables of white shell and crystal that were regarded as spiritually empowered.[6] As cultural translations, such material equivalencies can be more forgiving than the relatively more precise requirements of language. The ambiguity inherent in material translations can have advantages in intercultural contexts.

A recent statement by Peter Burke points to the potential value of linking the study of material forms to processes of cultural translation.

> Whether translators follow the strategy of domestication or that of foreignizing, whether they understand or misunderstand the text they are turning into another language, the activity of translation necessarily involves both decontextualizing and recontextualizing. Something is always 'lost in translation.' However, the close examination of what is lost is one of the most effective ways of identifying differences between cultures. For this reason the study of translation is or should be central to the practice of cultural history.[7]

Although Burke refers to language in this passage, I suggest that his point is also relevant to the realm of the material. The conjunction between translation and materiality has not yet been well worked out, and invites further investigation—ideally through comparative and interdisciplinary work. I offer a further Anishinaabe instantiation, not so much as a resolution or a conclusion, but as a contribution to such a future project.

Translating Thunderbirds

At the beginning of this chapter, I mentioned the disappearance of thunderbird imagery from Anishinaabe visual art during the middle decades of the nineteenth century. For centuries, Anishinaabe people have been representing these great hawk-like beings, who appear in the sky in spring, emitting the flashes of lightening that mark their powers and bringing rains, fertility, and other blessings to human beings. They appear on bags in the earliest collections from the Great Lakes, dating to the late seventeenth or early eighteenth century. They become even more numerous in later-eighteenth century collections made by British military officers who fought alongside Anishinaabe warriors during the wars for control of North America. That these images and the belief systems they reference are far older can be inferred from the many representations of raptorial birds that occur in the 2,000-year-old archaeological finds from Middle Woodland cultures in the Great Lakes.

With the influx of settlers into the central Great Lakes after the War of 1812, a period of rapid change began. Geometric and floral designs came to displace the images of the great manitous of the Anishinaabe cosmos by the middle of the century, and Anishinaabe women also invented a range of new weaving and embroidery techniques suited to the media of cloth and beads. Some Anishinaabe continued to observe the old spiritual practices, and, although the bags they wore looked different, the broad zigzag bands they display continued to evoke the lightning emanating from the thunderbird's eyes. Despite the near disappearance of thunderbirds from visual culture by the 1930s, anthropologist A. Irving Hallowell was still able to interview people who could hear thunderbirds talking and receive their protection. As recently as the 1990s,[8] Maureen Matthews was able to add further detail to Hallowell's classic account, providing a fascinating example of the survival of visual and material imagistic concepts in language. Although no examples of shoulder bags—floral or otherwise—had existed in Anishinaabe communities for decades, the grandson of one of Hallowell's informants used the image "one wears them"—gigshka-waa—to explain to her the closeness of the relationship between thunderbirds and people they "cherish."[9]

During the 1940s, an Ojibwa shaman named Moses Nanakonagos poured similar accounts into the receptive years of his grandson, Norval Morrisseau, and his stories stimulated in the younger man a determination to give these beings visual and material form once again through the medium of easel painting. Morrisseau's work, it could be argued, stretches the notion of translation. Arguably, his renderings become "prime objects," in George Kubler's terms, rather than resumptions of an interrupted series.[10] However that issue may be decided, this highly telescoped account illustrates the kinds of adaptations of imagery, materials, and techniques that characterize the artistic traditions of many colonized peoples. They are translational processes made necessary by deprivations and oppressions, but they are also made desirable by the stimulus of new artistic influences and materials. They illustrate, too, the slide of key cultural concepts into and out of material forms, and visual and verbal images. As such, they argue for the need to maintain the linguistic, the visual, and the material dimensions of expressive culture in tension in order to develop understandings adequate to the complexity of historical process.

NOTES

1. Madeleine Katt Theriault, *From Moose to Moosehide: The Story of Ka Kita Wa Pa No Kwe* (Toronto: Natural Heritage/Natural History, Inc., 1992), 59.
2. Madeleine Katt Theriault, *From Moose to Moosehide*, 61.
3. W. J. T. Mitchell, 1986, "What is an Image?," in *Studies in Iconology: Image, Text, Ideology* (Chicago: University of Chicago Press), 7–46.
4. See Margaret Dikoviskaya, *Visual Culture: The Study of the Visual after the Cultural Turn* (Cambridge, MA: MIT Press, 2005); and my essay "The Value of Disciplinary Difference: Art History and Anthropology at the Beginning of the Twenty-First Century," in *Anthropologies of Art*, ed. Mariet Westermann (New Haven, CT: Yale University Press and Clark Art Institute, 2004).
5. Martin Jay, *Downcast Eyes: The Denigration of Vision in Twentieth-Century French Thought* (Berkeley and Los Angeles: University of California Press, 1993).
6. George R. Hamell, "Trading in Metaphors, The Magic of Beads: Another Perspective on Indian-European Contact in Northeastern North America," in *Proceedings of the 1982 Glass Trade Bead Conference*, ed. Charles F. Hayes III (Rochester, NY: Rochester Museum and Science Center, 1983).
7. Peter Burke, "Cultures of Translation in Early Modern Europe," in *Cultural Translation in Early Modern Europe*, ed. Peter Burke and R. Po-Chia Hsia (Cambridge; Cambridge University Press, 2007), 38.
8. A. Irving Hallowell, "Ojibwa Ontology, Behaviour and World View," in *Culture in History: Essays in Honor of Paul Radin*, ed. Stanley Diamond (New York: Columbia University Press, 1960).
9. Maureen Matthews, *Repatriating Agency: Animacy, Personhood and Agency in the Repatriation of Ojibwe Artefacts* (PhD diss., Oxford University, 2010), 176.
10. George Kubler, *The Shape of Time: Remarks on the History of Things* (New Haven, CT: Yale University Press, 1962).

ELEVEN

The Antiquarian, the Collector, and the Cultural History of the Material World

Alain Schnapp

The notion of a cultural history of the material world is, without doubt, a sound strategy to avoid the contrived and problematic separations between disciplines, and thus manage the space between archaeology, art history, and social history. Those of my generation who had the opportunity to engage *l'école des Annales* have seen the value of an interdisciplinary approach to the historical event—both materially and immaterially. The reflections that follow are embedded within this mode of engagement.

The artifacts that one collects—the ruins, the discarded objects (to take Francesco Orlando's apt formulation)—these bring into relief the cultural history of the material world because they are solid, concrete. Their matter, their style, their age: these comprise their material density while their discarded nature, their disuse, separate them from the chains of production and use through which they come into existence, and thus render them also immaterial. The interest with which we approach these artifacts do not reveal an actual material world so much as our desire to understand, to listen, to see, to be enchanted. Discarded artifacts are a means to return enchantment to the world.

To collect rare objects—remote both in time and space—to explore ancient monuments, these are pursuits closely linked to the virtuosi of the Renaissance, who laid the foundations for an appreciation of the rare, the exotic, and the antique. This is a sensibility akin to the *cabinets de curiosités,* or the *Wunderkammer,* to use the term in vogue in the German courts. This type of collection associating *artificialia* with *naturalia*— the works of humankind, and those of nature—has been closely studied by numerous scholars, from Julius von Schlosser, to Walter Benjamin, to Krzysztof Pomian in his first major work. Yet from the fifteenth century, curiosity was no longer limited to princes and aristocrats, but became central to a shared culture linking the nobility with the bourgeoisie. Curiosity encompassed the past and the present, the near and far, nature and culture to the point that our modern disciplinary classifications cannot be easily placed within this complex topography of knowledge. Paleontology, archaeology, geography, ethnography, and other modern disciplines have their origins within this vast movement to explore both world and spirit. It is a movement of ideas embracing society from its intellectual to its economic practices, and contributes to the development of cosmology, topography, natural history, astronomy, physics, and medicine, and in turn influences political practices and national traditions.

This curiosity was not an invention of the Renaissance: there were collectors and antiquarians in the Middle Ages, and the portraits left to us by Catullus, Horace, and Cicero provide important evidence of the role played by collectors both in Hellenistic Greece and Ancient Rome. Moreover, the notion of the "Museum" of Alexandria clearly materializes this interest in human works—be they material or immaterial—and concerned with both the observation of nature and society. The act of collecting can be reduced to the extraction of a material object (either fashioned by human hands or produced by nature) from its milieu, and to its re-embedding within one framework or another. The traces of this collecting are revealed by the presence of "intrusive objects"; that is, different from those we use in our everyday lives and in religious ritual, found in stratified archaeological contexts or in monuments. When this type of object contains a label or inscription, as is the case in Egypt and Mesopotamia, then the intention is clear. In Mesopotamia, the practice of deporting the defeated enemy's cult images attests to the existence of collections seized from the vanquished and often quite ancient, carefully deposited in palaces and temples. These collections of objects and inscriptions, gathered for a reason not easy to determine—religious, intellectual, political—are well-known in several Mesopotamian cities, including Sippar and Babylon. How is this different, then, from the *Wunderkammer*? For the majority of historians of collecting, these are tied to an intellectual agenda: the exploration of the world, the establishment of classificatory schemata, the identification of the origin of objects, the description of their find-spot or place of excavation, the social and political use of objects, the "chamber of wonders" meant to reaffirm the owner's status. Samuel de Quicchelberg established the conventions for this type of collecting in 1565, in a system that extends to the world of things the classificatory practices of the world of ideas.

To organize objects is to organize the world. One does not need to see the *Wunderkammer* as a collection of inanimate objects; rather, the chamber of wonders is tied both to botanical and faunal collections of rare and exotic species, inheritors to the "paradise" of the ancient Persians. And, as emphasized by P. Falguières, the glory of these chambers of wonders is also deeply connected to a renewal in historical consciousness, in interest for the past: the genealogies of species, of works and families, were a means to reaffirm the kingdoms' identities, and to contribute to the writing of an ordered chronicle of past events. The chamber of wonders is also the material expression of a desire for knowledge and a mastery of the world proper to the prince yet not forbidden to the rich and the learned: the historical chronicle, much as the collection, thus becomes a political strategy. In 1452, the city of Augsburg was the first city in Europe to entrust, to a monk named Sigismond Meisterlin, the writing of a civic history. This work of local history, illustrated with original illuminations, was among the first to give us a prehistory of Europe based both upon Latin sources and the observation of place and customs.

The Poetics of Ruins as Knowledge of the Past in Ancient Egypt: *Stein und Zeit*

In ancient Egypt, the taste for the rare, the exotic, and the antique were counted among the sphere of pursuits appropriate to the pharaoh, as well as of his dignitaries and scribes. Khaemwaset (ca. thirteenth century BCE), son of Ramses II, is without doubt, among the best known and most visible of the antiquarians and restorers of monuments in ancient Egypt. From him comes one of the earliest surviving testimonies concerning a fortuitous discovery: engraved upon a statue of his distant predecessor Kaemois, Prince of Ka-Wab and son of Kheops, is an inscription testifying to the historical conscience and curiosity about the past that mark the true antiquarian. Through the centuries, the learned thus communicated the one with the other, addressing each other through these inscribed messages. The observation of monuments, the emphasis upon the interpretation of ancient inscriptions are pursuits familiar to scribes and those close collaborators of pharaoh who did not hesitate, in certain cases, to excavate the soil in order to discover monuments and restore them.

An interest in monuments, in ancient artifacts, in rare texts was not limited to pharaoh, but was also actively cultivated by the learned. This curiosity is intimately connected to a sense of history often manifest in annals, and in a dynastic conception of the past. Faced with crisis, the death of a sovereign, war, floods, battles, the scribe's immediate response was to turn to these annals in search of parallels and, if these were not found, to declare the uniqueness of the moment, and the extraordinary and exemplary action of the sovereign. The latter then sought to assert himself as a founder, yet a founder nonetheless respectful of the past as explored by these learned scribes. For the Egyptians, the sense of passing time seemed an immanent aspect of their self-consciousness that determined the special character of their perception of the past. The past was a means to understand the present—a reservoir of behaviors and actions that all men, priest or warrior—could invoke in due place. From this then comes the impetus to preserve it in the shape of rigorously interpreted texts and, of course, as monuments.

For what else could account for the Egyptian preoccupation with monuments if not this defiance of time? Jan Asmann has written on this theme in his aptly titled *Stein und Zeit*, where he asserts that stone (*Stein*) is indeed a form of being (*Sein*). Memory cannot exist without the perpetuation of sovereigns, of nobles, and elites: it becomes necessary then to master the written word, as well as monumentality, in their complementary roles. When the son of Ramses II, Khaemois, discovers in Memphis the statue of his distant predecessor Ka-Wab, he is not content merely to extract it from the earth, to read the inscription and restore the statue—he proceeds with a ritual of reinstallation and engraves upon it the circumstances of his discovery. To collect ancient inscriptions, discover monuments, to restore and interpret them were thus not simple pastimes, but the duties of the learned. This type of endeavor is a sign of a particular attitude and social engagement that as time passes continues to develop and to flourish.

Petosiris, a priest in the fourth century BCE, has bequeathed to us an extraordinary testimony: "the Temple of Heqat was found in ruins after much time. The Nile's water had shifted in the course of each year, so that the location of the structure was no longer in accord with the description entitled 'details of the Temple of Heqat,' as we call it . . . I called upon the scribe I found in the temple to this goddess. I gave him payment without measure to erect the monuments there on this day. I caused to be built a great colonnade surrounding the precinct to forbid the waters from being seized. I consulted each wise man about the proper nature of the ritual."

With the passing of time, a revolution was wrought upon the historical conscience of the Egyptians. Their will to scrutinize the past remained the same, but their point of view shifted. From the reign of Ramses an intellectual break becomes evident—a break between the past and the present. Tradition, Asmann states, is placed upon a pedestal. It is reified, yet in a manner that still permitted them to stand apart from it and critique it. Already by the Middle Kingdom, the famous Khâkhper-rêseneb set himself in opposition to tradition, repetition, and citation: "I commanded unknown expressions, original formulae, new turns of phrase that have not been overturned, that do not comprise any repetition, any oral traditional formulae as uttered by the ancestors." Faced with the crushing weight of tradition, of constantly repeated formulae, a dissident voice was elevated to reaffirm the autonomy and originality of writing. Despite the heavy weight of tradition, Egyptian civilization was nonetheless able to master time, to create the conditions for reflection and dialogue, to develop antiquarian practices different from those of the Renaissance, yet still highlighting the brevity of human existence, the fragility of empires, and the immensity of time. The Egyptians privileged stone: they erected structures both solid and monumental, and engraved majestic inscriptions to testify to their grandeur for subsequent generations. The Mesopotamians were more discreet, entrusting to their frail baked-brick constructions individual inscribed tablets with the aim of commemorating their munificence.

Combating Erosion in Its Own Domain: Tablets against Time

The sovereigns of great empires have all attempted to master time either by bequeathing to posterity ineradicable traces of their reigns or—and often for the same reasons—by establishing links to a particular place that in turn connects them to their predecessors. From this perspective, the ancient Egyptians, the ancient Mesopotamians, and the ancient Chinese all deployed an "Oriental despotism," if you will forgive the expression, which, in turn, appears rather a vast laboratory for domesticating the arts of memory.

Nevertheless, there are identifiable differences in comportment and technique. The pharaohs undertook to resist the erosion of time by deploying an indestructible mass of immense stone monuments. Mesopotamian sovereigns instead turned to a different solution: that of inserting into the foundations of their palaces and temples carefully buried brick inscriptions. These bricks bore inscriptions testifying to the glory of the sovereign ruler, to his piety, and his munificence. They constituted a message that each ruler sought to communicate to his descendants, even as they proclaimed his knowledge of the discoveries of his predecessors. This *savoir-faire*, nonetheless, was rather ironic: it was not the solidity of walls, the sumptuousness of painted and sculpted decorations, that were to testify to the grandeur of the sovereign, but rather the bricks of baked earth dried in the sun and carefully inscribed by scribes. Faced with the majestic stone monuments of the pharaohs, Mesopotamian rulers understood the fragility of their clay constructions, and so proclaimed loud and clear their grandeur with recourse to this very different means of communicating with the future. This subtle strategy rests upon inherited knowledge uniting scribes throughout the millennia; it presupposed a philological aptitude, an ability to master archaic scripts and the diplomatic traditions that characterized the early Mesopotamian scribes, who were collectors of inscriptions, as well as skilled translators. Egyptians and Mesopotamians thus showed the same faith and the same interest for the past, yet the means by which they explored this interest were quite different. Conscious of the fragility of their clay constructions, the Mesopotamians set out to combat erosion through knowledge: their palaces, quickly destroyed once no longer in use, still preserved their foundation bricks, now protected by the ruins. To communicate with the past, it was therefore not sufficient to inscribe messages piously deposited upon the soil, but to ensure throughout the passing of generations that kings and scribes would search this same soil and recover the indestructible traces of the past: the foundation bricks. This eagerness to explore the soil, to sift through previous layers, to date and interpret the walls, objects, inscriptions thus discovered, seem rather familiar to the modern archaeologist, who cannot but entertain in these explorers predecessors as passionate as themselves.

The study of the past is thus an exercise in piety that reclaims complex systems of knowledge. The king and his scribes must be capable of deciphering ancient inscriptions in order to validate their discoveries; they must recognize the traces of ancient temples, of sites of cult, of topography and climate, in order to uncover ancient sites. In short, antiquarian knowledge rests as a central function and practice of royalty—a means to affirm both the grandeur of the sovereign and his (or her) link to the divine.

Egyptians and Mesopotamians, much as our great Western antiquarians, knew how to engage in dialogue with the past, to locate and organize strategies of commemoration and preservation of the past. They elaborated these specific doctrines in order to manage the fragile equilibrium between memory and oblivion: to my eyes, the cultural history of materiality can thus contribute to better navigate the forest of signs, the fragile constructions aptly termed by Borges "los memoriosos."

TWELVE

Mountain as Material: Landscape Inscriptions in China

Robert E. Harrist, Jr.

"Cultural Histories of the Material World," as a line of inquiry, holds out the promise of innovative scholarship in which artifacts of all kinds—everything from portraits to pencil sharpeners—will be the shared focus of various branches of the humanities. For art historians, the word "material" has special resonance, as generally the first thing we consider in studying a work of art, or at least should consider, is the material from which it is made—marble, gold, bronze, oil on canvas, ink on paper, plexiglass—the familiar terms found in catalogue entries or museum labels. In many cases, identifying the material of a work of art illuminates the meanings it conveyed to an original community of viewers. One thinks of Michael Baxandall's work on the significance of pigments in fifteenth-century Italian painting, or Wu Hung's analysis of the ritual uses of jade and bronze in ancient China.[1] This chapter introduces another material of great importance in China—unquarried stone on mountains used as the surface for inscribed texts.[2] These inscriptions, which began to appear in the first century CE, are found at countless sites in China and constitute, like the writing system itself, one of the distinguishing features of Chinese civilization,

Embedded in the natural landscape, mountain inscriptions embody memory and knowledge in a network of language spread across the places they mark. They visually alter and demarcate terrain and generate meaning in the places where they are intended to be read, creating what might be called a "landscape of words." This is a landscape that must be experienced and understood as a dynamic interaction of language and

151

terrain. In his survey of stone inscriptions from the Roman world, Lawrence Keppie points out that "the most important thing to remember about any Roman inscription is that it is inscribed *on* something."[3] Keppie's observation refers to plinths, arches, temples, and other structures bearing carved Latin texts. Adapting his idea, I would argue that the most important thing to remember about any mountain inscription is that it is carved at some place, and the only way to fully understand its meaning is to go there.

Describing a landscape bedecked with carved texts, a seventeenth-century poet, Chen Yuanlong, said that "gazing at the mountains is like looking at paintings; traveling in the mountains is like reading history."[4] Much of the history embedded in mountain inscriptions consists of short records of visits to the sites where the texts appear. Consider an example carved on Mount Wu in Fujian Province that reads "Chen Xiuzhai was here," followed by a date corresponding to the year 1176 (fig. 1). In addition to whatever else we may know or learn about the mountain—Mr. Chen, a minor local official—saw to it that he became a part of its history, and he did so by producing an inscription that belongs to that universal genre of graffiti, "so and so was here." But unlike the scribblers and spray painters of modern times, or those who simply scratch their names on walls, Mr. Chen made sure his writing would last by having it carved on stone. Although the clerical script characters are not explicitly identified as Chen's own handwriting, the reader assumes that they were brushed on the stone by Chen himself and then carved to make them a permanent feature of the landscape. Interpreted as a piece of calligraphy—the most esteemed of all the arts in China—the writing would have been seen as a graphic expression of the mind and moral cultivation of the writer, as a form of self-revelation through which Chen presented himself to the world.

The word "graffiti" suggests violation and vandalism—mark making that is furtive and illicit.[5] But in writing his inscription, Chen Xiuzhai was participating in a venerable tradition of public writing sanctioned by the rulers of China themselves. Imperial inscriptions can announce that the writer visited a mountain, but emperors rarely limited themselves to simply recording their names. On the summit of Mount Tai, China's Sacred Mountain of the East, Emperor Xuanzong (r. 712–756 CE) of the Tang dynasty had carved on a polished granite cliff a long text that documents his successful performance of solemn rituals dedicated to the deities high Heaven and to his imperial ancestors (fig. 2). Although the emperor did not climb up ladders and scaffolding to brush the charac-

Fig. 1. "Chen Xiuzhai was here." Stone inscription, 1176. Mount Wu, Fujian Province. (Photo author.)

ters directly on the stone, the calligraphy was traced from his own hand-writing before being incised on the mountain and inlaid with gold. In addition to recording factual information about the reasons why he went to Mount Tai, the text includes hymn-like passages that voice for all eternity, the emperor hoped, his veneration of his ancestors. The scale of the writing—seventeen meters high, and its location—reachable only after many hours of climbing, also made the inscription a compelling form of political representation through which Xuanzong appropriated the ancient sanctity of the mountain to glorify his own reign.

In addition to commemorating past events—a private outing or an imperial progress—writing on mountains sanctified landscape by recording the names of deities and the words of sacred texts. On a cliff at Mount Hongding in Shandong Province, a Buddhist monk of the sixth century inscribed the name of the "Great Vacuity King Buddha" in characters over nine meters high (fig. 3). Overlooking a wide valley, the name imbued the landscape with the presence of this deity and likely was a focus of worship in its own right, approached with reverence and made the object of offerings and prayers. We know both from historical records and from observing religious practices of our own time that writ-

Fig. 2. Emperor Tang Xuanzong (r. 712–756). *Inscription for the Record of Mount Tai* (Ji Taishan ming). 726. Stone inscription inlaid with gold, total height 71.1 m. Mount Tai, Tai'an, Shandong Province. (Photo Author.)

Fig. 3. *Great Vacuity King Buddha* (Da kong wang Fo). 564. Stone inscription, total height 930 cm. Mount Hongding, Dongping County, Shandong Province. (Photo courtesy of Lis Jung.)

ing can function in this way. At the Nan Putuoshan Temple in southern Fujian Province, the giant character "Fo," or Buddha, is the object of veneration for worshippers who erected an altar in front of the carving and kneel before it to pray and offer incense, just as they might in the presence of a Buddhist image (fig. 4). Even those believers who are otherwise illiterate would be able to recognize the word "Buddha" and respond accordingly.

Depending on how they are displayed, inscriptions can promote a different type of religious experience by compelling a reader to move through space. On Mount Gang in Shandong Province, the text of a Buddhist sutra was transcribed in the sixth century on a sequence of boulders at progressively higher elevations (fig. 5). In order to read the sutra text, one ascends the mountain gradually, going from one inscribed passage to the next. Through this act of peripatetic reading, a pilgrim follows an itinerary that parallels the gradual attainment of enlightenment and entry into paradise that the text of the sutra describes.

Fig. 4. Worshipers before the inscribed character "Fo" (Buddha), Nan Putuoshan Temple, Xiamen, Fujian Province. (Photo author.)

Whether it is the emperor marking sites in his domains or a Buddhist monk invoking unseen deities by carving their names, writing on mountains asserts power over sites. The act of naming places in landscape is a special form of power through which peaks, boulders, or streams are wrested from the otherwise anonymous continuum of nature and given identities that have new meaning. Where once there was only land, inscribed site names produce landscape made up of places such the Sword Pond and Iron Flower Cliff on Tiger Hill outside the city of Suzhou, Cloud Peak Mountain in Shandong Province, the Stone Gate in Shaanxi, and countless others. Although such names simply may be carried in the minds of the inhabitants of a place or noted in the guidebooks of tourists, when they become part of the physical reality of a place, they give tangible form to the historical, political, or religious discourses that human beings bring to the experience of looking at nature.

One type of response to mountain scenery distilled in site names is triggered by the familiar, but complex, mental and visual habit of discerning likenesses within the shapes of geological formations: a process

Fig. 5. Passage from the *Laṅkvātāra Sutra*, ca. 580. Stone inscription, each character ca. 40 cm high. Mount Gang, Zou County, Shandong Province. (Photo courtesy of Lis Jung.)

that psychologists call "projection." In the contorted shape of a boulder or the irregular outline of a cliff, name-giving viewers have imagined all manner of real and fantastic beings, animals, birds, and manmade arti-facts. A rounded boulder on Tiger Hill has become the "Stone Peach" (fig. 6). A cliff with a pendant overhang on Mount Tai bears the inscribed words "Elephant Trunk Peak." And a rock on Mount Lao in Shandong bears three characters that proclaim it to be "The Lion Peak." Much as a title shapes or points to a particular reading of a work of art, these site names determine the way a viewer perceives the formations on which they appear. While different viewers might discern different likenesses, once a particular name is in place, like the flag of a colonizer claiming a territory, it fixes an act of nomination. These inscriptions also assert authority over landscape, and over a viewer, by establishing a vantage point from which a formation must be seen in order to discern the re-semblance. What the inscriptions imply is: "stand where you can read this to see the likeness the name evokes."

In addition to labeling and describing sites, writers of inscriptions—like critics evaluating works of art—assess and rank the attractions of landscapes. At several places on Mount Tai, inscriptions identify it as "Number one famous mountain under heaven." Similar expressions

Fig. 6. "The Stone Peach"
(Taoshi). Stone inscrip-
tion on Tiger Hill, Suzhou.
(Photo courtesy of Dr. Jane
Elliott.)

adorn hills, streams, and other topographical highlights throughout
China to express pride in local scenery. An inscription on Mount Tian-
ping in Jiangsu Province announces the location of the "Number one
stream in the state of Wu." Another inscription on the mountain identifies the location of "The number three stream," suggesting that two
others, even better, must be somewhere else. Inscriptions also prompt
specific forms of interaction with mountain scenery. On Mount Tai,
inscriptions urge travelers to "Listen to the stream," "Look up in admiration," or, beside a plunging cascade, "Look at the waterfall." Some
inscriptions on mountains offer encouragement to weary tourists. Four
characters carved on Mount Gu in Fujian Province urge those headed
upward, "Don't rest only half-way up the road!"

Mountain inscriptions consist of very different kinds of texts, but in
all cases they can be labeled by the Chinese term *moya*, which appears to
have been coined by the eleventh-century scholar and epigrapher Ou-

Fig. 7. Stele at the Temple of Mount Tai inscribed by Emperor Song Huizong (r. 1100–1125). 1124. Temple of Mount Tai, Tai'an, Shandong Province. (Photo author.)

yang Xiu (1007–1072). The literal meaning of the two characters is "polished cliff," or "to polish a cliff." This refers to the practice of smoothing stone to prepare it to receive carved characters, as was done for the imperial inscription on Mount Tai. The polished rectangular surface of such inscriptions recalls that of the most common of all epigraphic forms in China: the *bei* or free-standing stone stele (fig. 7). What makes the *moya* inscription different is the fact that the stone remains in place in its original geological setting. The term *moya* or "polished cliff" is also used, somewhat illogically I admit, to designate inscriptions carved on untreated, unsmoothed stone, for which the characters are adapted to the irregularities of the natural surface.

Producing any inscription required at least two steps: writing the characters with a brush and then carving them in stone. In the simplest and the most ancient method, called *shudan* or "writing in cinnabar," a calligrapher brushed characters directly on stone using red pigment to make them easier to see—a process that was distinct from adding colors to the finished inscription, which came later. After the writing was done, carvers completed the inscription by transforming the strokes into chiseled incisions. An inscription created in this way demanded that the

Fig. 8. "Inscribing a cliff" (Tibi tu). 1609. Woodblock illustrated from *Assembled Pictures of the Three Realms* (Sancia tuhui). (Photo courtesy of Starr Library, Columbia University.)

calligrapher go to the site, ideally with the help of a servant to carry his writing supplies. This act is depicted in Chinese pictorial art and was illustrated in the Ming dynasty encyclopedia *Assembled Pictures of the Three Realms* (*Sancai tuhui*) published in 1609 (fig. 8). This woodblock image is labeled *tibi* or "writing on a wall," but the wall is actually a stone cliff. Unlike a person seated at or standing before a writing table, bending over to produce calligraphy, the writer of a cliff inscription stands upright, his erect body parallel to the writing surface. This is why the contemporary scholar Guo Rongzhang describes this process of writing as a dialogue between the site in the landscape and the body of the calligrapher.[6]

According to a definition formulated by a nineteenth-century epigrapher, "to go to a mountain and carve it, this is called *moya*."[7] Implicit in this definition is the assumption that inscriptions were produced by a calligrapher standing outdoors, writing a text intended for a reader who would stand in the same place, It was not always necessary or practicable, however, for calligraphers to write directly on the stone where an inscription was to appear. Instead, they could brush characters on sheets of paper that were entrusted to expert craftsmen who transferred the calligraphy to stone using a clever transfer process. To do this, the original brush-written characters were traced on a sheet of translucent paper and outlined in pigments on the back. The paper was then pressed against the surface where the text was to appear and the outlines transferred to the stone. Carvers armed with mallets and chisels then set to work, just as they would if the characters had been brushed directly on the stone.

The transfer process just described sometimes resulted in carved calligraphy turning up on mountains where the writer never set foot. This has been especially common in modern times when local officials have appropriated the writing of famous people to ornament the parks and scenic areas they control. This happened on Mount Tai, where a large display of Chairman Mao's calligraphy in flowing cursive script appears on a stone about halfway up the mountain (fig. 9). The writing was enlarged from one of Mao's poetry handscrolls and then traced onto the stone. The text is a poem about the heroic Communist Long March of the 1930s that has nothing to do with Mount Tai, and Mao himself never visited the site.

Over the past few years, I have been asked more than once whether or not the writing is actually a defacement of the beauty of Chinese mountains—a complaint similar to that sometimes voiced about the Chinese habit of writing all over paintings. Doubts and reservations about writing on mountains are not new. Consider the complaints of Zhang Dai (ca.

Fig. 9. Mao Zedong (1893–1976). *Poem on the Long March*. Undated. Stone inscription based on a hand scroll transcribed in 1962. 85 × 280 cm. Munt Tai, Tai'an, Shandong Province. (Photo author.)

1597–ca. 1679), a writer of the seventeenth century who participated in a package-tour pilgrimage to Mount Tai and wrote an essay about his journey. Zhang was appalled by the coarseness of his fellow tourists and by the beggars he encountered on the mountain. He was disgusted also by the practice of visitors, as he put it, "inscribing on rocks such trite phrases as "Venerated by ten thousand generations" or "Redolence continuing for an eternity." While the beggars exploited the mountain for money," Zhang thundered, "the visitors leaving behind their inscribed names exploited Mt. Tai for fame."[8] Another harsh critic of stone inscriptions was the eighteenth-century scholar and editor Fang Bao (1688–1749), who complained bitterly about the "scraping and gouging of ignorant monks and vulgar scholars" who inflicted their names and poems on mountains.[9]

These doubters must be allowed their say, but Chinese concepts of the relationship between the eternal order of nature and the actions of human beings offer another way of thinking about the inscriptions. The eleventh-century philosopher Shao Yong (1011–1177) wrote: "that which completes heaven and earth and the myriad things is called a human being." In this view of the cosmos, the natural and the human are eternally joined, complementary forces. Writing on natural stone surfaces, calligraphers do not deface, but complement and complete the mountains of China.

Those who left writing on mountains availed themselves of what Mircea Eliade called "the hardness, ruggedness, and permanence of the material itself." In his book *Patterns in Comparative Religion*, Eliade muses on the relationship between human beings and stone.

> Above all, stone *is*. It always remains itself and exists of itself. Rock shows human beings something that transcends the precariousness of humanity; an absolute mode of being. Its strength, its motionlessness, its size and its strange outlines are none of them human; they indicate the presence of something that fascinates, terrifies, attracts and threatens, all at once. In its grandeur, its hardness, its shape and colour, stone represents a reality, and a force that belong to some world other than the profane world of which humans are a part.[10]

Like all products of the material world, writing is haunted by mortality: we sign a letter, or inscribe a landscape, and then pass from the scene. Perhaps it is the stark contrast between the durability of stone and "the precariousness of humanity" that lends a strange poignancy to inscriptions on mountains, where writers attempted to claim for their words something of the permanence of the earth itself.

NOTES

1. Michael Baxandall, *Painting and Experience in Fifteenth-Century Florence: A Primer in the Social History of Pictorial Style* (Oxford: Oxford University Press, 1972); Wu Hung, *Monumentality in Early Chinese Art and Architecture* (Stanford, CA: Stanford University Press, 1995).
2. For the early history of inscriptions on Chinese mountains, see Robert E. Harrist, Jr., *The Landscape of Words: Stone Inscriptions from Early and Medieval China* (Seattle: University of Washington Press, 2008).
3. Lawrence Keppie, *Understanding Roman Inscriptions* (Baltimore: Johns Hopkins University Press, 1991), 15.
4. Chen Yuanlong, "Longyin dong" (Dragon hiding cave), *Guangxi tongzhi* (Comprehensive gazetteer of Guangxi) 1781, *Siku quanshu* edition, 125.7a.
5. "Graffiti," *Oxford Art Online*. http://www.oxfordartonline.com/subscriber/.
6. Guo Rongzhang, *Shimen moya keshi yanjiu* (Research on the polished cliff

stone inscriptions at the Stone Gate) (Xi'an: Shaanxi meishu chubanshe, 1985), 16.

7. Feng Yunpeng and Feng Yunyuan, eds., *Jinshi suo* (Inquiry into metal and stone), *Shiku quanshu* edition, 1.1a.

8. Zhang Dai, "Daizhi" (Records of Mt. Tai.), in *Langhuan wenji* (Changsha: Yuelue shushe, 1985), 66–75; Wu Pei-yi, trans., "An Ambivalent Pilgrim to T'ai-shan in the Seventeenth Century," in *Pilgrims and Sacred Sites in China,* ed. Susan Naquin and Chün-fang Yu (Berkeley and Los Angeles: University of California Press, 1992), 65–88.

9. Cited by Richard Strassberg, *Inscribed Landscapes: Travel Writing from Imperial China* (Berkeley and Los Angeles: University of California Press, 1994), 401.

10. Mircea Eliade, *Patterns in Comparative Religion,* trans. Rosemary Sheed (Lincoln: University of Nebraska Press, 1996), 216.

THIRTEEN

Objects and History

Jaś Elsner

The place of material culture in relation to the writing of history has always been fraught. We know that Gibbon was a serious Grand Tourist, who knew his honored objects as well as the next man—in fact, probably rather better—but very few objects, most notably the Arch of Constantine, made it into his *Decline and Fall.*[1] And when the arch got there, the job it served was as the emblem of all that the book was itself about—a perfect and monumental summary of decline.[2] Gibbon got his model (not only the specific discourse on the arch as archetype of artistic decadence, but even the terms in which he could characterize its embodiment of the fall) from great predecessors—Vasari and Raphael himself.[3] But he translated their use of the emblem (as a paradigm of artistic decadence in the retreat from classical styles and naturalism in late antiquity) to an historical usage as the epitome of a decline that was much grander in concept than just in the visual arts (though, of course, the arch's use by Gibbon was proof that this decline included the arts too). Gibbon bequeathed the miseries of the Arch of Constantine as emblem for the woes of the world to numerous successors—of whom Bernard Berenson is the most interesting. Written in 1941, in a work only published in Italian in 1952 and in English in 1954, Berenson's excoriations of the Arch of Constantine as exemplar of all things in chaotic collapse read like a rant that is entirely out of control if one sees it in relation to the monument; they can only be understood as a commentary on his own time and context as a Jew caught in Italy, and observing firsthand the dismantlement of all that he held precious in European civilization on a scale never experienced before (except perhaps when the Huns and Vandals ravaged the Roman Empire roughly around the time the arch was put up).[4] In Berenson's hands—some of the most distinguished hands in the history of art history writing—the arch is effectively entirely removed from its contextual historical reality as an honorific monument for a triumphant emperor and turned into a pure symbol of all that is worst in the demise of Western culture, a harbinger of the Dark Ages, both medieval and contemporary.

Now the point of this swift canter through a monument's most unfortunate historiography—actually *the* most unfortunate (and some might say also undeserved) historiography of any monument in the history of Western art—is to stress the strangeness of the entry of any material culture into history. For to be discussed within an argument, objects must first be translated out of their nontextual being (as two- or three-dimensional works of art, as fragments or relics or spoils, or whatever) and turned into a descriptive piece of prose—a process that is always and inevitably tendentious in that the translation is done to suit the purpose and needs of the context into which the object is being inserted, and to suit the ends and arguments of the person who has done the translating. Second, they must bear much more weight within the given argument than any poor bit of material culture really deserves to bear: however impressive and sturdy the Arch of Constantine may be, it cannot carry the weight of cultural claims placed upon it by its historiography from Raphael to Berenson. Third—and most interesting for our purposes here, as well as most problematic—monuments in the process of translation into verbal discourse have a tendency to take on an emblematic resonance, which in the case of the Arch of Constantine comes to signal the collapse of all civilization as we know it.[5]

It may be that all of this is just to say that when history finds itself dealing with material culture, it is forced to turn from its more usual rhetorical and discursive methods to ekphrasis—which has been, since antiquity, the specific trope of vivid rhetorical description. Ancient ekphrasis, according to the rhetorical handbooks probably produced for generations of Greco-Roman schoolchildren (our earliest is first century AD),[6] need not be about art (despite the way the word "ekphrasis" is used in most modern practice).[7] Indeed, the handbooks cite Thucydides's description of a night battle as a classic case,[8] and that is, of course, an occurrence within a paradigmatic example of history. But, even in antiquity and through a series of purple passages spanning the Middle Ages and modernity, ekphrasis of works of art has been a privileged form of the genre in which the writer may pause and examine his or her own artistic practice, poetics, potential readings of his or her bigger project by means of the metaphor of a work of art described in the text, and evoking varieties of emotions and responses within the fictive world of the text.[9] That is, the long history of writing about works of art (whether fictional, like the shields of Achilles in the *Iliad* and Aeneas in the *Aeneid,* or actual, like Josephus's account of the Temple in Jerusalem) is inextricably tied up with the tendency to turn the object into an emblem and the urge to see it as a metaphor. How consciously this pattern of emblematic tendentiousness in the ekphrasis of material culture was present in the minds of Raphael, Vasari, Gibbon, or Berenson when each launched his rhetorical torpedo against the Arch of Constantine, is impossible to say, but in a sense it is unnecessary to ask, for the pattern is written into what we might call the rhetorical unconscious when it comes to the practice of ekphrasis.

All this has got me round to saying that objects make the narrative flow of history stumble. They should do—for against our speculations about motives and character, actions and causes in the past, they place a material obstacle (of course, an obstacle voiced rhetorically) that alludes within the discursive patterns of writing to an actuality or thereness exterior to the written. Objects affect narratives in two ways, which are frequently not in perfect harmony: they are inevitably part of whatever story, agenda, theme they have been summoned to help on its way, but they are also reminders of real and tangible things, things we know or can conjure in our imaginations from a space of real-life experience outside the narrative. What matters here is their appeal "outside the narrative," as well as within it. For it is in that space—whether a Marxist materialist reality check, a relic's or icon's material link into a spiritual realm greater than mere history, the German phantasm of *Bildung* as developed through the experience of high culture and great art—that the ideological phantasmagoria which I have evoked by means of the Arch of Constantine can come into powerful play.

The challenge of executing a series of cultural histories of the material world might be thought the reverse of the process of summoning images and objects to do their bit for history. It is the attempt the make history out of the material world. But we have to be doubly careful. For that means the adaptation of discourses principally created for the appropriation of textual documents to materials which do not signify in the ways that texts do. Indeed, we do not even have any kind of general agreement as to how objects mean, how they signify, whether they communicate at all. We have very few studies of the varieties of materiality—the ways imitation, replication, miniaturization, enclosure, invagination, inscription, texture, volume, etc., let alone issues of function and instrumentality—direct the beholder's (often the holder's) attention and imagination. We may, if we are sensitive to this, have some sense of how a work of art or music may affect us (one day—but is it the same or remotely similar the next?), but to what extent is any of this transferable to how other people—or the generality of people—may respond? And is it the case that all categories of material culture actually signify in the same ways—from high art in two dimensions (e.g., painting) via high art in three dimensions (e.g., sculpture) via high art in three dimensions which encloses a beholder's space (e.g., architecture) via every other form of non-high art from ancient archaeological artifacts to all kinds of modern packaging and ephemera—from books as artifacts themselves to the illustrations within them—and so forth. The question is analogous on the level of text to whether a poem means in the same ways as a will, or an epitaph, or a political speech—let alone a historian's narrative. What I mean by all this is that the cultural history of the material world—meaning the world of man-made artifacts at specific times and across time—is a great experimental adventure in which few rules have yet been written, and many pitfalls and heffalump traps remain to be fallen into.

Now it might be fairly claimed that at least we have some selected historiographic models to help our enterprise along: examples of good histories of material culture and— perhaps even more usefully—examples of bad ones, roads better left untraveled. But here again I am skeptical. The history of art—an area where one might reasonably expect to find such models—has largely been a series of ideologically charged discussions of objects tied into a scheme borrowed from history and coordinated—through most of the twentieth century at least—by a specially constructed jargon around questions of style and form. Berenson's *The Arch of Constantine or the Decline of Form* may stand as a particularly mad, fascinating, and extreme example, from a giant among art historians. The model of Warburg—of great current critical interest—has frequently been adduced. But here we have a further problem, which has rarely been articulated, but is essential to the challenge.

We work and write at a time when the products of high art—especially literature, music, and the visual arts—no longer have the same cultural standing across Western culture as a whole (let alone in the context of globalization) that they did for Warburg, or indeed for anyone brought up and trained in the values that predominated before the Second World

War, which includes most practitioners within the academy—which has been conservative in preserving those values—both after the war, and until today. The reason for the collapse of those values in the culture generally may be traced fundamentally to the breaking of what I would call the "cultural contract" that prevailed in the 150 years before the Nazi government in Germany. This contract affirmed that great art was, above all, valuable because it created the conditions for *Bildung*—the intellectual, ethical, and philosophical formation of human beings to make them better people—and that the fostering of *Bildung* itself led to the generation of more great art in new and experimental forms, as well as scholarship, humanism, and human development. Of course, the values and arenas to which the products of *Bildung* extend are larger than the fine arts—including at least music and literature, in all of which criteria such as beauty might be seen to resonate. But there is little doubt that Winckelmann's seminal art historical project of the 1760s not only helped to inaugurate the formulation of a series of canonical master-pieces on which *Bildung* could be based, but also prompted much of the great scholarly explosion of the later eighteenth and nineteenth centuries in which the project of *Bildung* was developed.[10] Although *Bildung* is supremely a German enterprise, many of its values and assumptions were shared and remain implicit—if no longer fully or wholeheartedly believed—in the other Western cultures.

The orchestras that played Mozart as the cattle cars were emptied, and their occupants marched to the gas chamber have broken forever the fantasy that art can deliver anything by way of *Bildung*, and that *Bildung* has any certainty of making a man a better man. I know this personally. My mother's piano teacher, who lived in Krakow before the war, and in London after the war—Natalya Karpf—survived Auschwitz by playing Chopin for Amon Goeth. The point is that the appreciation of art has no effect at all on the capacity of a man to conduct genocide on a daily basis. No amount of education in any of the great achievements of humanism necessarily makes any difference. But the problem with the breaking of the cultural contract is that most people who believe in it—or want to do so—are either in denial, or enter apologetic mode. Most art histori-cal writing—especially by the best art historians after the War—is, in my view, both interestingly and highly problematically caught in apology as it tries to find ways of justifying value which can no longer have a basis, and as far as wider contemporary culture is concerned, do not.[11]

The cultural history of the material world in our time cannot be caught in apologetics and must, therefore, be wary and skeptical about its debts to earlier traditions. It must, of course, absolutely not be art historical in the old-fashioned sense, in that its focus must be on a much wider range and remit of material culture than just high art. But the challenge is not made easier by the lack of models from which to start, and the lack of much conceptual understanding of how objects in all their variety may make meaning in their cultural settings. My hunch is that we need to get a lot more material and hands-on in our approaches—just at a historical juncture when museums are making it that much more difficult to handle anything, and as our students, tied more than ever before to a high sophistication of the two-dimensional image as delivered on the flat screen of a computer, are less literate than ever before in questions of three-dimensional materiality. We need, therefore, to be both closer to our objects in understanding their materiality, and more theoretical than we have so far been about how that materiality and its decorative semiotics translate into cultural meanings, both in their periods of production and over longer trajectories of time and reception. That theoretics needs to be materially grounded in the ways objects themselves exist spatially and chromatically; the turn to forms of theory rooted in linguistics and literary criticism, which dominated art history in the 1980s and 1990s, is not particularly helpful here. In fact, I do not think much is obvious about how we should proceed, but some things are clear about how we should not.

NOTES

1. See F. Haskell, *History and Its Images* (New Haven, CT: Yale University Press, 1993), 186–91.
2. See E. Gibbon, *The History of the Decline and Fall of the Roman Empire* (1776), ed. J. B. Bury (New York: The Limited Edition Club, 1946), 331; or ed. D. Womersley (London: Allen Lane, 1994), vol. 1, 428.
3. The text of Raphael's letter of 1519 is in E. Camesasca and G. Piazza, eds., *Raffaello, Gli Scritti* (Milan: Rizzoli, 1994), 257–322; with discussion and translated in R. Goldwater and M. Treves, *Artists on Art* (London: Kegan Paul, 1945), 74–75; the discussion of Vasari is in G. Vasari, *Le vite de' piu eccellenti pittori, scultori ed archittetori,* ed. G. Milanesi (Florence: Barbèra, 1878 [1568]), 224–25 (*Proemio delle Vite,* 5). On the stylistic rhetoric running these accounts, see J. Elsner, "Style," in *Critical Terms for Art History,* 2nd ed., ed. R. Nelson and R. Shiff (Chicago: University of Chicago Press, 2003), 98–109. On Gibbon's debt to "written sources," see Haskell, *History and Its Images.*
4. See B. Berenson, *L'arco di Costantino o Della decadenza della forma* (Milan:

Electa, 1952); and *The Arch of Constantine or the Decline of Form* (London: Chapman and Hall, 1954); see the discussion of J. Elsner, "Berenson's Decline, or his *Arch of Constantine* Reconsidered," *Apollo* 148 (July 1998): 20–22.

5. This paragraph summarizes a much longer argument in J. Elsner, "Art History as Ekphrasis," *Art History* 33 (2010): 8–33.

6. These handbooks (the so-called *Progymnasmata*) are conveniently translated and introduced by G. Kennedy, *Progymnasmata: Greek Textbooks of Prose Composition and Rhetoric* (Atlanta: Society of Biblical Literature, 2003). For discussion, see R. Webb, *Ekphrasis, Imagination and Persuasion in Ancient Rhetorical Theory and Practice* (Aldershot, UK: Ashgate, 2009), 39–60.

7. See Webb, *Ekphrasis, Imagination, and Persuasion*, 1–3, 61–86.

8. See Theon, *Progymnasmata* 7; Hermogenes, *Progymnasmata* 10; see Aphthonius, *Progymnasmata* 12; respectively in Kennedy, *Progymnasmata*, 46, 86, 117.

9. Useful recent discussions include S. Goldhill, "What is Ekphrasis For?" *Classical Philology* 102 (2007) 1–19; V. Cunningham, "Why Ekphrasis?" *Classical Philology* 102 (2007) 57–71; Webb, *Ekphrasis, Imagination, and Persuasion*, 167–92 (on the poetics of Ekphrasis).

10. On Winckelmann, one might start with A. Potts, *Flesh and the Ideal: Winckelmann and the Origins of Art History* (New Haven, CT: Yale University Press, 1994); E. Décultot, *Johann Joachim Winckelmann: Enquête sur la genèse de l'histoire de l'art* (Paris: Presses universitaires de France, 2000); and E. Pommier, *Winckelmann, inventeur de l'histoire de l'art* (Paris: Gallimard, 2003); on his place at the origins of the German cultural obsession with Greece, see S. Marchand, *Down From Olympus: Archaeology and Philhellenism in Germany 1750–1970* (Princeton, NJ: Princeton University Press, 1996), 7–16; C. Güthenke, *Placing Modern Greece: The Dynamics of Romantic Hellenism 1770–1840* (Oxford: Oxford University Press, 2008), 25–32.

11. The history of the effect of the breaking of the cultural contract across all the arts (not just material culture, but also music and literature), and in all the scholarly disciplines of humanism, remains to be written. The topic is not only vast but by no means simple—differently modulated among Germans and German-Jewish émigrés, among the other nations of Europe (with various degrees of collaboration and resistance to Nazi rule, and various degrees of postwar guilt, most of it suppressed or expressed mutedly), in the most significant receivers of postwar Jewish emigration—namely, the United States and Israel. It cannot be wholly differentiated from colonialist/imperialist assumptions about civilization, which were again differently modulated among the great imperial powers of the nineteenth and twentieth centuries (including the United States).

FOURTEEN

Beyond Representation: Things—Human and Nonhuman

Ittai Weinryb

> There is a gallery in Rome where I take myself
>   while wandering about;
> Looking for new things, I found a sapphire vase.
> The ignorant vendor was selling incense with
>   the sapphire;
> My companion bought the incense for thrice
>   three pennies
> And I lavishly bought the vase for three and a
>   half shillings.
> Since I was concerned about carrying it with-
>   out jarring it,
> I paid the price of an elegant wicker box.
> The vase was put in whole, I remember about
>   that, brought out cracked:
> I feel very sad and unhappy about that.
> If it had been carried in among court nobles
> As it had been put in then, it would have been
>   of high value.
> But the porter pressed down on it—may no
>   day be prosperous for him![1]

In an imaginary stroll through the streets of Rome, while looking for new things (*res,* which usually signifies an object, but could also be understood as matter or material), the bishop and poet Marbod of Rennes (1035–1123) reveals a hitherto concealed aspect of the early twelfth-century attitude toward the material world. A newly purchased vase was broken on the way home. Noting the crack it now bore, Marbod comments that if the damage had been made in the past, it would be acceptable. In fact, an historical crack would have delighted Marbod, for it would have made the precious vase even more valuable. Since cracks bore witness to an object's historicity, he saw, in a calculated manner, that broken objects could have value in the Middle Ages.[2]

The poem likely narrates a fictional journey. Modern scholars have stressed the importance of such journeys as exegetical, and as exemplars of mnemonic contemplative practice. But in addition to this, however, the poem reveals that Rome, for the Frenchman Marbod, was a place of difference, and even alterity. In the heart of this foreign region, as in the essence of the poem, lies an understanding that the value of objects, particularly ones with temporal marks postdating their fabrication, extended far beyond their material form.[3]

As a broken *res*, the vase offered, apart from a promise of a form that was now lost, a material presence that bore formidable significance. The poet's understanding that the vase was once whole, and his subsequent dismay due to the porter's mishandling of it, are simply echoes of a contemplative notion. According to Marbod, as an object combines its material form with marks of its "history," its wholeness is transformed so that the material presence of the broken vase exceeds, in a sense, its functional value.

For a medievalist, especially one who developed his scholarly outlook in an art history department, the reality that there was a material world in the Middle Ages, and that this material world is not with a collection of pictorial representations, is of extreme importance. Until now, the study of medieval art has focused almost exclusively on the analysis of pictorial representations: it is the disembodied representation that bears meaning, especially when it is combined with networks of text, primarily those relating to the Holy Scriptures. From this point of view, all images produced in the Middle Ages are seen to either participate in—or to be in discourse with—other types of representation. Thus, conventionally, the material world is only engaged insofar as it provides a potential surface for studying such representations.[4]

Marbod's poem offers a rare glimpse into medieval object lore, for it considers an object's material state as a primary component of its significance. Here, materiality conveys not representation, but presence. The "being" of the object is not necessarily perceived by sight as the primary tool of cognition, but rather through networks of significations that lie beyond the visible. This is to say that pictorial representation, if it existed on the vase, would have been of secondary importance to Marbod. Based on this story, at least, we might propose that, in the study of interactions between humans and objects, it is not the study of the representation, but rather the rigorous assessment of the presence of an object that is— or ought to be—of significance to historians.

While examining pictorial representation has been the primary method used to scrutinize objects, Marbod's poem provides something substantial that cannot necessarily be understood through a conflation of text and image. The poem demonstrates that meaning lies beyond a mere understanding of "things" as allusions to this or that text. The poem suggests that the merit of an object lies in its material presence, where text—or at least text in its direct referential function—is not critical to an understanding of the object. The "histories of things" of the Middle Ages are sometimes written as histories of materials. At present, this constitutes a growing field of research where the symbolism of materials is determined largely by looking to texts that derive from the Scriptures and their commentaries. Sometimes known as the "Iconology of Material," this mode of analysis assumes that physical matter has a certain metaphorical value, which is constituted by texts that are independent of, and unrelated to, the object itself. It is the meaning of the material in the text that enhances an understanding of an object made from a specific material.[5]

Marbod's engagement with the broken sapphire vase, and in a sense his preoccupation with its materiality, is not about the metaphorical value of the sapphire. His interest in the vase lies primarily in his "discovery" of it. Marbod, a foreigner in Rome, realized the vase had been displaced from the site of its fabrication—or at least the place where its material substance was excavated. This awareness thus produced the possibility of imagining the locale where the sapphire originated. With the understanding that material cannot be created *ex nihilo*, but must always be made or brought from somewhere else, materials were always designated as either "local," or extraterritorial. This foreign place could be a geographical location or an imagined site. Yet, in both cases they were understood as elsewhere—a place unreachable at present, if ever. This precondition has generated several studies relating to materials and their significance, particularly in the field of spolia studies, where the reuse of specific, geographically dislocated materials is understood as an indication of political or religious ideology.[6] In both the case of spolia studies, as in Marbod's poem, foreignness is a prerequisite for a discussion of materials and their representation. It is only when Marbod is away from his native habitus that he discovers the material presence of the vase and makes note of its cracks.

Other works written by Marbod additionally underscore his interest in materials. Notably, he wrote the first medieval "book of gems," or lapidary. His manuscript, penned in hexameter and based on an Aristotelian model, discusses the secrets of sixty different stones, while also assessing their medicinal qualities. The property of each stone—which Marbod does not locate in the stone's decorative potential, nor in its representational value—is embedded in the material itself. Marbod's lapidary marks a shift in the interests of the monastic and clerical community.[7] Scholars such as Gerald Bond have suggested that the lapidary demonstrates a revival of naturalism indicative of a "Twelfth-Century Renaissance."[8] I would like to claim more than that, for the interest here is in the power of material. Marbod touches upon this at the onset of his lapidary.

Their different kinds, their varying hues I teach,
What land produces, what the power of each . . .
For sure, the hidden powers of gems to know,
What great effects from hidden causes flow,
A science this to be confines and viewed with admiration by
    mankind.[9]

In this passage Marbod insists that the different origins of materials and the concealed knowledge of their power are cause for their admiration. Indeed, knowledge of the qualities of organic entities like the gems was known only to few, who understood the material presence of each stone only through its apparent magical power. Attesting to his connoisseurship, Marbod presents himself reflexively in the poem, insisting on the legitimacy of his knowledge. A few lines earlier, he remarks that the book's readership ought to be tightly restricted: "whoever vulgarizes mysteries reduces majesty, and things known to the crowd do not remain secret."[10] There is knowledge in matter, in its materiality, and in what comprises material culture. He attributes powers—even vitalism—to nonhuman objects. It is this his belief in this knowledge that might have motivated, at least in part, Marbod's purchase of the vase, as well as his endeavor to classify the marvelous gems of the world.[11] Marbod seems to believe that a nonhuman object can possess power independent of its appearance because of its material, and that this power could affect humans and nonhumans alike.[12] A few decades after Marbod described his

Fig. 1. The vase of red porphyry was made in Egypt or imperial Rome. The mount of gilded silver in the form of an eagle was added before 1122 in the Abbey of Saint Denis under Abbot Suger (1081–1151). MR. 422. Louvre, Paris, France. (Photo: Erich Lessing/Art Resource, New York.)

fictional purchase, another vase (fig. 1), still extant, was sought by Suger, Abbot of St. Denis, as is mentioned in his *De Administratione* (1147).[13] This particular object was an antique Egyptian vase, a spoliated work acquired by Suger. He embellished the vase with the head, feet, and wings of an eagle—all made of gold.[14] The container, made of porphyry, was transmogrified into an elaborate sculpture. Yet, as Suger commemorated in an inscription appended to the neck of the vase, the original material was still fundamental to the transformed object.

> This stone deserves to be enclosed in gems and gold. It was marble, but in [these] settings it is more precious than marble[15]

Scholars dealing with this well-known object usually emphasize its liturgical function within Suger's newly expanded treasury. In doing so, they highlight the symbolic character of the porphyry as related to royalty.[16] The vase is also frequently cited as an example of the interest in spolia within the "treasury culture" of the Middle Ages.[17] Aside from the vase, Suger commissioned bronze doors for St. Denis, which have an inscription stating that the "work suppresses the material" (*materiam suberabat opus*). Recently, both the vase and the doors have been the center of a debate about whether the work referred to in the inscription relates to the creative capabilities of the artist, or whether it refers to the devotional work of the worshipper—in this case, Suger, whose belief is stronger and more valuable than the preciousness of the material. In comparing Marbod's vase with that of Suger, we see that both men were invested in the object not as a representation of form, nor as a representation of a certain temporal past, but rather as an integral part of a network of meaning that extends beyond the formal appearance of the object.[18]

In transforming the vase into an eagle, Suger bestowed upon it the features of an animal and, in doing so, the object was imbued with an animate spirit—that is, with vitality. This process of enlivening an object is also found in the material essence of the sapphire vase in Marbod's poem.[19] In his book of gems, Marbod associates the precious qualities of the sapphire with kings and nobles, presenting it as a material that also enlivens the body, binds the soul of a loved one, and even breaks prisoner's chains.[20] Such ascriptions were recently conceptualized by Jane Bennett as "thing-power"—by which she means that the inherent vitalism of material is not the result of efficacy, nor does it aspires to affect; rather, it grants independence to materials and objects. Their meaning lies beyond the definition that their makers or users give them.[21]

The inscription Suger placed on his vase seems to suggest that the vase was transformed purely for financial enrichment: it was worth more when embellished with gold and gems. Indeed, the inscription might be read as a calculated assertion of vase's absolute monetary value. Marbod likewise seems to view his purchase in monetized terms. Yet, in his lapidary, Marbod forwards the argument that the functional value of a stone is its essence, and that this value has an impact on the natural world. Suger, too, presents the porphyry's materiality as something living, thus inserting it into the natural world. Curiously, Marbod and Suger express surprisingly similar attitudes toward material presence in their terminology: Marbod endeavors to look for things (*res*), while Suger's inscription refers to the vase as stone (*lapis*).

Objects, for both Marbod and Suger, exist as embodiments of materials, not as forms, and the meaning of these materials lies beyond pictorial representation. In a passage of his manuscript, *De Administratione,* Suger describes looking at both a screen reliquary, known as the *crista,* and the jeweled Cross of St. Eloi.

> Then I say, sighing deeply in my heart: every precious stone was thy covering, the sardius, the topaz, and the jasper, the chrysolite, and the onyx, and the beryl, the sapphire, and the carbuncle, and the emerald. To those who know the properties of precious stones it becomes evident, to their greatest wonder (*admiratione*), that none of these is missing except the carbuncle, but that they abound most copiously.[22]

As in Marbod's book of gems, Suger emphasizes that the meaning of stones lies beyond representation—a meaning that is knowable only to a chosen few *cognoscenti*—the same intellectual elite for whom Marbod wrote his book.[23] Viewing materials as representations induces this response; "things" are approached as if they were living, animated objects. Both Suger and Marbod explicitly differentiate between humans and nonhumans—a division in which nonhumans are not presented as figural representations, but as "things" whose meaning extends beyond representation.[24]

What I suggest is that a certain type of vitality begins to be ascribed to the materiality of objects in the early twelfth century.[25] Outlining the multiplicity of reasons for this development is well beyond the scope of this chapter. However, to understand this ontological change, one needs only to think of the formation of Salerno's medical school in the second half of the eleventh century, and the translation of Arabic knowledge into Latin, which elicited a new conceptualization of the human body, particularly in regard to blood circulation and the function of the humors.[26] Similarly, the translation of scientific texts by Constantine the African at Monte Cassino and his successors likewise promoted new ways of conceiving the material body.[27]

These movements ought to be viewed both synchronically and diachronically. More specifically, the translation of texts from Arabic and Greek to Latin seen alongside the commentary on Marbod's vase and Suger's transformation of his vase are critical to interpreting the reception of both texts and the objects. This movement promoted an understanding of both humans and stones as made of minerals. An equality of materials is at play: sapphire, agate, and porphyry are as human as flesh, bones, and blood. Conversely, these materials should be regarded as nonhuman. In the early to mid-twelfth century, both humans and nonhumans embodied an animation whose origins were not found in figural representation, but rather in the vitalism assumed in their material essence—the magical and spiritual properties of which were beyond the boundaries of any pictorial display. During this period, the interaction between humans and objects was conceived of as an interaction between two material-based entities, whose distinction in relationship to humanity was not necessarily as obvious as it is to our twenty-first-century minds. At the onset of the twelfth century, the material world and the world beyond representation collapsed: materiality—as opposed to the impression of forms—motivated interaction between humans and objects.[28]

A rigorous examination of the notion of materiality, shared between humans and nonhumans of diverse historical periods and geographical regions, defines what could well be called the cultural history of the material world. Given the current questions concerning stem-cell research, DNA replication, and material cloning, the thoughts of men such as Marbod and Suger, both of whom humanized the inanimate world, should well illuminate our own moral dilemmas.[29] Men and women of the twelfth century were constantly engaged in understanding their immediate surroundings, while simultaneously coming to terms with their place in the world. Their relationship with things—as much as, or even more than, their social fellowship—was a core aspect of cultural production of the period. The objects and minerals considered as *res* demand new interpretive historical and art-historical methods and frameworks that we have yet to uncover, but which we certainly will grow closer to establishing in this new series.[30]

NOTES

1. *Porticus est Roma, quo dum spatiando fero me/ Res quaerendo novas, inveni de saphyro vas/ Institor ignotus vendebat cum saphiro thus/ Thus socius noster tres emit denatorios ter/ Vas tribus et semi-solidis ego prodigus emi / Hoc inconcussum dum tollere sollicitus sum/ Pro cofino mundo de viminibus pretium do/ Ponitur introrsum sanum vas, inde memor sum,/ Extrahitur fissum, tristis miser inde nimis sum./ Inter convivas magni foret hoc pretii vas/ Si foret allatum, sicut positum fuerat tum/ Lator at hoc pressit, cui prospera nulla dies sit* (PL 171.1685). I follow Gerald A. Bond's excellent translation. See also Gerald A. Bond, *The Loving Subject: Desire, Eloquence and Power in Romanesque France* (Philadelphia: University of Pennsylvania Press, 1995): 94–95. See also Charles Witke, "Rome as 'Region of Difference' in the Poetry of Hildebert of Lavardin," in *Papers of the Twentieth Annual Conference of the Center for Medieval and Early Renaissance Studies,* ed. Saul Levin and Aldo S. Bernardo (Binghamton, NY: Center for Medieval & Early Renaissance Studies, 1990), 403–11. Witke interprets Rome in the poem he studies as an imaginary place rather than the actual, visited city.

2. This popular poem, which survives today in fifteen distinct copies, exhibits an overlooked relationship between people and objects in the Middle Ages. Traditionally, the poem is interpreted as a self-reflective, almost meditative piece, and is often compared with the passage: "I am forgotten as one dead from the heart. I am become a broken vase" (Psalms 30:13, *oblivioni traditus sum quasi mortuus a corde factus sum quasi vas perditum*). In this chapter, however, I present a different interpretation. See Gerald A. Bond, *The Loving Subject,* 95.

3. Exile as a process that leads to of discovery because of its potential to alert the senses, is a concept best described by literary scholars such as Edward Said, especially in his discussion of Erich Auerbach. See Edward Said, *Reflections on Exile and other Essays* (Cambridge, MA: Harvard University Press, 2000), 173–86. For recent arguments on issues of exile and discovery as related to questions of cultural mobility, see Stephen Greenblatt, ed., *Cultural Mobility: A Manifesto* (Cambridge, MA: Harvard University Press, 2009); Finbarr B. Flood, *Objects of Translation: Material Culture and Medieval "Hindu-Muslim" Encounter* (Princeton, NJ: Princeton University Press, 2009).

4. For various assessments of the "state" of the field, see Herbert L. Kessler, "On the State of Medieval Art History," *Art Bulletin* 70 (1988): 166–87; Herbert L. Kessler, "Medieval Art as Argument," in *Iconography at the Crossroads,* ed. Brendan Cassidy (Princeton, NJ: Princeton University Press, 1993), 59–73; Herbert L. Kessler, *Seeing Medieval Art* (Peterborough, ON: Broadview Press, 2004); Jeffrey F. Hamburger, "The Place of Theology in Medieval Art History: Problems, Positions, Possibilities," in *The Mind's Eye: Art and Theological Argument in the Middle Ages* ed. Jeffrey F. Hamburger and Anne-Marie Bouché (Princeton, NJ: Princeton University Press, 2006), 11–31; Jeffrey F. Hamburger, "The Medieval Work of Art: Wherein the 'Work'?; Wherein the 'Art'?," in *The Mind's Eye: Art and Theological Argument in the Middle Ages,* 374–412. See also the articles in Conrad Rudolph, ed., *A Companion to Medi-*

eval Art: Romanesque and Gothic in Northern Europe (Oxford: Blackwell, 2006).

5. Thomas Raff, *Die Sprache der Materialien: Anleitung zu einer Ikonologie der Werkstoffe* (Munich: Deutscher Kunstverlag, 1994); Günther Bandmann, "Bemerkungen zu einer Ikonologie des Materials," *Städel-Jahrbuch* 2 (1969): 75–100; and Wendy Stedman Sheard, "Verrocchio's Medici Tomb and the Language of Materials: with a Postscript his Legacy in Venice," in *Verrocchio and Late Quattrocento Italian Sculpture: Acts of Two Conferences Commemorating the Fifth Centenary of Verrocchio's Death,* ed. Steven C. Bule (Florence: Casa Editrice Le Lettere, 1992), 63–90. Herbert L. Kessler, *Seeing Medieval Art,* 19–42; Bruno Reudenbach, "'Gold ist Schlamm': Anmerkungen zur Materialbewertung im Mittelalter," in *Material in Kunst und Alltag,* ed. Monika Wagner and Dietmar Rübel (Berlin: Akademie Verlag, 2002), 1–12; and Hans-Rudolf Meier, "Ton, Stein und Stuck: Materalaspekte in der Bilderfrage des Früh- und Hochmittelalters," *Marburger Jahrbuch für Kunstwissenschaft* 30 (2003): 35–52; Friedrich Ohly, "On the Spiritual Sense of the Word in the Middle Ages," in *Sensus Spiritualis: Studies in Medieval Significs and the Philology of Culture,* ed. Samuel P. Jaffe (Chicago: University of Chicago Press, 2005), 1–30. More generally, see Monika Wagner, Dietmar Rübel, and Sebastian Hackenschmidt, *Lexikon des künstlerischen Materials: Werkstoffe der modernen Kunst von Abfall bis Zinn* (Munich: Beck, 2010), Dietmar Rübel, Monika Wagner, and Vera Wolff, *Materialästhetik: Quellentexte zu Kunst, Design und Architektur* (Berlin: Reimer, 2005).

6. Dale Kinney, "Rape or Restitution of the Past?: Interpreting 'Spolia,'" in *The Art of Interpreting,* ed. Susan C. Scott (University Park: Pennsylvania State University Press, 1995), 52–67; Dale Kinney, "The Concept of 'Spolia,'" in *A Companion to Medieval Art: Romanesque and Gothic in Northern Europe,* ed. Conrad Rudolph (Oxford: Blackwell, 2006), 233–52; Philipe Buc, "Conversion of Objects," *Viator* 28 (1997): 99–143; Anthony Cutler, "Reuse or Use? Theoretical and Practical Attitudes Toward Objects in the Early Middle Ages," in *Ideologie, pratiche e reimpiego nell'alto Medioevo, XLVI Settimana di Studio del Centro Italiano di Studi sull'Alto Medioevo* 46 (1999), 1055–79; Avinoam Shalem, *Islam Christianized: Islamic Portable Objects in the Medieval Church Treasuries of the Latin West* (Frankfurt: Peter Lang, 1998); Beat Brenk, "Spolia from Constantine to Charlemagne: Aesthetics Versus Ideology," *Dumbarton Oaks Papers* 41 (1987): 103–9; and also Rebecca Müller, *Sic hostes Ianua frangit: Spolien und Trophäen im mittelalterlichen Genua* (Weimar: VDG-Verlag und Datenbank für Geisteswissenschaften, 2002).

7. The literature on early medieval lapidaries is not extensive: see Joan Evans and Mary S. Serjeantson, *English Mediaeval Lapidaries* (Oxford: Oxford University Press, 1933); Robert Halleux, "Damigéron, Evax et Marbode: l'héritage alexandrin dans les lapidaires médiévaux," *Studi medievali* 15, no. 1 (1974): 327–47; Paul Studer, *Anglo-Norman Lapidaries* (Geneva: Slatkine Reprints, 1976); William Holler, "Unusual Stone Lore in the Thirteenth-Century Lapidary of Sidrac," *Romance Notes* 20 (1979): 135–42; Stefano Pittalunga, "Marbodo e Teofilo," in *Latin Culture in the Eleventh Century: Proceedings of the Third International Conference on Medieval Latin Studies Cambridge, September 9–12, 1998,* ed. Michael W. Herren, C. J. Mcdonough, and

Ross G. Arthur (Turnhout: Brepols, 2002), 302–16; and Serenella Baggio, "Censure Lapidarie," *Medioevo romanzo* 11, no. 2 (1986): 207–28. See also Sharon Farmer, "Low Countries Aesthetics and Oriental Luxuries: Jacques de Vitry, Marie de Oignies, and the Treasures of Oignies," in *History in the Comic Mode: Medieval Communities and the Matter of Person*, ed. Rachel Fulton and Bruce Holsinger (New York: Columbia University Press, 2007), 205–22. Jeffrey Jerome Cohen recently published an article dealing with Marbod's book of stones: "Stories of Stone," *Postmedieval: a Journal of Medieval Cultural Studies* 1 (2010): 56–63.

8. Gerald A. Bond, *The Loving Subject*. Among the extensive bibliography, see Charles Homer Haskins, *The Renaissance of the Twelfth Century* (Cleveland: The World Publishing Co., 1967); Robert L. Benson and Giles Constable, "Introduction," in *Renaissance and Renewal in the Twelfth Century*, ed. Robert L. Benson and Giles Constable (Toronto: University of Toronto Press, 1991), xvii–xxx; R. N. Swanson, *The Twelfth Century Renaissance* (Manchester: Manchester University Press, 1999), 1–11; Melve Leidulf, "'The Revolt of the Medievalists': New Directions in Recent Research on the Twelfth Century Renaissance," *Journal of Medieval History* 32, no. 3 (2006): 231–52; Sara Ritchey, "Rethinking the Twelfth-Century Discovery of Nature," *Journal of Medieval and Early Modern Studies* 39, no. 2 (2009): 225–55.

9. *Hoc opus excerpens dignum componere duxi/ Aptum gestanti forma breviore libellum . . . Scilicet hinc solers mediocrum cura juvantur/ Auxilio lapidum morbos expellere docta.* John M. Riddle, ed., *Marbode of Rennes' De Lapidibus: Considered as a Medical Treatise with Text, Commentary, and C.W. King's Translation, Together with Text and Translation of Marbode's Minor Works on Stones* (Wiesbaden: Steiner, 1977), 34.

10. John M. Riddle, ed., *Marbode and Rennes' De Lapidbus*, 34.

11. On medieval wonder and the "wonder" as an object, see Jaques Le Goff, "The Marvelous," in *The Medieval Imagination,* trans. Arthur Goldhammer (Chicago: University of Chicago Press, 1988): 27–46; Lorraine Daston and Katharine Park, *Wonders and the Order of Nature*, 1150–1750 (New York: Zone Books, 1998), 13–87; Caroline Walker Bynum, "Wonder," *American Historical Review* 102, no. 1 (1997): 1–17; *Metamorphosis and Identity* (New York: Zone Books, 2001), 37–76; and, most recently, Robert Bartlett, *The Natural and the Supernatural in the Middle Ages* (Cambridge: Cambridge University Press, 2008).

12. In this respect, the medieval nonhuman can be regarded also as an automaton—a functional and efficacious machine of some sort. On medieval automata, see Kurt Weitzmann, "The Greek Sources of Islamic Scientific Illustrations," in *Archaeologica orientalia in memoriam Ernst Herzfeld,* (New York: Augustin, 1952), 244–66; Alfred Chapius and Edmond Droz, *Automata: A Historical and Technological Study,* trans. Alec Reid (Neuchatel: Editions du Griffon, 1958); Derek J. de Solla Price, "Automata and the Origins of Mechanism and Mechanistic Philosophy," *Technology and Culture* 5 (1964): 9–23; Reinhold Hammerstein, *Macht und Klang: Tönende Automaten als Realität und Fiktion in der alten und mittelalterlichen Welt* (Bern: Francke Verlag, 1986); Elspeth Whitney, *Paradise Restored: The Mechanical Arts from*

Antiquity through the Thirteenth Century (Philadelphia: American Philosophical Society, 1990); and Elly Rachel Truitt, "From Magic to Mechanism: Medieval Automata 1100–1550" (PhD diss., Harvard University, 2007).

13. Susanne Linscheid-Burdich, *Suger von Saint-Denis: Untersuchungen zu seinen Schriften "Ordinatio", "De consecratione", "De administratione"* (München: Saur, 2004); Andreas Speer, "L'abbé Suger et le trésor de Saint-Denis: une approche de l'expérience artistique au Moyen Age," in *L'abbé Suger, le manifeste gothique de Saint-Denis et la pensée victorine: colloque organisé à la Fondation Singer-Polignac, le mardi 21 novembre 2000,* ed. Dominique Poirel (Turnhout: Brepols, 2001), 59–82; Lindy Grant, *Abbot Suger of St-Denis: Church and State in Early Twelfth-Century France* (London: Longman, 1998); Andreas Speer, "Art as Liturgy: Abbot Suger of Saint-Denis and the Question of Medieval Aesthetics," in *Roma, magistra mundi: itineraria culturae medievalis,* ed. Jacqueline Hamesse (Louvain-La-Neuve: Collège Cardinal Mercier, 1998), 855–75; Conrad Rudolph, *Artistic Change at St-Denis: Abbot Suger's Program and the Early Twelfth-Century Controversy over Art* (Princeton, NJ: Princeton University Press, 1990); and Gabrielle M. Spiegel, *The Chronicle Tradition of Saint-Denis: A Survey* (Brookline, MA: Classical Folia Editions, 1978).

14. For basic bibliography on the vase, see *Le Trésor de Saint-Denis: Musée du Louvre, Paris, 12 mars 17 juin 1991* (Paris: Bibliothèque nationale, Réunion des musées nationaux, 1991), 184–87; Danielle Gaborit-Chopin, "Suger's Liturgical Vessels," in *Abbot Suger and Saint-Denis: A Symposium,* ed. Paula Lieber Gerson (New York: Metropolitan Museum of Art, 1986), 283–93. See also George T. Beech, "The Eleanor of Aquitaine Vase, William IX of Aquitaine, and Muslim Spain," *Gesta* 32, no. 1 (1993): 3–10.

15. *Include gemmis lapis iste meretur et auro. Marmor erat, sed in his marmore carior est.* In *Abbot Suger on the Abbey Church of St.-Denis and its Art Treasures,* trans. and ed. by Erwin Panofsky, 2nd ed. by Gerda Panofsky-Soergel (Princeton, NJ: Princeton University Press, 1979), 78–79; see also Peter Cornelius Claussen, "Materia und opus: mittelalterliche Kunst auf der Goldwaage," in *Ars naturam adiuvans: Festschrift für Matthias Winner zum 11. März 1996,* ed. Victoria V. Flemming and Sebastian Schütze (Mainz am Rhein: von Zabern, 1996), 40–48. More recently, Jeffrey Hamburger associated the inscription with the Middle Ages' complex relationship between physical objects and spiritual devotion, "The Medieval Work of Art; Wherein the 'Work'?; Wherein the 'Art'?," 374–412.

16. Josef Deér, *The Dynastic Porphyry Tombs of the Norman Period in Sicily* (Cambridge, MA: Harvard University Press, 1959); Thomas Raff, *Die Sprache der Materialien,* 134–41; and Michael Greenhalgh, *Marble Past, Monumental Present: Building with Antiquities in the Mediaeval Mediterranean* (Leiden: Brill, 2009), 144–52.

17. Beat Brenk, "Sugers Spolien," *Arte Medievale* 1 (1983): 101–7; and Beate Fricke, *Ecce Fides: die Statue von Conques, Götzendienst und Bildkultur im Westen* (Munich: Fink, 2007), 281–310; and Pierre Alain Mariaux, "Collecting (and display)," in *A Companion to Medieval Art: Romanesque and Gothic in Northern Europe,* ed. Conrad Rudolph (Oxford: Blackwell, 2006), 213–32.

18. See Martin Büchsel, "Die von Abt Suger verfaßten Inschriften: gibt es eine

ästhetische Theorie der Skulptur im Mittelalter?," in *Studien zur Geschichte der europäischen Skulptur im 12./13. Jahrhundert*, ed. Herbert Beck (Frankfurt: Henrich, 1994), 57–73; and Peter Cornelius Claussen, "Materia und opus: mittelalterliche Kunst auf der Goldwaage," in *Ars naturam adiuvans: Festschrift für Matthias Winner zum 11. März 1996*, ed. Victoria von Flemming (Zabern: Mainz am Rhein, 1996), 40–49. See also, as part of a more extensive trend of shifting Suger from a Panofskian art lover to a zealous image-theologian, the various editions and translations made under the direction of Andreas Speer, especially the collected writings and translations: Andreas Speer, Günther Binding et al., eds., *Abt Suger von Saint-Denis. Ausgewählte Schriften: Ordinatio, De consecratione, De dministratione* (Darmstadt: Wissenschaftliche Buchgesellschaft, 2005). Recently, on this debate, see Jeffrey F. Hamburger, "The Medieval Work of Art: Wherein the 'Work'?; Wherein the 'Art'?" On the significance of work, material, and their relations, see Peter Cornelius Claussen, "Materia und opus," 40–49. On the phrase *materiam suberabat opus* in relation to material iconology in the Middle Ages, see Thomas Raff, "'Materia superat opus': Materialien als Bedeutungsträger bei mittelalterlichen Kunstwerken," *Studien zur Geschichte der europäischen Skulptur im 12./13. Jahrhundert*, ed. Herbert Beck and Kerstin Hengevoss-Dürkop (Frankfurt: Henrich, 1994), 17–28; and Thomas Raff, *Die Sprache der Materialien: Anleitung zu einer Ikonologie der Werkstoffe* (München: Deutscher Kunstverlag, 1994), 27–49.

19. On enlivenment, see primarily these studies: David Freedberg, *The Power of Images: Studies in the History and Theory of Response* (Chicago: University of Chicago Press, 1989); Hans Belting, "Image, Medium, and Body: A New Approach to Iconology," *Critical Inquiry* 31 (2005): 302–19; Horst Bredekamp, *Theorie des Bildakts* (Berlin: Suhrkamp, 2010).

20. *Nam corpus vegetat, conservat et integra membra.* John M. Riddle, ed., *De Lapidus*, 42.

21. Jane Bennett, *Vibrant Matter: a Political Ecology of Things* (Durham, NC: Duke University Press, 2010), 1–38. See also Manuel De Landa, *A Thousand Years of Nonlinear History* (New York: Zone Books, 1997), 11–103.

22. See *Abbot Suger on the Abbey Church of St.-Denis and Its Art Treasures*, 63.

23. From the endless bibliography, see Lorraine Daston and Katharine Park, *Wonders and the Order of Nature, 1150–1750* (New York: Zone Books, 1998), 13–66.

24. I cannot but evoke the work of Bruno Latour, especially in regard to the Actor-Network Theory. See Bruno Latour, *Reassembling the Social: an Introduction to Actor-Network-Theory* (Oxford: Oxford University Press, 2005); and John Law and John Hassard, eds., *Actor Network Theory and After* (Oxford: Blackwell, 1999).

25. Many things are ascribed to the twelfth century, and the notion of the "twelfth-century Renaissance" has long been an over-encompassing frame aimed at dealing with that "change" that took place in the twelfth century, see Robert L. Benson and Giles Constable, "Introduction," in *Renaissance and Renewal in the Twelfth Century*, ed. Robert L. Benson and Giles Constable (Toronto, University of Toronto Press, 1991), xvii–xxx; and R. N.

Swanson, *The Twelfth-Century Renaissance* (Manchester: Manchester University Press, 1999), 1–11. Most recently see Melve Leidulf, "'The Revolt of the Medievalists': New Directions in Recent Research on the Twelfth Century Renaissance," *Journal of Medieval History* 32, no. 3 (2006): 231–52. Animation and Vitalism could be regarded as another aspect of the "twelfth-century Renaissance."

26. Paul Oskar Kristeller, "The School of Salerno: Its Development and its Contribution to the History of Learning," *Bulletin of the History of Medicine* 17 (1945): 151–57; Charles Singer, *From Magic to Science: Essays on the Scientific Twilight* (New York: Dover Publishing, 1958); Ilse Schneider, "Die Schule von Salerno als Erbin der antiken Medizin und ihre Bedeutung für das Mittelalter," *Philologus: Zeitschrift für klassische Philologie* 115 (1971): 278–91; Morris Harold Saffron, "Maurus of Salerno twelfth-century 'Optimus Physicus' with his commentary on the prognostics of Hippocrates," *Transactions of the American Philosophical Society* 62, no. 1 (1972): 5–104; Gerhard Baader and Gundolf Keil, *Medizin im mittelalterlichen Abendland* (Darmstadt: Wissenschaftliche Buchgesellschaft, 1982); Monica H. Green, "The *De genecia* Attributed to Constantine the African," *Speculum* 62, no. 2 (1987): 299–323; Brian Lawn, *The Prose Salernitan Questions: An Anonymous Collection Dealing with Science and Medicine Written by an Englishman c. 1200, with an Appendix of Ten Related Collections* (Oxford: Oxford University Press, 1979); Gerhard Baader and Gundolf Keil, *Medizin im mittelalterlichen Abendland* (Darmstadt: Wissenschaftliche Buchgesellschaft, 1982); Tony Hunt, *Anglo-Norman Medicine I: Roger Frugard's "Chirurgia", the "Practica Brevis" of Platearius* (Woodbridge: Boydell Brewer, 1994); Monica Green, *The Trotula: A Medieval Compendium of Women's Medecine* (Philadelphia: University of Pennsylvania Press, 2001); Paolo Delogu and Paolo Peduto, eds., *Salerno nel XII secolo: Istitutzioni, società, cultura: atti del convegno internazionale, Raito di Vietri sul Mare Auditorium di Villa Guariglia 16/20 giugno 1999* (Salerno: Centro Studi salernitani "Raffaele Guariglia," 2004); Peter Murray Jones, "Image, Word, and Medicine in the Middle Ages," in *Visualizing Medieval Medicine and Natural History, 1200–1550,* ed. Jean A. Givens, Karen M. Reeds, and Alain Touwaide (Aldershot, UK: Ashgate, 2006), 1–24; Danielle Jacquart and Agostino Paravicini Bagliani, eds., *La Scuola Medica Salernitana. Gli autori e i testi. Convegno internazionale Università degli Studi di Salerno 3–5 novembre 2004* (Florence: Sismel-Edizioni del Galluzzo, 2007); Noga Arikha, *Passions and Tempers: A History of the Humours* (New York: Ecco, 2007). For an overview of these issues, see David C. Lindberg, *The Beginnings of Western Science* (Chicago: University of Chicago Press, 1992), 321–56.

27. On Constantine the African, see Dominique Haefeli-Till, *Der Liber de oculis des Constantinus Africanus: Übersetzung und Kommentar* (Zürich: Juris-Verlag, 1977); Charles Burnett and Danielle Jacquart, *Constantine the African and Ali ibn al-Abbas al-Magusi: The Pantegni and Related Texts* (Leiden: Brill, 1994); Fuat Sezgin, *Constantinus Africanus (11th cent.) and his Arabic Sources: Texts and Studies* (Frankfurt: Institute for the History of Arabic-Islamic Science at the Johann Wolfgang Goethe University, 1996); and Thomas Ricklin, *Der Traum der Philosophie im 12. Jahrundert: Traumtheorien zwischen Constantinus*

Africanus und Aristoteles (Leiden: Brill, 1998). On the translation movement of the twelfth century, see Marie-Thérèse d'Alverny, "Translations and Translators," in *Renaissance and Renewal in the Twelfth Century*, ed. Robert L. Benson and Giles Constable (Cambridge, MA: Harvard University Press, 1982), 421–62; Charles Burnett, *The Introduction of Arabic Learning into England: The Panizzi Lectures, 1996* (London: The British Library, 1997); Charles Burnett, "The Coherence of the Arabic-Latin Translation Program in Toledo in the Twelfth Century," *Science in Context* 14 (2001): 249–88; Charles Burnett, "A Group of Arabic-Latin Translators Working in Northern Spain in the mid–twelfth Century," *Journal of the Royal Asiatic Society* (1977): 62–108; Charles Burnett, "Arabic into Latin in Twelfth-Century Spain: The Works of Hermann of Carinthia," *Mittellateinisches Jahrbuch* 13 (1978): 100–134; Charles Burnett, "Some Comments on the Translating of Works from Arabic into Latin in the Mid-Twelfth Century," in *Orientalische Kultur und europäisches Mittelalter*, ed. Albert Zimmerman (Berlin De Gruyter, 1985), 161–71; Charles Burnett, "The Translating Activity in Medieval Spain," in *The Legacy of Muslim Spain*, ed. Salma Khadra Jayyusi (Leiden: Brill, 1992), 1036–58; and Jeanette Beer, *Translation Theory and Practice in the Middle Ages* (Kalamazoo, MI: Medieval Institute, 1997). For an overview of these questions, see David C. Lindberg, *The Beginnings of Western Science*, 193–225. To my knowledge, the issues promoting a blurriness in the distinctions between animate-inanimate and human-nonhuman did not exist in the original Arabic and Greek texts, but resulted from the conflation of different texts arriving from different sources, and from their interpretation through Latin commentaries.

28. This development should be viewed as a phenomenon developing side by side with anthropomorphic three-dimensional sculpture, which served either as shrines for relics or as cult images. See recently Beate Fricke, *Ecce Fides*.

29. W. J. Thomas Mitchell, "The Work of Art in the Age of Biocybernetic Reproduction," *Modernism/Modernity* 10, no. 3 (2003): 481–500; Jeffrey Jerome Cohen, *Stories of Stone*.

30. In 1994, when asked to comment on the future of medieval art, Michael Camille argued that if the cathedral nave was read by scholars in the nineteenth century as a book, as a "summa in stone," then scholars of the twenty-first century would regard the very same nave as a computer interface. What I describe suggests a further development, beyond the computer desktop dotted with icons signifying pictorial representations to which Camille alluded, into the domain of virtual reality and artificial intelligence. See Michael Camille, "Art History in the Past and Future of Medieval Studies," in *The Past and Future of Medieval Studies*, ed. John Van Engen (Notre Dame, IN: University of Notre Dame Press, 1994), 362–82.

FIFTEEN

Materialities of Culture

Bill Brown

It seems to be a propitious time for a monograph series to unfold under the rubric of "The Cultural History of the Material World." Several disciplines—history, art history, the history of science and science studies, literary studies, anthropology, political science, media studies, even philosophy—these have taken a "material turn" of one sort or another. The editors of *The Handbook of Material Culture* (2006) begin their introduction by asserting that "studies of material culture have undergone a profound transformation during the past twenty years and are now among the most dynamic and wide-ranging areas of contemporary scholarship in the human sciences."[1] And with unbridled excitement, the editors of *The Object Reader* (2009) report that "the study of objects is intensifying across the arts, humanities, and social sciences": "it seems that everywhere one looks in the academy, objects abound."[2] More dispassionately, I noted, in my introduction to *Things*, a special issue of *Critical Inquiry* (2001), that "these days you can read books on the pencil, the zipper, the toilet, the banana, the chair, the potato, the bowler hat"—a list to which one could now add (among other things) the cell phone, the Twinkie, corn, nylon, salt, beans, the iPod, and the toothpick.[3] A Victorianist literary critic publishes *Ideas in Things* (a history of calico curtains, of mahogany furniture, of "Negro Head" tobacco as these inform the novels of Gaskell, Brontë, and Dickens), and a critic of the eighteenth century in England publishes *The Things Things Say* (an account of property law, object autobiographies, and slave narratives); one philosopher argues on behalf of *Thing Knowledge* (the effort to develop a materialist epistemology that recognizes instruments as the bearers of knowledge that themselves shape science), and another argues on behalf of *Guerilla Metaphysics: Phenomenology and the Carpentry of Things* (an "object-oriented philosophy" that has no truck with the analytic and continental traditions); historians of science and of art converge to contribute essays to *Things That Talk* (isolating particular objects to investigate how matter means).[4] Forty years ago, Jean Baudrillard could lament (and denounce) the way that the object, considered "only the alienated, accursed part of the subject," had been rendered unintelligible, "shamed, obscene, passive."[5] But by the turn of the twentieth century, figures such as Michel Serres, Bruno Latour, and Jacques Rancière described a kind of ontological democracy where persons and things—the human and the nonhuman—can be understood as living together and as speaking to one another.[6] Bringing its audience *in medias res*, "Cultural History of the Material World" may help us perceive the complications, equivocations, and possible destinations of that "democracy" (present, past, and future). At the very least, the current frisson of fascination with the inanimate object world presents this project with unusual possibilities, and with particular problems.

For on the one hand, there is now a much broader scholarly audience for the history of material culture; there is a materialist longing unsatisfied by Marx's historical materialism, eager to discover aesthetic and semantic dimensions of the material world which economic attention tends to elide, and no less eager to convey the sense (and sensations) of the human encounter with the physical environment. But on the other hand, scholars trained neither in history nor in material culture (as taught within art history, anthropology, or archaeology) might very well lay claim—consciously or unconsciously—to practicing the cultural history of the material world. How, then, does a publishing project make use of the transdisciplinary energy that has newly catalyzed the interpretive focus on objects while simultaneously insisting on the discipline (or the specific interdisciplinarity) that distinguishes this series from any number of publications seemingly devoted to both materiality and culture? It did not take long for anthropology to develop an allergic reaction to cultural studies, with the sense that its central concept had been poached. It did not take long for art history to develop an allergic reaction to visual studies, with the sense that its central object threatened to blur. How does the cultural historian of the material world produce an (abstract) object of analysis and a mode of analysis that establishes knowledge claims that distinguishes this practice from others? How does a series that is not invested in stabilizing an academic field, but rather in recognizing an epistemological field that has emerged from distinct disciplines—say art history, design history, history, anthropology—achieve coherence? What kind of historiographical and methodological self-consciousness will energize (or enervate) the series? To borrow from what I tend to call the post-postprocessual moment in archaeology, what strategies can be marshaled for remaining empirical without being empiricist? What certainties about the terms "culture," "history," and "the material world" should be shared? Which uncertainties should be staged?

The cultural history of the material world can hardly help but evoke its inverse—the material history of the cultural world—which may mean little more than pausing to think about the mutual mediation of culture and materiality. Culture—as it is studied and as it is lived—is materially mediated, and materiality is mediated culturally. However casually one thinks about Athenian culture, ca. 500 BCE; or Kwakwaka'wakw culture, ca. 1900; or New York culture, ca. 2010, the thought will no doubt involve some image of the object world—of built space, of dress, of practical things, and of decorative things. Within ethnology, the culture concept as such emerged from curatorial questions about how to display objects: when Franz Boas decided to abandon the exhibition of artifacts within a technological history (of knives or baskets or pots), and to exhibit them instead within a dioramic scene of their use, the coherence of the scene depended on recognizing and organizing cultural specificity.[7] Even though he abandoned museum work, unconvinced that culture could be apprehended through objects alone—without attention to language, for instance—culture remains, nonetheless, the medium through which we understand material artifacts to attain meaning and value.

In both ordinary and specialized language, materiality can refer to different dimensions of experience, or dimensions beyond or below what we generally consider experience to be. Like many concepts, materiality may seem to make the most sense when it is opposed to another term: the material serves as a commonsensical antithesis to the spiritual, the abstract, the ideal, the phenomenal, the virtual, and the formal, let alone the immaterial. Still, Epicurean or Spinozan convictions about the materiality of the imagination would seem to have resurfaced within neurophysiology. And yet materiality has achieved a specificity that differentiates it from its superficial cognates, such as physicality, reality, or concreteness. When one admires the materiality of a lead-glazed earthenware bowl, one is admiring something about its look and feel, not sim-

ply its existence as a physical object. These days, within the melodrama
of besieged materiality, digitization has been cast as the most likely vil-
lain. Describing the "dematerialization of material culture," Colin Renfrew laments the current separation "between communication and substance," the image having become increasingly "electronic and thus no
longer tangible." Because "the electronic impulse is replacing whatever
remained of the material element in the images to which we became
accustomed," the "engagement with the material world where the material object was the repository of meaning is being threatened." All told,
by Renfrew's light, "physical, palpable material reality is disappearing,
leaving nothing but the smile on the face of the Cheshire Cat."[8] Nonetheless, media history, media theory, and cybercultural studies now draw
attention to the "materiality of the medium," the "materiality of information," and the "materiality of communication," ranging from a focus
on the material substratum of media, to a focus on the human body's
interaction with technology, to a focus on the socioeconomic systems
which support that interaction.[9] Moreover, within the history of media
aesthetics, Walter Benjamin and Siegfried Kracauer (among others) insisted that new media—specifically, photography and film—can disclose
a material world that remains otherwise inapprehensible.[10] A digital project devoted to the cultural history of the material world will have to face
the contemporary cultural fact that the digital and the material have
become—for many people—antagonists. Which is only to say that some
participants in the project will probably need to reiterate the Benjamin-
ian point—that new technologies can enrich the perceptual field, dis-
closing new details and new structures of the material world.

In his contribution to an anthology of essays on material culture,
History from Things, Robert Friedel points to what Aristotle designated
the "first cause" of things—the material cause, as that which has been
elided in studies of material culture that emphasize instead the design,
the maker, and the purpose. "It is ironic," Friedel writes, "that studies
of material culture should so neglect the actual materials that go into
creating culture." Using the example of two teapots—one manufactured
from tin, the other from blown glass—he insists on what might be considered obvious: that only by considering the material of each object can
we begin to understand the cultural significance of each.[11] A striking
example of such consideration appears in the overture of Eric Slauter's
study of the cultural origins of the U.S. Constitution, *The State as a Work
of Art.* He begins by drawing attention to the mahogany speaker's chair
of the Constitutional Convention in Philadelphia, to the iconography

invoked by Benjamin Franklin in what Madison recorded as the final
words of the constitutional debates: the painting of a half-eclipsed sun,
whose ambiguity (as a rising or a setting sun) had troubled Franklin during the convention until, at last, he "had the happiness to know that it is
a rising sun." But Slauter concentrates not just on the iconography of the
chair that George Washington occupied as he presided over the sessions
of debate. He concentrates as well on the history of the chair's fabrication by John Folwell, which includes the chair's material constitution:
"That Folwell fashioned this symbol of liberty [a liberty cap atop a pole]
from a wood harvested by slaves in Central America and the West Indies
was a material fact that would not have registered with many contemporary viewers, black or white, who found themselves in the Pennsylvania
State House. To them, the chair would have symbolized the revolution-
ary promise that the rise of liberty could be as natural as the rising sun."
What Slauter calls the "material fact" of the chair's origin in the log-
ging of mahogany (at the close of what Percy Macquoid, the historian
of English furniture, designated the "Age of Mahogany," ca. 1720–1770)
amounts to a cultural history congealed within the material that is at
odds with the cultural history of the object.[12] Scholars from different
disciplines have shown how particular objects more legibly stage a nego-
tiation between different cultures.[13]

In her inspiring essay, "Beyond Words," Leora Auslander argues that
"historians of all periods should be attentive to, and train themselves in
the use of, material culture" because "people have always used all five of
their senses in their intellectual, affective, expressive, and communicative practices"; because "objects not only are the product of history, they
are also active agents in history"; and because "most people for most of
human history have not used written language as their major form of expression."[14] Even within my own remote sphere—literary studies—from
which the linguistic turn gained such serious momentum, it has become
possible to glimpse a circle that only some cultural history of our material
world will be able to bring into focus. The history of the book is a subfield
that may seem to provide literary criticism with historical, archaeological
relief from theory. But one could argue instead that the field has, in fact,
affirmed the very concerns raised by the most iconic of theorists: concerns about paratexts, frames, folds, borders, margins, authorship and
authority, typing and printing, gathering and dispersion, . . . the "materiality of the signifier."[15] In turn, it is hard to imagine a scholar in the
distant future being able to write a history of what was once called theory
without providing a short history of the material components of the em-

bodied text, such as paper: "the basis of the basis, the base figure on the basis of which figures and letters are separated out," as Jacques Derrida wrote in "Paper or Me."[16] How else to explain the moment in 1967 when, questioning the unity of the book—of his books—Derrida gestured toward the rematerializing fantasy of stapling *Writing and Difference* between the two parts of *Of Grammatology* with *Speech and Phenomena* appended as a "long note."[17] Thirty years later, he was willing to assert that he had "never had any other subject" than "paper, paper, paper," the subject—if not the substance—that precipitated the themes of the mark, the trace, the fold, all circulated within an overarching "tenacious certainty . . . that the history of this 'thing,' this thing that can be felt, seen, and touched, and is thus contingent, paper, will have been a brief one."[18] Even as Derrida points out how theory, too, inhabits the cultural history of the material world—things felt, seen, and touched—we must be ready to sense how and when cultural history summons its own theorization.

NOTES

1. Chris Tilley et al., eds., *Handbook of Material Culture* (London: Sage, 2006), 1.
2. Fiona Candlin and Raiford Guins, eds., *The Object Reader* (London: Routledge, 2009), 3.
3. Bill Brown, "Thing Theory," *Critical Inquiry* 28 (Autumn 2001): 2. This special issue was expanded and republished as a book, *Things* (Chicago: University of Chicago Press, 2004).
4. Elaine Freedgood, *The Ideas in Things: Fugitive Meaning in the Victorian Novel* (Chicago: University of Chicago Press, 2006); Jonathan Lamb, *The Things Things Say* (Princeton, NJ: Princeton University Press, 2011); Davis Baird, *Thing Knowledge: A Philosophy of Scientific Instruments* (Berkeley and Los Angeles: University of California Press, 2004); Graham Harman, *Guerilla Metaphysics: Phenomenology and the Carpentry of Things* (Chicago: Open Court, 2005); Lorraine Daston, ed., *Things That Talk: Object Lessons from Art and Science* (New York: Zone, 2004).
5. Jean Baudrillard, *Fatal Strategies,* trans. Phillip Beitchman and W.G.J. Niesluchowski (New York: Semiotext(e), 1990), 111–12.
6. See, in particular, Bruno Latour, *We Have Never Been Modern,* trans. Catherine Porter (Cambridge, MA: Harvard University Press, 1993); *Pandora's Hope: Essays on the Reality of Science Studies* (Cambridge, MA: Harvard University Press, 1999); and, more recently, "Objects Too Have Agency," in *Reassembling the Social: An Introduction to Actor-Network-Theory* (Oxford: Oxford University Press, 2005), 63–86.
7. On Boas, see George Stocking Jr., "Franz Boas and the Culture Concept in Historical Perspective," *Race, Culture, and Evolution: Essays in the History of Anthropology, 1883–1911* (Chicago: University of Chicago Press, 1982), 195–

233. On objects and the culture concept in both anthropology and literature, see Bill Brown, "Regional Artifacts," *A Sense of Things: The Object Matter
of American Literature* (Chicago: University of Chicago Press, 2003), chapter
3; and Brad Evans, *Before Cultures: The Ethnographic Imagination in American
Literature, 1865–1920* (Chicago: University of Chicago Press, 2005).

8. Colin Renfrew, *Figuring It Out* (London: Thames and Hudson, 2003), 185–
86.

9. See, for example, Hans Ulrich Gumbrecht and K. Ludwig Pfeiffer, eds.,
Materialities of Communication, trans. William Whobrey (Stanford, CA: Stan-
ford University Press, 1994); Timothy Lenoir, ed., *Inscribing Science: Scientific
Texts and the Materiality of Communication* (Stanford, CA: Stanford University
Press, 1998); and Robert Mitchell and Phillip Thurtle, eds., *Data Made Flesh:
Embodying Information* (New York: Routledge, 2004).

10. See, for instance, Walter Benjamin, "Little History of Photography," trans.
Edmund Jephcott and Kingsley Shorter, in *Walter Benjamin: Selected Writ-
ings, vo. 2, 1927–1934,* ed. Michael W. Jennings, Howard Eiland, and Gary
Smith (Cambridge, MA: Harvard University Press, 1999), 512; and Siegfried
Kracauer, *Theory of Film: The Redemption of Reality* (Princeton, NJ: Princeton
University Press, 1997).

11. Robert Friedel, "Some Matters of Substance," in *History from Things: Essays
on Material Culture,* ed. Steven Lubar and W. David Kingery (Washington,
D.C.: Smithsonian Institution Press, 1993), 41–50.

12. Eric Slauter, *The State as a Work of Art: The Cultural Origins of the Constitution*
(Chicago: University of Chicago Press, 2009), 1–5. Percy Macquoid, *The Age
of Mahogany* (London: Lawrence and Bullen, 1906).

13. Nicholas Thomas, *Entangled Objects: Exchange, Material Culture, and Colonial-
ism in the Pacific* (Cambridge, MA: Harvard University Press, 1991); Ruth B.
Phillips, *Trading Identities: The Souvenir in Native North American Art from the
Northeast, 1700–1900* (Seattle: University of Washington Press, 1999); Laurel
Thatcher Ulrich, *The Age of Homespun: Objects and Stories in the Creation of an
American Myth* (New York: Vintage, 2002).

14. Leora Auslander, "Beyond Words," *American Historical Review,* October
2005. http://www.historycooperative.org/journals/ahr/110.4/auslander.
html.

15. On the history of the book, see, for instance, among his many books, Roger
Chartier's *Inscription and Erasure: Literature and Written Culture from the Eleventh to the Eighteenth Century,* trans. Arthur Goldhammer (Philadelphia: University of Pennsylvania Press, 2008); and see Adrian Johns, *The Nature of
the Book: Print and Knowledge in the Making* (Chicago: University of Chicago
Press, 1998). For the literary-critical deployment of this history, see Leah
Price, "Reading Matter," *PMLA* 121, no. 1 (2006): 9–16. This is her introduction to *PMLA*'s special issue on the history of the book.

16. Jacques Derrida, *Paper Machine,* trans. Rachel Bowlby (Stanford, CA: Stanford University Press, 2005), 53.

17. Jacques Derrida, *Positions,* trans. Alan Bass (Chicago: University of Chicago
Press, 1981), 4.

18. Jacques Derrida, *Paper Machine,* 40.

PART 4

Future Histories

SIXTEEN

Toward a Cultural History of the Material World

Juliet Fleming

> Analytical bibliography: the study of books as
> physical objects; the details of their produc-
> tion, the effects of the method of manufacture
> on the text. When Sir Walter Greg called
> bibliography a science of the transmission of
> literary documents, he was referring to analyti-
> cal bibliography. Analytical bibliography may
> deal with the history of printers and booksell-
> ers, with the description of paper or bindings,
> or with textual matters arising during the pro-
> gression from writer's manuscript to published
> book.
>
> —Terry Belanger[1]

> *Of Grammatology* is the title of a question: a
> question about the necessity of a science of
> writing, about the conditions that would make
> it possible, about the critical work that would
> have to open its field and resolve the epistemo-
> logical obstacles; but it is also a question about
> the limits of this science.
>
> —Jacques Derrida, *Positions*[2]

The best contribution I can make to this project is to offer a rationalized
prospectus of the book I am currently writing, and to sketch in brief its
concern with how, within literary studies, we might newly address the material world. I know next to nothing about the discipline and traditions

of cultural history, so excuse myself from that part of our task—although what I imagine must be the fundamental questions of cultural history, "how do things move us? And how are those movements of the mind or heart transmitted?" are also questions at the center of my own concerns.

My first book, *Graffiti and the Writing Arts of Early Modern England,* led me to be identified, with Peter Stallybrass and others, as a "new materialist," and a contributor to what is sometimes, and unfortunately, called "the new history of the book."[3] But I think the term "material" as used in such work is often an alibi for concepts that, however useful they may be in practice, have not been rigorously scrutinized, and I continue to believe that if there is something consequential to be achieved within a renovated history of the book we will find it only by pushing further with the question of what, theoretically rather than practically, we can know about writing and its materials. My current project is to read Derrida's *Of Grammatology* (1967) against the grain of even its most positive reception, and to find within it the outlines of an intellectual practice that should markedly sophisticate what is currently being called, within literary studies, "the new materiality."

The book I am currently writing, "Counter-productions: Analytical Bibliography after Derrida," takes as its leading term a neologism coined by Sebastiano Timpanaro, the Italian critic whose professional interests ranged from philology and cultural history to the theory and practice of materialism. In *The Freudian Slip: Psychoanalysis and Textual Criticism,* Timpanaro took issue with Freud's proposition that the unconscious was the agent of linguistic errors by referring the immediate cause of such errors to the material properties of the language systems within which they occurred, as when a hard term is replaced by one more familiar, when phonically or semantically similar words are transposed, or when words are repeated, omitted, or introduced from elsewhere in the text.[4] Drawing on his experience as a proofreader, Timpanaro demonstrated that many instances of what Freud judged to be linguistic parapraxes (that is, actions bungled when conscious intentions were derailed by the interference of unconscious thoughts) were, on the contrary, typical scribal or typographical errors, and that what Freud regarded as *Begunstigungen*— circumstances that favored, but did not cause the slip of tongue, pen, or memory—were themselves the sufficient conditions for many of the errors in question.

Timpanaro called such errors "counter-productions," a term that happily underlines what appears to be their double nature, for slips of the pen are both held to be accidents and judged to have a thoroughly material cause. As Timpanaro defined them counter-productions occur outside the conscious mind, and can therefore be said to frustrate its wishes, but their cause must be referred, not to the deeper intentions of unconscious thought, but to the neurophysiological processes of the brain. Even when they concern the substitution of one extant word or phrase for another, counter-productions are thus not words, at least as that concept is commonly understood, for the substituted term represents the trace of a perception rather than the expression of a conscious or unconscious thought. So where, for Freud, verbalization is always linked with the bringing of something to consciousness, for Timpanaro it is a process that can be referred, instead, to the physiological mechanisms of memory, forgetfulness, and concentration.

Timpanaro's analysis has given me fruitful pause for three reasons (none of them having to do with the status of psychoanalysis as a theory or practice):

1. It picks up a question that briefly interested Derrida, and continues to interest me—the question as to what Freud was really up to when, in *The Psychopathology of Everyday Life*, he first adduced and then overrode the issue of slips of the pen.
2. It raises the issue of chance and its links with determinism. For here the fact that chance, being always materially determined, is not chance at all, is no longer surprising. Counter-production comes about because the material world is not an external force that oppresses human actors but is inside us: it is the grounds of our agency. Furthermore, as the unpredictable appearances of counter-production can remind us, the material world is not implacable, massive, and recalcitrant, but in motion, volatile, and reactive: its events are unpredictable not because they are set against human intention but because they are the outcome of an incalculable number of material variables—including human actions—as these adapt and respond to each other. A properly "new materiality" would now recognize that the humans sciences have, at least since the nineteenth century, always been addressed to the problem of human life as it unfolded in the middle of environmental affordances, and would continue to develop the work done there in order to describe the feedback relations between the material and the social worlds. Thus, it would not accord priority to nature over thought, or to the biological over the socioeconomic or cultural levels, but would do away with

these divisions as it worked to read human practices of all sorts as responses to the complexities of the real material process. In literary studies, a new materiality could then work to develop, as something that illuminated the rest of our work, a sense of language in its various forms as the intercommunication of forces and sensations felt in a continuous process of psychogenesis.

3. As described by Timpanaro, counter-production is a writing practice so thoroughly alienated from anything that usually goes by that name, and yet so intimately bound to it, that it renders writing enigmatic. As I see things, it is from just such a position, of having unlearned or forgotten what writing is, that we can best approach *Of Grammatology*.

When, in later life, Derrida looked back at *Of Grammatology* he saw it as the "seed-bed" of his subsequent intellectual career. But it may also be said to contain a path not taken. Gayatri Spivak, whose dazzling and influential introduction to her English translation of the work appeared in 1974, and has since continued to dominate its Anglophone reception, certainly thought so. As Spivak saw it, *Of Grammatology* is a work of Derrida's intellectual apprenticeship, marked by the overprominence within it of the topic of writing "in the narrow sense." Noting that part 1 is an expanded version of Derrida's earlier review of three books—Madeleine V. David's *Le débat sur l'écritures et l'hiéroglyphe aux xviii siècles,* André Leroi-Gourhan's *Le geste et la parole,* and the papers of a colloquium called "L'ecriture et la psychologie des peuples"—Spivak wondered "if all this overt interest in an account of writing in the narrow sense—rather than the interpretation of texts—is not simply due to the regulating presence of the books to be reviewed." Arguing that "in the *Grammatology* . . . we are at a specific and precarious moment in Derrida's career," when "'writing' so envisaged is on the brink of becoming a unique signifier and Jacques Derrida's chief care," Spivak noted with relief that "arche-writing" and "other important words in the *Grammatology* do not remain consistently important conceptual master-words in subsequent texts," but are replaced by other terms, while Derrida "quietly drops the idea of being the authorized grammatological historian of writing in the narrow sense."[5]

I do not think Spivak was wrong to conclude as she did. Considering the comparatively early date of her translation there is much in its preface that is remarkable for its prescient grasp of Derrida's consequence.

And yet, with hindsight we can see that Derrida, who described himself as never wanting to let anything go, retained to the end of his career an interest in writing "in the narrow sense," as is attested by a late collection of essays, published in 2001 and translated in 2005 as *Paper Machine*. More consequentially, I think that Derrida continued to worry—albeit in oblique ways—the path not taken in *Of Grammatology*, holding it in reserve as a line of inquiry that might have led, not to a newly sophisticated history of writing "in the narrow sense," but to the articulation of an entirely new discipline. Reading *Of Grammatology* under the guidance of Spivak's preface and through the prism of her pathbreaking but overly literal translation, English readers have been led away from one of Derrida's most audacious thought experiments—and from an idea whose moment has perhaps now come.

The new discipline would have been a science of writing conceived and prosecuted at two levels: grammatology, and cultural graphology. At the level of its most radical and necessary generality, grammatology could not, thought Derrida, be one among the sciences of man. Rather, it would be the science of man, and, before that, it would be at the root of all sciences. Following the lead of paleoanthropologist André Leroi-Gourhan, grammatology would understand man as an epiphenomenon in the history of the program or "natural technology" that is the progression of life on earth. Derrida called this program writing in its largest sense, and it is as the science of this writing that grammatology could be imagined. Had the two disciplines ever been established, cultural graphology would have been the regional science of grammatology. But again, it could not have behaved as just one among the regional sciences. For its subject, which Derrida envisioned as the investigation of all the "investitures" to which the forms and substances of writing are submitted by and within the collective mind of peoples, could not have been contained within a traditional understanding of writing, nor could the concepts of ideality and objectivity, which underpin the study of writing in the narrow sense, have proved an adequate foundation for its researches.

Sketching the outlines of the new discipline in twenty rarely read pages of the *Grammatology*, Derrida could only announce its prohibitive difficulties—only the most decisive of which was that it would have "to stop receiving its guiding concepts from other human sciences or, what nearly always amounts to the same thing, from traditional metaphysics." It is such formulations that have licensed Spivak and others to see the topic of writing in Derrida's work as an early and local manifestation of his larger commitment to the questions of being and presence. But in

Writing and Difference—a collection of essays published in the same year as *Of Grammatology,* and conceived as part of that work—Derrida seems to have been, for the space of two pages, almost sanguine about the chances of a new science of writing. "Such a radicalization of the thought of the trace would," he speculated, "be fruitful, not only in the deconstruction of logocentrism, but in a kind of reflection exercised more positively, in different fields, at different levels of writing in general, at the point of articulation of writing in the current sense and of the trace in general."[6]

At that point of articulation, cultural graphology could presumably address writing in the narrow sense as a privileged site where, within our traditions of thought, the problem of being (or, what for Derrida is the same thing, the effect of différance) had been encountered, noted, dissimulated, and dismissed, without being understood. Its first contours might therefore lie in those places where common sense and the academic disciplines had already tried and failed to account for writing, and Derrida went so far as to indicate four fields where it might begin its work. Three of these are: a history of writing that resisted its own tendency to privilege phonocentrism; a literary theory newly attentive to the "originality of the literary signifier," rather than to nonliterary signified meanings; and a "psychoanalytic graphology" that would draw on the work of Melanie Klein to explain how it is that, "on the stage of history," writing has been regarded both as food that nourishes and as the letter that kills. The fourth field, which appears first on Derrida's list, and which (at least at first appearance) has a more local dimension than the other three, would have comprised "a psychopathology of everyday life in which the study of writing would not be limited to the interpretation of the lapsus calami, and, moreover, would be more attentive to this latter and to its originality than Freud himself ever was."

Having said so much, Derrida fell silent. After 1967 he never pursued either part of the grammatological project by name, and although his later work makes signal contributions to the question of what—in its widest and narrowest senses—writing could be said to be, he said no more concerning the pursuit of cultural graphology as a unified field. I do not doubt that Derrida knew what he was doing, any more than I doubt that he continued the work of grammatology elsewhere, otherwise, using the opportunities that everywhere presented themselves to his extraordinary reach. Nevertheless, in the years in which I have been teaching and thinking about *Of Grammatology* I have found myself wondering if the seam he abandoned might not contain enough riches to reward further exploration, and for the past few years I have been following the most general form of his "ghost" discipline, engaging topics in litera-ture, psychoanalysis, and the history of writing in order to discover the consequences of recombining them under the single aegis of cultural graphology.

NOTES

1. Terry Belanger, "Descriptive Bibliography," in *Book Collecting: A Modern Guide,* ed. Jean Peters (New York and London: R. R. Bowker, 1977), 97–101.
2. Jacques Derrida, *Positions,* trans. Alan Bass (Chicago: University of Chicago Press, 1981).
3. Juliet Fleming, *Graffiti and the Writing Arts of Early Modern England* (Philadel-phia: University of Pennsylvania Press, 2001).
4. Sebastiano Timpanaro, *The Freudian Slip: Psychoanalysis and Textual Criticism* (London: NLB, 1976).
5. Jacques Derrida, *Of Grammatology,* trans. Gayatri Spivak (Baltimore: Johns Hopkins University Press, 1976).
6. Jacques Derrida, *Writing and Difference,* trans. Alan Bass (Chicago: University of Chicago Press, 1978), 230

SEVENTEEN

Thoughts on Cultural Histories of the Material World

Nancy J. Troy

> Let us suppose that the idea of art can be
> expanded to embrace the whole range of man-
> made things, including all tools and writing in
> addition to the useless, beautiful, and poetic
> things of the world. By this view the universe
> of man-made things simply coincides with
> the history of art. It then becomes an urgent
> requirement to devise better ways of consider-
> ing everything men have made. This we may
> achieve sooner by proceeding from art rather
> than from use, for if we depart from use alone,
> all useless things are overlooked, but if we take
> the desirableness of things as our point of de-
> parture, then useful objects are properly seen
> as things we value more or less dearly.
>
> —George Kubler, *The Shape of Time*

As a scholar trained in the history of modern art, I have worked primarily on the late nineteenth and early twentieth centuries in Europe. More
specifically, I have focused, in turn, on the art, architecture and design
of the Dutch De Stijl movement, modernism and the decorative arts in
France between 1895 and 1925, and the conjunction of art and fashionable women's clothing in early twentieth-century Paris. Although I have
always identified myself and the core concerns of my research with the
history of art as a discipline, it gradually became clear that my intellectual trajectory could not be located on the conventional map of modern-

ist art history that is embodied, for example, in the chart drawn up by Alfred Barr in 1936, in conjunction with his groundbreaking exhibition at the Museum of Modern Art, *Cubism and Abstract Art.*

De Stijl figured prominently in the narrative of modernism that Barr was tracing, but decorative art was anathema at MoMA, where industrial design in the Bauhaus mold was collected and praised instead, and contemporary fashions figured at the museum only when its galleries became the setting for photo shoots ordered up by advertisers or the editors of women's magazines. Thus, despite Barr's diverse and surprisingly eclectic interests, MoMA's focus developed more narrowly—mirroring his chart more faithfully—than its founding director might originally have wished.

Given my departure from the paradigm of modern art secured and promoted by the dominant institution in the field, I should not have been surprised when my books were catalogued by the Library of Congress, which saw to it that each seemed to stray further than the last from the history of art as a discipline—no matter where I thought they ought to be situated. MoMA's multimedia, yet insistently formalist model of modernism's development had ceded ground to a socially grounded history of art by 1983, when *The De Stijl Environment* appeared, and my study of the interaction between painters and architects could therefore be located at the heart of the discipline, if one were to judge by Library of Congress cataloguing categories.

Indeed, the categories applied to that book corresponded closely to a conventional history of art defined by styles (neoplasticism), articulated in the writings of artists (the journal *De Stijl*), and located, generally, in place and time ("Art, Modern—20th century—Netherlands"). That my second book, *Modernism and the Decorative Arts in France: Art Nouveau to Le Corbusier,* occupied a different position, outside the center of art historical gravity, was evident from its first two Library of Congress cataloguing categories, organized around what most historians of modern art dismissed as the mere decorative arts (against which many modern artists had oriented their work), while the third category, "Modernism (Art)—France," recognized the fine-art quotient of the book, though only parenthetically. In 2003, the categories applied to my third book, *Couture Culture: A Study in Modern Art and Fashion*—ranging from costume design to the clothing trade—seemed alien to my own knowledge base; art made an appearance only once, and then not as a self-sufficient category, but only in relation to fashion.

What now seems worth remarking about this trajectory outward to the margins of art history is that it was not a deliberately selected path: I never tried to aim my practice anywhere other than at the center of what I regarded, perhaps naively, as a fairly flexible disciplinary discourse capable of embracing multiple points of view and a disparate array of material objects. I embraced Kubler's suggestion that "the universe of man-made things simply coincides with the history of art," and saw no need to distinguish between objects of use, and those destined for contemplation. This was the spirit in which I approached the discipline's flagship journal, the *Art Bulletin*, during the years I was its editor. (The fact that I was selected for that post may be taken as a sign that the conventional distinctions were anyway loosing their force, at least to some of those at the discipline's center.) As editor, I sought to publish a range of viewpoints and invited contributions representing widely divergent theoretical perspectives. Far from seeing my goals as subversive, I thought art history was capable of celebrating difference and I wanted the *Art Bulletin* to embody change—made especially visible in relation to the status quo that many art historians thought the journal represented.

As far as my own work was concerned, I was unnerved when the Library of Congress cataloguers repeatedly overlooked the art historical dimension of *Couture Culture*, acknowledging my attention to fashion while ignoring my discussions of such staples of modernist art history as cubism and the work of Marcel Duchamp. The cataloguers seemed oblivious to the fundamental premise of my book—namely, that art and fashion were more similar than different, insofar as they were organized according to a common logic, a parallel structure of copying, and innovation. Fashion, it could therefore be argued, was actually not marginal at all.

Yet when I saw the Library of Congress' cataloguing-in-publication data for *Couture Culture*, I worried that my scholarship might not become visible to many of those who I considered to be my intellectual interlocutors—my primary audience. Few, if any, of their books would be retrieved by a subject search of fashion designers, much less of fashion merchandising or costume history, where my work was being located. However, I was aware that ambitious research was being devoted to fashion—in several cases, by costume historians who knew how to interrogate the material specificity of a dress—which I did not. Indeed, my knowledge of costume history was, and remains, fairly narrow, and my interest in the field is correspondingly limited. I did not particularly seek to be in sustained dialogue with costume historians, from whom, nevertheless, I had learned an enormous amount in the course of preparing my book.

If writing about early twentieth-century fashion and the decorative arts threatened to make my work peripheral to art history as typically practiced—even by those with whom I wanted to be in dialogue—my training, professional experience, and intellectual commitment to the discipline also made it awkward when I found myself identified with costume history or the history of the decorative arts. For example, when potential graduate students would ask about the possibility of working with me in those fields, I felt compelled to explain that my approach to both decoration and couture was through the history of art; I focus on visual materials and images, issues of representation, and the discursive construction of art and other visual objects in social and institutional contexts, studying those other media and practices in order to illuminate conditions and practices germane to the history of art. I would not be capable of training a student in the material history of fashionable clothes or the decorative arts, nor am I interested in trying to do so.

While my work has sometimes been marginal to conventional art historical practice, and I nevertheless cling to my disciplinary roots, nowadays I find myself aligned with those who study visual culture—a field that is, according to Vanessa Schwartz and Jeannene Pryzblyski, "constituted less by its topical repertoire and more to the degree that it produces a discursive space where questions and materials that have been traditionally marginalized within the established disciplines become central."

The study of visual culture accommodates works of art, but concentrates more on images or materials that typically circulate outside the realm of art, cannot be evaluated according to aesthetic criteria, and are therefore alien to the philosophical traditions that have underwritten the hierarchies on which modernist-art discourse was based. This is both the promise and the problem of visual-culture studies, insofar as the field has been, to some degree, shaped by attacking or rejecting the elitism of art and its institutions, as well as the history of art as a disciplinary practice. I have trouble recognizing the caricature that this construction of art history has produced. While I believe good art history can be written about bad art (or furniture, or clothing), I continue to learn from those who insist on studying the so-called masters of modernism, and I would not want to sacrifice the attention to specific formal, theoretical, and material issues that they bring to this work. Simple high/low, insider/outside dichotomies are too limiting when applied to the disciplines, whose boundaries, as Svetlana Alpers once remarked, ought to be a subject of investigation, rather than either reification or denial. With this in mind, I can embrace the interdisciplinary potential of visual- and material-culture studies, which are capable of producing cultural analysis that is rigorously grounded historically and intellectually.

Where has this led me in my scholarly practice today? In a sense, I have come full circle because I am once again working on the De Stijl painter and theorist, Piet Mondrian. This time, however, I am studying the historical construction of the artist that took place after his death in New York City in 1944. I aim to demonstrate that the understanding of Mondrian was not simply given in the artist's paintings or his writings about them, nor was it the result of disinterested scholarship or the straightforward exhibition of his work. Instead, Mondrian's place in the narrative of modernism was contested, shaped, and in some ways transformed as his work was conserved, copied, collected, displayed, studied, described, marketed, and publicized in a wide variety of venues ranging from art museum exhibitions to the pages of women's magazines—none of which were neutral or disengaged factors in the process. I plan to show that while Mondrian's international reputation as a master of high modernism was being secured in posthumous exhibitions and publications, his work simultaneously followed a parallel trajectory in the realm of popular culture, where his signature abstract style became instantly recognizable as a result of its appropriation by graphic designers, couturiers, and hotel owners, among many others. In fact, it is misleading to speak of parallel trajectories, because these were intertwined and mutually reinforcing rather than discrete or distinct from one another. Mondrian's work accrued value in the marketplace not only because it was recognized in the museum, but also because it was circulating widely in the popular sphere. My interest, then, lies in the discursive as well as the actual construction—and reconstruction—of Mondrian's oeuvre, which should be attributed not only to the artist and his contemporaries, but also—and arguably just as importantly—to the many others, myself included, who have engaged with his work in scholarly, elite, commercial, or popular contexts during the nearly seventy years since his death. Far from collapsing the differences between the various constituencies who have had a stake in Mondrian's work, I want to illuminate the degree to which they are mutually dependent and cumulatively ramifying precisely because they approach the discursive space in which Mondrian is constantly being constructed from different historical positions and highly differentiated points of view.

What can we learn from this example about the history of the material world and how it might be written? First of all, we should recognize that history is always in a process of being written and revised—and not only, or even principally, by scholars who self-consciously seek to do so. One way to imagine how we could write a history of the material world would be to inquire into how material objects and processes become historically relevant to us. This, it seems to me, involves both the ways in which they are constructed historically, and the ways in which we discover them in relation to that constructed narrative. Objects are not simply intrinsically meaningful, apart from their discursive environment and culturally imbedded circumstances, including their reception and circulation in time. Instead, they resonate within historically specific discursive conditions that we cannot afford to ignore. What the most exciting scholarship brings to this process is an insight into the character of the historical discourse, an ability to tease out the kinds of questions that may profitably be posed with respect to particular theoretical perspectives, and a sure sense of what is at stake in changing, or at least challenging, received paradigms. In this context, the disciplinary perspective of art history continues to be useful, even indispensable. Yet, it seems to me to be impossible to prescribe how a compelling history of the material world should be written, and what methods would be appropriate—or not. The material world is much too unwieldy to be tamed by any single methodological framework, and it is in the nature of intellectual inquiry to question any absolute or overarching structure—whether disciplinary or not. What we can do, I think, is work within, and against, the constraints of the (art) historical narratives we have received, analyzing and expanding them in ways that challenge us to think differently about things in the world—historically, and in the present.

EIGHTEEN

The History of Science
as a Cultural History
of the Material World

Pamela H. Smith

One of the most powerful manifestations of human culture today is the combination of science and technology that has come to be codified in the natural sciences.[1] This manner of human engagement with nature has brought into being structures and systems of knowledge, belief, education, and of communities, and has come to provide a means of arbitrating competing knowledge claims. Nothing like the system that exists today to produce knowledge about the natural world—a system that includes structures of education and research, and a generally standardized method of obtaining and presenting knowledge—ever existed on a similarly global scale in previous ages. Many historians view this new mode of producing knowledge as having emerged in Europe in the early modern period during the Scientific Revolution (ca. 1400–1700), although components of this revolution can be traced back to Greco-Roman antiquity, and even to ancient Babylon. These historians view this revolution culminating in the nineteenth century during the Industrial Revolution when techno-scientific research came to be regarded as the basis of material progress and national strength, and then coming to full flowering with the military sponsorship of scientific research in the Second World War and the boom in industrial and state-sponsored research in postwar society.

This conventional narrative of the growth of science is Western, tracing the development of the theoretical and mathematical sciences (astronomy and physics) from ancient Mesopotamia, to Greece, to Europe (often neglecting altogether the Roman and Islamic periods, or viewing them as constituting only reproductive transmission, and translation, or as being overly focused on applied science), and, finally, diffusion out to the European colonies from European metropoles during the nineteenth century. This, of course, neglects huge swaths of the world—Africa, China, and the Americas—and it creates hierarchies closely correlated to the ideology of nineteenth-century European imperialists. Moreover, it entirely neglects material factors such as, for example, the centrality of new energy regimes for human interaction with, and control over, the immediate environment: the shift from wood energy to fossil fuels—first coal in the 1780s, then petroleum in the early twentieth century, and nuclear energy in the mid-twentieth century.[2]

With eighteenth-century philosophical positivism, and on into the nineteenth and early twentieth centuries, if science was seen to have a history at all, it was viewed as the history of truth (or Truth). Truth's history was told as the slow revelation and accumulation of an ever more accurate reflection of nature in the mirror of the human mind, expressed by individuals in theories about the natural world. Philosophical positivists viewed the growth of science as an inevitable process of discoveries about the natural world, which allowed increased scientific-technological human capabilities, a greater control over natural processes, and revealed an ever more accurate picture of the natural world. The truth of the scientific world picture was viewed as the result of a unique method that involved a combination of theory, experiment, and observation. Scientific knowledge was regarded as trustworthy because it relied upon replication and recording of evidence in unbiased circumstances, often by use of instruments, and because the subjective experience of the observer/theorizer was strictly separated from the objective process of the method.[3] This history of truth gave way in the 1920s and 1930s to a new view of the scientific enterprise which, while still realist in its view of the relationship of scientific theories to nature, regarded ideas about the universe that later came to be viewed as outmoded—such as the geocentric model of the universe—not so much as the errors of past individuals, but the results of a different worldview based on less precise or less use-oriented categories. For example, Aristotle's philosophy of nature was viewed by Alexandre Koyré as based on the dictates of commonsense experience.[4] At the same time, other authors came to see the development of a mode of knowledge making that combined theory and experiment—informally known as the scientific method, or by some authors as the "experimental philosophy"—as a story of human civilization itself.[5] The interwar period was very fertile for the history of science, for it was also at this time that Ludwig Fleck put forward his famous idea of a *Denkkollectiv* (thought collective), which exercised such influence through its articulation in Thomas Kuhn's *The Structure of Scientific Revolutions* (1962).[6] Kuhn no longer saw scientific knowledge as emerging inexorably and progressively only by means of the scientific method properly employed, but rather viewed natural knowledge and the methods of obtaining it as contingent upon, and constructed within, particular communities and their place in social and intellectual structures, as people make use of ideas, information, and techniques available in that society.[7] Since the publication of Kuhn's book, sociologists and anthropologists of science have put forward a picture of science that is ever more human, seeing science as not set apart from other everyday human cognitive functions or from other kinds of human practice. In the current view of historians and sociologists of science (if not of the public at large), science is not, then, something apart from human society and the material world, but very much intertwined in both.[8] Starting, then from this point, this chapter offers two possible versions of the history of science as a cultural history of the material world: (1) a sketch of the "deep" history of science and technology, based on the definition of science as active engagement with the natural world, and (2) a view of the relatively recent development of a standardized scientific method as the result of material and commercial exchange.

Deep History of Science

All human societies interact in a variety of ways with their environment for survival and, out of the experience gained through that interaction, certain skills and knowledge emerge.[9] Taking an expansive perspective, we can see that this engagement with nature and the resulting accumulation of skills and knowledge has occurred throughout the long human past. The emergence of tool use in the Paleolithic era may have led to the development of language, which took on written form about 5,000 years ago, apparently growing out of commercial exchange and the need for keeping track of trade goods. The discovery of the uses of fire among early hominids allowed the manipulation of materials such as clay and native metals, whereas the ability to control fire itself led to high temperature furnaces in which minerals could be smelted (e.g., bronze—a mixture of copper and tin—ca. 3,500 BCE, and iron ca. 1,500 BCE), and glass produced (ca. 1,500 BCE), which led to the use of progressively sturdier artificially produced materials. The domestication of plants during what has been called the Neolithic Revolution, about 10,000 years ago, and of animals further in the past,[10] and their subsequent cultivation and breeding for food, medicine, textile production, and other survival uses was based on long-term systematic observation of patterns in nature, which led to a significant increase in skills and knowledge. So too did the accumulation of celestial observations evident first in Neolithic grave and religious monuments, and then emerging in calendrical form (often pictorial, or monolithic constructions such as Stonehenge) at various times in Africa, ancient Mesopotamia, Asia, Europe, and the Americas, and eventually in written form in Egypt and Babylon. These observations enabled the codification of a planting schedule divorced from immediate meteorological observations, and, by this means, numbers, arithmetic, and the calculation and prediction of celestial events emerged.

Such skills—sometimes referred to as crafts[11]—grew out of a collective interaction with the material world—sometimes apparently emerging spontaneously in different places, and at other times traceable as they spread throughout various regions by means of trade. Some see the modern scientific and technological capability of human beings as essentially different from these earlier developments, but there is no reason to regard the present development and accumulation of techniques and knowledge by means of the natural sciences as radically different from the very long-enduring human engagement with the environment. There is a difference in the quantity and speed at which knowledge is accumulated, as the system of knowledge production that we call science now involves many people and exists in a highly networked world where information travels very fast.

Some observers might point to the recent history of science and the discoveries of individual scientists as evidence of new processes of knowledge production occurring since the advent of modern science, but such a view grows out of a limited perspective on human history arising from historians' overwhelming reliance upon the written word. The existence of a written record for the exceedingly short recent present of human history—only about 7,000 of the approximately 200,000 years since Homo sapiens emerged—gives historians the sense that they can pin scientific discoveries and inventions to individuals. Upon further investigation, however, those discoveries are found to have been the result of collective and collaborative processes[12]—much like those that produced bronze, writing, glass, and moveable type—to name a few examples.

One such discovery was of the Gulf Stream in the eighteenth century—often ascribed to Benjamin Franklin, but actually the common knowledge of whalers (and mariners before them). Timothy Folger, Franklin's cousin and a Nantucket whaleboat captain, informed Franklin of the existence of the Gulf Stream, and mapped it for him.[13] There is no doubt that the transition of knowledge from oral to written form as happened in this case is an extremely important step, but writing is not necessary to transmit knowledge from one generation or region to another, although it can be more efficient. Innovation, intelligence, and creativity (sometimes labeled "genius") have often been thought about as located in, and manifested by, individual brains, but in reality, they emerge and occur within social fields. Of course, individuals can still be important in developing particular aspects of innovations, in focusing ideas and methods emerging out of the social field, and in giving written form to ideas or methods, as we see in the case of the Gulf Stream. Reliance by historians on written records and on identifiable individuals (whose papers or works are still extant) living in the recent human past has had the effect of misleading us about the collective and distributed nature by which all knowledge, but especially knowledge of our natural environment, is produced. Moreover, recent institutions such as the Nobel Prize have reinforced the view that science develops by means of discrete inventions and discoveries made by individuals.

The results of this perceptual and technical engagement with the environment are often codified, especially in relation to health and the prediction of agricultural or hunting cycles. Such codification has been recorded in texts, tables, and taxonomies in some societies, such as Mesopotamian cuneiform tablets containing the risings and settings of the stars and planets brought together in the library at Nineveh in the seventh century BCE. In others, this knowledge has been encoded in myths, songs, or rituals, such as the oral songs and mnemonic devices by which Polynesian peoples transmitted from one generation to the next the knowledge needed to navigate thousands of miles over the open ocean.[14] Human beings are also tool users, and human societies often manipulate natural materials—such as minerals, metals, plants, and animals—in order to produce useful effects and products. The manipulation of natural materials is also codified, although it is more often transmitted from master to apprentice or via rituals and the spoken word, rather than by texts. And its transmission is often facilitated or organized by the body politic, as in the case of state intervention in agriculture throughout the two millennia of imperial rule in China (221 BCE–1911 CE),[15] or in mining, controlled in Egypt by the pharaohs as early as the third millennium

BCE. The codification of this knowledge often leads to the creation of certain culturally specific identities, such as shamans, medical doctors, and craftspeople, and, today, scientists and engineers. Such codification has also been used as a marker of more general cultural identity and character, expressed in such contrasts as those often drawn between Chinese and Western medicine, between modern and premodern modes of understanding, and between universal and local ways of knowing. Sometimes, problematically, the possession of scientific knowledge has also been viewed as indicating a superior intellectual capacity or way of life.

Human engagement with nature has also led to the construction of views of the cosmos, often undertaken as a means of determining agricultural cycles, or arising out of the processes of manipulating natural materials. Historians have usually labeled such attempts to understand the cosmos and nature as "science," and the manipulation of natural materials as "technology," while the attempt to understand human health and disease has been called "medicine." In premodern societies, these spheres of culture were generally not separate from each other, and some historians of science and technology argue that these three realms are still deeply imbricated today. One recent historian sees science, technique, and technology as functioning together as parts of a whole to produce knowledge about the natural world. Science, she says, is "knowledge about natural, material processes expressed in declarative, transmissible form; its representations generally aspire to be authoritative beyond the time and place of their production." In other words, it is the knowledge about nature usually written down in texts that claims to be valid at all times, and in all places. Techniques are the "skilled practices that go into the material production of knowledge as well as the production of artifacts." These are the skills by which nature is manipulated, knowledge is gained, and objects are produced. On the other hand, technology can be thought about as an entire system involving a variety of people, practices, machines, raw materials, and institutions by which knowledge is both made and applied. In her view of the production of knowledge, the three areas of science, technique, and technology are "not separate kinds of activity but rather overlapping phases of an organic process of knowledge production."[16] Moreover, they are not separable from social relations and human institutions, but rather are embedded within them. Indeed, at a more general level, if we conceive of techniques as arising at the interface of the human senses and human body with the natural environment, even the material world and human culture cannot be separated.[17]

Building on this insight, we can propose an even more deeply material history of science, in which all science begins in matter. Matter possesses particular properties that enable the manufacture of certain kinds of materials and objects by means of specialized practices and technologies. Humans assign meanings to these practices and objects, and these meanings are both embedded within, and help to extend, systems of belief—or theories—about the matter, practices, and objects they incorporate. This forms a reciprocal dynamic by which matter gives rise to practices and objects, which themselves produce systems of belief, which in turn inform ideas about materials and practices. Analysis of this dynamic could form the stuff for a research program aimed at providing a framework for a history of science as the deep history of human engagement with natural materials.

An example of this flow from materials to ideas can be provided by the deep red pigment, often called vermilion, manufactured by heating mercury and sulfur together at a high temperature for a long period of time. As these substances combine, they go through dramatic color changes, which result in a bright-red powder deposited around the rim of the heating vessel. Vermilion had been made in Europe since the early Middle Ages; the technique of combining sulfur and mercury apparently moving east from China through the Islamic realms.[18] In China, sulfur and mercury were central medicinal agents, used for their heating and cooling properties, and the making of vermilion was viewed as part of an esoteric system of belief and practice.[19] In Europe, vermilion was especially associated with the blood of Christ; scribes and illuminators marked with a cross the places where vermilion was to be used in their manuscripts.[20]

In the Islamic world, the same ninth- and tenth-century scholar practitioners who experimented with mercury compounds also began to articulate a theory about the basic composition and transformation of metals that came to be called alchemy.[21] This theory, which explained the substance and properties of metals, taught that sulfur and mercury were the two fundamental components of all metals; mercury embodying the liquefiable nature of metals, and sulfur their flammable nature. This theory was taken up avidly in twelfth-century Europe, where scholars and practitioners began to manipulate these materials, and elaborate alchemical theory in their studies and workshops.[22] Clearly, aspects of vermilion production and alchemical theory overlapped—most obviously, of course, in their common bases in the two metals—sulfur and mercury. In addition, a central component of the sulfur-mercury theory of metals was the possibility of transforming a base metal, such as lead, made from impure sulfur and mercury into noble silver or gold by eliminating the impurities from the two elemental metals. Such a process was described as subjecting the metal to a process of putrefaction and regeneration, which brought about a series of color changes not unlike those observed in the making of vermilion. The metal mass was described as black in the putrefaction stage, and bright red just before it transmuted into gold. Some alchemical writers believed that it might be possible to derive a substance that could effect this purification of base metals instantaneously. This "philosopher's stone," which was theoretically capable of transmuting a mass of base metal into shining gold through a dramatic series of color changes, was often described as a red powder, like vermilion. Thus, pigment making and alchemical theory appear to have been intimately related in more ways than one. Not only were the two principles of metals in alchemical theory also the ingredients of vermilion production, but the outward manifestations of both processes of combination also involved spectacular transformations, which bore strong resemblances.

The practice of vermilion production everywhere predated the articulation in texts of a theory of metals. It would appear, then, that the sulfur-mercury theory of metals emerged from the practices of making vermilion—from the work of craftspeople manipulating materials with certain properties to produce a substance with particular cultural resonance associated with spectacular transformation, with gold, and with the vital substance of blood. In other words, one of the most pervasive and long-enduring metallurgical theories of matter and its transformation—the alchemical sulfur-mercury theory—flowed from the making of a valuable material.[23] Here is an instance of materials giving rise to practices that produced objects, which in turn shaped theories. These complexes of ideas then fostered more practical work with those substances, which further articulated the knowledge system while it simultaneously shaped further the products of that practice both as objects of study, and as objects of material exchange.

The Development of Scientific Method as the Result of Material Exchange

While the process of interacting with nature, developing skills, and building theories about natural processes has been constant from the advent of recorded history to the present day—although the resultant practices and theories have varied markedly—the development of a explicit and codified method through which nature is investigated and understood by means of the exercise of reason and practice can be traced to a quite specific beginning point: in Europe, between the fifteenth and nineteenth century. During this period, scholars and practitioners alike put forth a new method of philosophizing that was intended to bring about material, spiritual, and intellectual reform. While many elements of this new method can be found in earlier times and places, European scholars of the seventeenth and eighteenth centuries asserted its superiority over all other methods of gaining natural knowledge, and it was consolidated in rhetoric about European distinctiveness and institutionalized in scientific societies. And it spread across the globe with European political and institutional hegemony in the following centuries.

While many early modern and modern European scholars have viewed the construction of this new method of science as purely a European creation, it is better seen as a process of amalgamation as novel ideas, techniques, inventions, scholarly manuscripts, and books entered Europe through diverse routes of world trade.[24] Arabic numerals (actually Hindi numerals) began to be used by European merchants in the fifteenth century, and sophisticated mathematics and astronomy entered Europe from the Islamic world. Gunpowder, papermaking, and the use of the compass, among other crucial technologies, endured complex routes of transmission that stretched back to Asia, while tales of marvels that helped to legitimize curiosity as a motor of discovery were transmitted by literature from South Asia. The movement of peoples and the search for commodities fostered new modes of collecting information in unfamiliar environments by means of observation and testing.[25] New attitudes to nature arose as a result of viewing natural objects as commodities convertible into monetary values that could be sent around the world. In the process, these natural goods were decontextualized and shorn of their original religious and cultural significance. World trade also brought about the dominance of Europe by the nineteenth century, as European nations established colonies, in which cultural forms, such as the pursuit of science, were constructed as superior modes of knowing that distinguished the modernity of the European colonizer from the "primitive" colonized subject. In colonial India, for example, the pursuit of science functioned as a dividing line between colonizer and colonized, as individuals of Indian extraction were not allowed to be members of the Asiatic Society in Mumbai (founded in 1830)—the premier scientific institution in South Asia.[26]

In the Middle Ages, the idea had solidified that learning was obtained only at university by means of reading and engaging with texts, but this began to be challenged about 1400, as new arenas of action opened up for all kinds of practitioners who had not been trained at university. The rapidly growing cities and territorial courts throughout Europe from the fifteenth through eighteenth centuries became places to which claimants to natural knowledge—such as craftspeople, alchemists, architects, and practitioners of all sorts—came to assert new standards of proof, and make new claims about their ability to obtain certainty in natural knowledge.[27]

As cities in the global backwater that was Europe in the twelfth and thirteenth centuries burgeoned, a new group of people emerged in European society—city dwellers. These urban dwellers, making their living as craftspeople and merchants, gained power in city governments throughout Europe. As their social and political power increased, it raised their intellectual status and that of their de facto epistemology, in which practices such as observation, repeated trial and error testing, and demonstration and proof by producing things that worked, often counted for more than texts and textual authorities. Craft could not generally be taught by texts, as observation and experience were more important in building the skills required to respond to the variability of materials and forces involved in producing goods. Similarly, the merchant required news of markets, information about goods, the ability to discern among products, and a working knowledge of mathematical functions. As for knowledge of natural things, merchants viewed knowledge as a product that could travel and be converted into units of value, and their natural commodities were treated in this way. Historians have recently argued that this created a new type of objectivity in the early modern period because natural objects were stripped of their polyvalent meanings and religious significances to become interchangeable units of information and value—a reductionist and nonreligious approach to nature that became typical of modern science.[28]

This attitude to natural knowledge became especially prevalent as the commercial and territorial expansion of Europe and the Ottoman Empire, and the formation of long-distance trading networks in East and Southeast Asia in the early modern period led to an unprecedented movement of individuals, objects, and trade goods. The search for commodities and the investigation of nature went hand in hand on the European voyages of navigation and conquest. These voyages—often joint enterprises between merchants and the emerging territorial powers of Spain, Portugal, the Netherlands, France, and England—certainly encouraged the viewing of nature as the source of material gain, and even the material improvement of society. Moreover, navigation itself, which had brought knowledge of a new continent to Europeans, was seen by them, along with the printing press and gunpowder, as proof of the moderns' superiority over the ancients. This novel idea of progress took hold from the seventeenth century, and the knowledge of nature was viewed as a motor of that progress. In the mid-seventeenth century, societies imbued with these notions of material reform and progress, such as the Royal Society of London for the Improvement of Natural Knowledge, and the Académie Royale des Sciences in Paris, were established, and began to sponsor information gathering of all kinds. These institutions were allied directly with the centralized territorial powers, and proclaimed their method as a means to arbitrate disputes about natural questions.

The model of knowledge making promoted by these societies was collective and cumulative, and it involved the gathering and partial testing of particular facts, rather than posing general theories. They advocated both skepticism in the face of received wisdom and textual authorities, and empirical work of observation and hands-on experiments in the laboratory. Indeed, the laboratory became the hallmark of the new method of philosophizing promoted by these societies. The laboratory, as a space where nature was investigated by engaging with the material world itself and getting the hands dirty, can be traced back to the workshops of craftspeople and to the hands-on activities of alchemy.[29] Laboratories existed in noble courts in Europe and in medical faculties up through the late eighteenth century, and, although they were a centerpiece of a new model of knowledge making, they were mainly used for the demonstration of already-established facts of nature rather than for research into the unknown. It was not until the early nineteenth century that scientific research was instituted at the most elite universities, first in Justus von Liebig's (1803–1873) chemical laboratory at the university at Giessen in Hesse-Darmstadt, and then in the French and Anglo-American spheres. The presence of original scientific research continues to be a measure of academic quality today.

By the end of the seventeenth century, then, the knowledge of nature, mediated by European men who called themselves new experimental philosophers, was becoming a tool of centralizing territories seeking wealth through commercial projects, including colonies and manufactories. In distinction to past ages, these natural philosophers viewed knowledge of nature as cumulative, and continually refined and improved by new methods rather than contained in a fixed corpus of texts, and, importantly, one that was productive of material goods. In other words, natural knowledge had come to be seen as active, not contemplative: a way of doing that involved manual work in the laboratory, and tangible products. It was as certain as human knowledge could be, but it also produced effects, thus turning inside out Aristotle's tripartite schema of theory, practice, and technē that had endured for a millennium. Natural knowledge was now believed to be capable of bringing into being useful inventions and knowledge that would contribute to a limitless progress of humanity and its material and intellectual culture. Since the mid-twentieth century, scientific research has been carried out in industry- and state-sponsored institutions, including universities and corporate laboratories for the purposes of war, medicine, and commodity production. Natural philosophy—once of interest to a very limited group of individuals—has come to be of intense interest to the entire body politic, and its material and productive aspects are now viewed as possessing great national importance.

Conclusion

By focusing on the material dimensions of the human engagement with matter over the deep human past, and by following the flows of material objects and techniques as well as the flows of ideas, we can provide a picture of science as it emerged out of material, social, and cultural fields. Such a focus can work to integrate the narratives of material and intellectual culture that have remained separate in the overarching narratives of the history of science. A history of science and technology that traces not only the reciprocal process by which the mundane production of material things (involving the manipulation of matter and natural forces) informed and transformed theoretical formulations of knowledge, but also the ways that the transfer of practical techniques across space fostered new ways of controlling both nature and other people, will make clear the means by which the flows of goods and the people who mined, produced, transported, and consumed them helped to constitute the social, cultural, and medical complexes of belief that structured and fostered this exchange. Such a view has the potential to transform the history of more recent engagement with nature from a Eurocentric master narrative to a history that takes into account the movement of knowledge, things, and practices—not only over geographic space, but also over the epistemic distance between the knowledge systems of different social and cultural groups.

NOTES

1. For the purposes of this essay, I am defining "science" as the combination of technology and science that historians have recently labeled "techno-science." In the interests of length, I have provided only a bare minimum of references below. Parts of this essay appear in somewhat different form in my essay "Science," in *The Oxford Companion to History*, ed. Ulinka Rublack (Oxford: Oxford University Press, 2011), 268–97. For a fuller account of the deep history of science, see that essay.

2. Jack A. Goldstone, "The Problem of the 'Early Modern' World," *Journal of the Economic and Social History of the Orient* 41, no. 3 (1998): 249–83.

3. The precise meaning of "objectivity" has varied over the centuries. See Lorraine Daston and Peter Galison, *Objectivity* (New York: Zone Books, 2007).

4. Alexandre Koyré, "Galileo and the Scientific Revolution," *Philosophical Review* 52, no. 4 (1943): 333–48.

5. George Sarton, "East and West," in *The History of Science and the New Humanism* (New York: George Braziller, 1956), 59–110.

6. Ludwig Fleck, *Entstehung und Entwicklung einer wissenschaftlichen Tatsache: Einführung in der Lehre vom Denkstil und Denkkollectiv* (Basel: Benno Schwabe and Co., 1935), translated by Fred Bradley and Thaddeus J. Trenn as *Genesis and Development of a Scientific Fact* (Chicago: University of Chicago Press, 1979).

7. A founding introduction to the place of the community in making science can be found in Thomas Kuhn, *The Structure of Scientific Revolutions* (Chicago: University of Chicago Press, 1962), and the recent understanding of the social nature of science is treated by Jan Golinski, *Making Natural Knowledge: Constructivism and the History of Science* (Cambridge: Cambridge University Press, 1998).

8. This short sketch compresses much work in the history, sociology, and anthropology of science. Some of the most important shifts came through the work of Harry Collins, Bruno Latour, Michael Callon, John Law, Simon Schaffer, and Steven Shapin. See, for example, Harry Collins, *Changing Order: Replication and Induction in Scientific Practice* (London: Sage, 1985); Bruno Latour, *Science in Action* (Cambridge, MA: Harvard University Press, 1987); Michael Callon, "Some Elements of Sociology of Translation: Domestication of the Scallops and the Fishermen of St. Brieuc Bay," in *Power, Action and Belief: A New Sociology of Knowledge*, ed. John Law (London: Routledge, 1986), 196–233; John Law, "Technology and Heterogeneous Engineering," in *The Social Construction of Technological Systems: New Directions in the Sociology and History of Technology* ed. Wiebe E. Bijker, Thomas P. Hughes, and Trevor Pinch (Cambridge, MA: Harvard University Press, 1987), 111–34;

and Steven Shapin and Simon Schaffer, *Leviathan and the Air-Pump: Hobbes, Boyle and the Experimental Life* (1985), 2nd ed. (Baltimore: Johns Hopkins University Press, 2011). See also Ian Hacking, *Representing and Intervening* (Cambridge: Cambridge University Press, 1983); Andrew Pickering, ed., *Science as Practice and Culture* (Chicago: University of Chicago Press, 1992); and Andrew Pickering, *The Mangle of Practice: Time, Agency and Science* (Chicago: University of Chicago Press, 1995).

9. Tim Ingold, *The Perception of the Environment: Essays in Livelihood, Dwelling and Skill* (London and New York: Routledge, 2000). This is a view that owes much to pragmatism and Heidegger's view of technology. Interestingly, this view has resonance with that expressed by George Sarton, the founder of the History of Science Society and its journal *Isis*. In a 1931 essay, Sarton called for a view of science as a part of human cultural evolution. He believed that the accumulation of techniques and ideas throughout human history in various cultures had brought about the progress of humankind over the very long durée. His history of science was the history of human civilization itself. George Sarton, "East and West." Sarton's call for a long history of science as the slow accumulation of techniques and ideas was neglected by subsequent generations of historians.

10. Richard W. Bulliet, *Hunters, Herders, and Hamburgers: The Past and Future of Human-Animal Relationships* (New York: Columbia University Press, 2005).

11. Howard Risatti, *A Theory of Craft: Function and Aesthetic Expression* (Chapel Hill: University of North Carolina Press, 2007). See especially chapter 6.

12. Several decades ago, Robert K. Merton pointed out the phenomenon of multiple scientific discoveries: Robert K. Merton, "Singletons and Multiples in Scientific Discovery: a Chapter in the Sociology of Science," *Proceedings of the American Philosophical Society* 105 (1961): 470–86. Reprinted in Robert K. Merton, *The Sociology of Science: Theoretical and Empirical Investigations* (Chicago: University of Chicago Press, 1973), 343–70. In recent years, there have been both scholarly and popular accounts of the collective nature of invention and innovation. For example, see Arnold Pacey, *The Maze of Ingenuity*, 2nd ed. (Cambridge, MA: MIT Press, 1992); Clifford D. Conner, *A People's History of Science: Miners, Midwives, and "Low Mechanicks"* (New York: Nation Books, 2005); Keith Sawyer, *Group Genius: The Creative Power of Collaboration* (New York: Basic Books, 2007).

13. Joyce E. Chaplin, "Knowing the Ocean: Benjamin Franklin and the Circulation of Atlantic Knowledge," in *Science and Empire in the Atlantic World,* ed. James Delbourgo and Nicholas Dew (New York and London: Routledge, 2008), 73–96.

14. Helen Watson-Verran and David Turnbull, "Science and Other Indigenous Knowledge Systems," in *Handbook of Science and Technology Studies,* ed. Sheila Jasanoff, Gerald E. Marble, James C. Peterson, and Trevor Pinch (London: Sage Publications, 1995).

15. Francesca Bray, "Science, Technique, Technology: Passages between Matter and Knowledge in Imperial Chinese Agriculture," *British Journal for the History of Science* 41 (2008): 319–44.

16. Francesca Bray, "Science, Technique, Technology," 320–21. Thomas P.

Hughes was influential in introducing the view of technology as a system, especially in *Networks of Power: Electrification in Western Society, 1880–1930* (Baltimore: Johns Hopkins University Press, 1983). On the definition of technology, see also David Edgerton, "From Innovation to Use: Ten Eclectic Theses on the Historiography of Technology," *History and Technology* 16, no. 2 (1999): 111–36.

17. Ingold, *The Perception of the Environment,* and Bruno Latour, *We Have Never Been Modern,* trans. Catherine Porter (Cambridge, MA: Harvard University Press, 1993).

18. Daniel V. Thompson Jr., "Artificial Vermilion in the Middle Ages," *Technical Studies in the Field of the Fine Arts* 2 (1933–34): 62–70. See also R. D. Harley, *Artists' Pigments 1600–1835,* 2nd ed. (London: Archetype Publications, 2001), 127. I have published more on this in "Vermilion, Mercury, Blood, and Lizards: Matter and Meaning in Metalworking," in *Materials and Expertise in Early Modern Europe: Between Market and Laboratory,* ed. Ursula Klein and Emma Spary (Chicago: University of Chicago Press, 2010), 29–49.

19. Edward H. Schafer, *The Golden Peaches of Samarkand: A Study of T'ang Exotics* (Berkeley and Los Angeles: University of California Press, 1963), 219; and Joseph Needham and Lu Gwei-Djen, *Science and Civilization in China,* vol. 6, part 6: Medicine, ed. Nathan Sivin (Cambridge: Cambridge University Press, 2000), 38–45. See also Joseph Needham and Lu Gwei-Djen, *Science and Civilization in China,* vol. 5, part 2 (Cambridge: Cambridge University Press, 1974); Joseph Needham, Ho Ping-Yü, and Lu Gwei-Djen, *Science and Civilization in China,* vol. 5, part 3: *Chemistry and Chemical Technology* (Cambridge: Cambridge University Press, 1976); and Fabrizio Pegadio, *Great Clarity: Daoism and Alchemy in Early Medieval China* (Stanford, CA: Stanford University Press, 2006).

20. John Gage, "Colour Words in the High Middle Ages," in *Looking through Paintings: The Study of Painting Techniques and Materials in Support of Art Historical Research (Leids Kunsthistorisch Jaarboek XI),* ed. Emma Hermens (Baarn: Uitgeverij de Prom, 1998), 35–48, 39.

21. Georges C. Anawati, "Arabic Alchemy," in *Encyclopedia of the History of Arabic Science,* vol. 3, ed. Roshdi Rashed (London and New York: Routledge, 1996), 853–85.

22. Robert Halleux, "The Reception of Arabic Alchemy in the West," *Encyclopedia of the History of Arabic Science,* vol. 3, ed. Roshdi Rashed (London and New York: Routledge, 1996) 886–902.

23. For more on vermilion, see Pamela H. Smith, "Knowledge in Motion: Following Itineraries of Matter in the Early Modern World," in *Cultures in Motion,* ed. Daniel Rogers, Bhavani Raman, and Helmut Reimitz (Princeton, NJ: Princeton University Press, 2013).

24. As Geoffrey Lloyd and Nathan Sivin, in *The Way and Word,* express it: "the cosmopolitan blend of Syriac, Persian, ancient Middle Eastern, Indian, East Asian, and Greco-Roman traditions that formed in the Muslim world. This blend entered Europe beginning about A.D. 1000. . . .", xiii. See also the early articulation in Sarton, "East and West."

25. Antonio Barrera-Osorio, *Experiencing Nature: The Spanish American Empire*

and the Early Scientific Revolution (Austin: University of Texas Press, 2006); and Londa Schiebinger and Claudia Swan, eds., *Colonial Botany: Science, Commerce, and Politics in the Early Modern World* (Philadelphia: University of Pennsylvania Press, 2005).

26. David Arnold, *Science, Technology and Medicine in Colonial India* (Cambridge: Cambridge, 2000), 31.

27. Edgar Zilsel, "The Sociological Roots of Science," *American Journal of Sociology* 47 (1942): 544–62; Edgar Zilsel, "The Origin of William Gilbert's Scientific Method," *Journal of the History of Ideas* 2 (1941): 1–32; and Edgar Zilsel, *The Social Origins of Modern Science,* ed. Diederick Raven, Wolfgang Krohn, and Robert S. Cohen (Dordrecht: Kluwer Academic Publishers, 2003). See also Paolo Rossi, *Philosophy, Technology, and the Arts in the Early Modern Era,* trans. Salvator Attanasio (New York: Harper and Row, 1970 [published in Italian in 1962]); Arthur Clegg, "Craftsmen and the Origin of Science," *Science and Society* 43 (1979): 186–201; A. C. Crombie, "Science and the Arts in the Renaissance: The Search for Truth and Certainty, Old and New," *History of Science* 18 (1980): 233–46; Reijer Hooykaas, "The Rise of Modern Science: When and Why?" *British Journal for the History of Science* 20 (1987): 453–73; J. V. Field and Frank A. J. L. James, eds., *Renaissance and Revolution: Humanists, Scholars, Craftsmen and Natural Philosophers in Early Modern Europe* (Cambridge: Cambridge University Press, 1993); and *Rethinking the Scientific Revolution,* ed. Margaret J. Osler (Cambridge: Cambridge University Press, 2000); and Pamela H. Smith, *The Body of the Artisan: Art and Experience in the Scientific Revolution* (Chicago: University of Chicago Press, 2004).

28. Harold Cook, *Matters of Exchange: Commerce, Medicine, and Science in the Dutch Golden Age* (New Haven, CT: Yale University Press, 2007).

29. See Pamela H. Smith, "Laboratories," in *The Cambridge History of Science, Vol. 3: Early Modern Europe,* ed. Lorraine Daston and Katharine Park (Cambridge: Cambridge University Press, 2006), 290–305.

NINETEEN

Reflecting on Recipes

Deborah L. Krohn

Among the most famous recipes in English literature is that found in act 4, scene 1 of Shakespeare's *The Tragedy of Macbeth*. Three witches circle a cauldron as they add a series of ingredients.

> Fillet of a fenny snake,
> In the cauldron boil and bake;
> Eye of newt and toe of frog,
> Wool of bat and tongue of dog,
> Adder's fork and blind-worm's sting,
> Lizard's leg and howlet's wing,
> For a charm of pow'rful trouble,
> Like a hell-broth boil and bubble.

The refrain of their incantation is well known.

> Double, double toil and trouble;
> Fire burn, and cauldron bubble.

And more ingredients follow.

> Scale of dragon, tooth of wolf,
> Witches' mummy, maw and gulf
> Of the ravin'd salt-sea shark,
> Root of hemlock digg'd i' th' dark,

Liver of blaspheming Jew,
Gall of goat, and slips of yew
Silver'd in the moon's eclipse,
Nose of Turk and Tartar's lips,
Finger of birth-strangled babe
Ditch-deliver'd by a drab,
Make the gruel thick and slab:
Add thereto a tiger's chawdron,
For th' ingredience of our cau'dron.

This is a recipe for disaster, as becomes clear in the course of the play. But it crystallizes several characteristics of recipes that I would like to discuss.

On the most basic level, a recipe is a list of ingredients. The word in English is actually an imperative form derived from the Latin *recipere* (to take), and is what still appears at the beginning of a doctor's prescription, abbreviated in good notarial shorthand as the Rx symbol, as in "take two aspirin and call me in the morning." The French term *recette* is also derived from the same Latin verb, though in a different form: the past participle. In English, the word "receipt" is still used today.

It is worth noting that both English and French uses of the vernacular of this Latin verb to refer to what we call a recipe are first noted in the High Middle Ages. As scholars of medicine, food, the arts, and material culture concur, this is when broad shifts in the transmission of knowledge about how to deploy the natural world to advantage begin to be discernible in Europe. From the rise of pharmacopeia and the flourishing medical cultures of Salerno and Montpellier, to Theophilus's treatise *De diversis artibus*, generally dated to the first half of the twelfth century,[1] to the earliest surviving postclassical culinary compilations,[2] recipes are an important index of the rise of the documentation of empirical knowledge, and link together an array of physical manifestations.

But recipes are also a form of magic, as the citation from *Macbeth* demonstrates. As the witches throw the grisly ingredients into their cauldron, they return to a kind of refrain: "Double, double toil and trouble; Fire burn, and cauldron bubble." Words and things join together to seize mastery over matter. Language is the accomplice of agency in the transformation of discrete ingredients into a powerful substance that will dictate action. For the spell to work, words are just as important as ingredients. The recipe is understood as both word and deed, both a noun and a verb, to echo the two forms for the term in the *Oxford English*

Dictionary. Though the witches' spell in *Macbeth* is a real-time demonstration of the creation of the potion, and thus includes the acting out of the recipe, most recipes are in the imperative form: take your capon, take your herbs, etc. They embody the voice of experience, commanding the user to act in prescribed ways to achieve the desired end.

The witches' power in *Macbeth* is harnessed to effect a kind of bloody diplomacy, but it harks back to an archaic fear of latent female power, as visible, for example, in Hans Baldung Grien's *Witches Sabbath* (1510). The combination of odd ingredients wielded by the witches can be contextualized in a variety of ways in late Renaissance Europe.[3] Beyond the obvious nod to the periodic outbreaks of witchcraft and the attempts by official culture to control it, Shakespeare's witches may have reminded an early seventeenth-century audience of the genre of books of secrets that proliferated in the course of the sixteenth century: a topic upon which William Eamon has written extensively.[4] Books of secrets, as the genre is widely called, contained a dizzying selection of recipes for everything from hair care, to stain removers, to fertility enhancers. The most famous example was the *Secreti del reverendo donno Alessio Piemontese,* first printed in 1555, which became an international best-seller and model for countless other similar books. The title page for Giovanventura Rosetti's *Notandissimi secreti de l'arte profumatoria* from 1555 indicates that it will enable the reader to make oils, waters, pastes, pomades, etc. the way it's done in Naples, Rome, and Venice. The Italian *secreti* might also be translated simply as "recipes."

The genre spread across Europe as the printed book became economically profitable and socially desirable, and as numbers of readers—i.e., literacy, increased.[5] Many of the more popular tracts, which went into multiple editions, were translated into several European languages. If the first stage of the rise of the recipe can be identified in the pharmacopeia and cookery compilations of the High Middle Ages, the next stage must be the rise of these ironically titled "books of secrets" which were not always proper books, but often pamphlets or booklets, and certainly anything but secret. What they traded on was their appeal as keys to understanding materials and processes, and the mastery over matter. They also enabled regular folks to practice craft skills and techniques that were available previously only to professional artisans, making manifest what has been called tacit knowledge.

Another example of the rise of the recipe might be a treatise written in the 1550s by Cipriano Piccolpasso (1524–1579), called the *Arte del Vasaio* (The Art of the Potter). Though it was the first comprehensive description of the manufacture of pottery since Abu'l Qasim of Kashan's 1301 treatise, it was not published until the nineteenth century. Like Baldassare Castiglione's courtier, Piccolpasso was more a virtuoso than a craftsman, and spent much of his life in the service of aristocracy. His interest in pottery was related to his role as military and civil engineer, inspecting the fortifications along the Adriatic coast which were maintained by the duke of Urbino. He was also a founding member of the *Accademia del Disegno* in Perugia in 1573—one of the earliest artistic academies in Italy.

The *Arte del Vasaio* was commissioned by the Cardinal de Tournon, Archbishop of Lyons, who had spent time in Piccolpasso's native Castel Durante, a major center of majolica production. Tournon was interested in stimulating the pottery industry in Lyons, and intended to publish the treatise so that the secrets of the Italian masters could be disseminated. The treatise included information on the composition of clays, kilns, patterns, and recipes for glazes—in some cases, even regional variations of the same glaze. Had it been published for the Lyons craftsmen in the sixteenth century, as was planned, it would be possible to talk about its influence on ceramic production since it would probably have enjoyed wide distribution. But since it was not, it now has a different role in the historiography of Renaissance ceramics. Clearly a luxury manuscript— from its size, to its copious illustrations, it represents a stage in the process of professionalization for artisans such as potters who achieved this status, counterintuitively, through the dissemination of knowledge and its packaging in discrete formulae in the recipe.[6]

Culinary culture offers important insights into the material culture of the recipe. Bartolomeo Scappi's *Opera,* first published in 1570, was by no means the first Italian recipe collection to be printed, but it was the first cookbook to feature a series of technical illustrations to supplement the procedural instructions provided in the recipes. Scappi's publishers, in underwriting an illustrated cookbook that paralleled texts like Giorgius Agricola's *De re metallica* (1556), or Agostino Gallo's *Vinti Giornate* (1564) must have grasped the transformation from the magical to the scientific that was in the air.

Early cookbooks—pretty much without exception—did not provide measures or indications of time, but simply, ingredients that were to be used for a particular dish, and some indication of how to combine or prepare them for mixing or blending. The earliest postclassical culinary recipe collections grew out of medical or nutritional guides such as the eleventh-century treatise compiled in Baghdad, and which entered the

European arena as the *Tacuinum Sanitatis,* known primarily now from several luxury manuscripts illuminated in and around the Milanese court in the late fourteenth century.[7] Food was considered a therapeutic substance that could be manipulated to influence human nature and health, based on Aristotelian and Galenic humoral theory from the ancient world. Ingredients were tempered or blended to produce the desired effects in conjunction with age, gender, season, and weather conditions. By the middle of the sixteenth century, recipe collections were frankly cut loose from this moral and medical tradition, and were clearly more about taste and spectacle. The need to specify instructions concerning how much or how long would come much later, as empirical science moved on from the purely visual, and developed methods of fine measurement that enabled degrees of heat to be calibrated by thermometers, or time to be measured by individuals in their own domestic spheres rather than by communal clocks or church bells.[8]

Until the modern period, few recipes actually provided enough information—either in the form of ingredients, or instructions—to create the object for anyone other than a skilled craftsman, or someone who had already received training. They functioned as a kind of shorthand for the workshop, or as a record of practice.

Peppered in the literature of recipes, one can also find allusions to the failure of the system, to moments when the instructions were not adequate, or things just went wrong. The first three recipes in the *Viandier of Taillevent,* a recipe collection attributed to Guillaume de Tirel (d. 1395), chef to King Charles V, were for correcting errors: how to fix a soup that was too salty, or to take away the burnt taste from a stew that had perhaps lingered too long on the fire.[9] An anecdotal example of a recipe that did not work out as planned comes from Benvenuto Cellini's autobiography, where he describes in breathless detail the casting of the *Perseus* in molten bronze. As Cellini's carefully constructed system begins to fail, he retreats in fever to bed. He then reemerges to take over the process after being told that the metal was curdling. Instructions for his assistants were not adequate, whether in written form or not. Cellini affirms the importance of personal intervention.

> When I had got my clothes on, I strode with soul bent on mischief toward the workshop; there I beheld the men, whom I had left erewhile in such high spirits, standing stupefied and downcast. I began at once and spoke: "Up with you! Attend to me! Since you have not been able or willing to obey the directions I gave you, obey me now

that I am with you to conduct my work in person. Let no one contradict me, for in cases like this we need the aid of hand and hearing, not of advice.[10]

In this literary version of the failed recipe, there is no handbook to follow—he attempts to raise the temperature of the molten bronze by tempering the alloy, flinging in all of his household pewter dishes to achieve the goal.

As in many forms of knowledge, the availability and increased standardization of print changed the role of the recipe. In looking briefly at a range of examples, from Cellini to Shakespeare, as well as at a few culinary recipe collections, I think we can begin to outline a shift in the cultural significance of the recipe between late medieval and early modern Europe. Once a recipe is available in written form, it becomes a thing. Once printed, its material life can be mapped through time and space. Recipes are also a key to understanding process, and allow us to cut through the traditional social hierarchies that tend to organize the way objects are created, collected, and displayed. They take us back to the first instance in the creative cascade, to the moment when materials are gathered and organized, and the workshop is prepared for the labor of making. Recipes exist as conceptual elements whether or not they are recorded in any kind of permanent form—either in workshop notes, or a printed text. They span the transition period from script to print. It is an ongoing debate on just how this shift affected the status of the recipe. Did fixing it in a more-or-less static form inhibit the process of innovation, or did it instead lead to greater competition through the availability of knowledge and its diffusion? Finally, how does studying the evolution of the way knowledge is transmitted give us insight into the knowledge itself? Discussed a great deal by people who study the history of science, this question is also of great relevance for the histories of the decorative arts and material culture.

NOTES

1. *Theophilus, De diversis artibus,* ed. G. R. Dodwell (London, Edinburgh, Paris: Thomas Nelson and Sons, Ltd., 1961), xxxiii. A compilation of earlier artisanal recipes, possibly dating to the 600 C.E., in manuscripts from the ninth century onward, is known as the *Mappae clavicula.* See C. S. Smith and J. G. Hawthorne, *Mappae clavicula: A Little Key to the World of Medieval Techniques* (Philadelphia: American Philosophical Society, 1974).

2. *Libellus de arte coquinaria: An Early Northern Cookery Book,* ed. and trans. by Rudolfe Grewe and Constance B. Hieatt (Tempe: Arizona Center for Medieval and Renaissance Studies, 2001).

3. On witches and witchcraft, see Keith Thomas, *Religion and the Decline of Magic* (New York: Scribner, 1971). For a more recent study of witches in art with a feminist perspective, see Linda C. Hults, *The Witch as Muse: Art, Gender, and Power in Early Modern Europe* (Philadelphia: University of Pennsylvania Press, 2005).

4. William Eamon, *Science and the Secrets of Nature. Books of Secrets in Medieval and Early Modern Culture* (Princeton, NJ: Princeton University Press, 1994).

5. See William Eamon, *Science and the Secrets of Nature,* esp. chapter 3, where he discusses print culture and the genre of the *Kunstbüchlein,* 93–133.

6. Cipriano Piccolpasso, *The three books of the potter's art. I tre libri dell'arte del vasaio: a facsimile of the manuscript in the Victoria and Albert Museum, London,* trans. Ronald Lightbown and Alan Caiger-Smith (London: Scolar Press, 1980), xi–xxiv.

7. The illustrated manuscripts were most likely created between 1390 and 1410. See Cathleen Hoeniger, "The Illuminated Tacuinum Sanitatis Manuscripts from Northern Italy c. 1380–1400: Sources, Patrons, and the Creation of a New Pictorial Genre," in *Visualizing Medieval Medicine and Natural History, 1200–1550,* ed. Jean A. Givens, Karen Reeds, and Alain Touwaide (Aldershot, England: Ashgate, 2006), 51–81.8.

8. See Carlo M. Cipolla, *Clocks and Culture 1300—1700* (New York: W. W. Norton, 1967), especially chapter 1.

9. Taillevent, *Viandier of Taillevent: An Edition of All Extant Manuscripts,* ed. Terence Scully (Ottawa: University of Ottawa Press, 1988), 35–56.

10. *The Autobiography of Benvenuto Cellini,* trans. John Addington Symonds (New York: P. F. Collier and Son, 1910), 379.

TWENTY

Music in the Material World: Cultural Traces and Historical Cases

Elaine Sisman

Played by material instruments, sung by voices emanating from bodies, heard live in specially constructed rooms or acousmatically through speakers, music fills a span of time and then vanishes, leaving only intangible traces on its shaken and stirred auditors. If nearly every way we can describe music is metaphorical—the height of pitch, the thickness of sonority, the darkness of minor mode, the texture woven of melodic strands, the painting of its accompanying text—its effects are not, as the motions of the music both mirror and direct the motions of the listening body, while the dynamics can make us strain to hear, grip us during a crescendo, or assault us with nearly material force. "Immaterial" sonic vibration, like the invisible wind, can knock us around some.

Music's materiality has always been regarded with admiration and suspicion, and its cultivation, as well as its effect on human emotion and behavior has been the subject of philosophical and political critique since ancient times. Plato feared powerful musical modes and suggested their social control; Aristotle offered an intrinsic class distinction between (low) virtuosic technicians and (high) judges of quality; Augustine wrestled with the morality of music's pleasure even as he understood its necessity in worship. As a mirror of the harmonic perfection of the cosmos, "number made audible," music was embedded in the history of science, astronomy, and mathematics until the birth of romanticism preferred its mysteries to its clarities. But science also allowed sound to become newly material in the nineteenth and twentieth centuries, as developments in physiology of the ear, sound-spectrum studies, and the development of

technologies to create new sources of sound allowed for a kind of laboratory focus on sound's materials. Timbres were deconstructed and reconstituted; electronic instruments changed the nature of composition,
performance, and listening, as well as the relationship between timbre
and the other elements of music, acoustic and acousmatic instruments;
spectral composers today invent new sonorities based on the sound spectrum. As if to emphasize their materiality, real-world sounds subject to
electronic manipulation were collectively termed *musique concrète*.

Considered historically, music's resonance in culture emerges from
every aspect of its production, including composition, performance, and
publication, and its reception, whether by writers, by the public, or in
the home. Aspects as disparate as the secular afterlife of Handel (which
began a valorization of the past in new communal events previously unknown outside the church), and the beginnings of a musical canon in
the late eighteenth century, the emerging interest in collecting (and
later studying) composers' sketches and manuscripts in the nineteenth
century, and the recovery of the sound of earlier music instruments in
the twentieth century, suggest that more or less self-conscious interpretations of the materials of music's cultural history have always been with
us, but without the theoretical frame and impetus of the project under
discussion.

Encouraged by a framing device that conjures with culture, history,
material, and world, I offer a few historical cases of the materiality of
music's performance intersecting, at times colliding, with cultural pre-
occupations. The time is the eighteenth century, the culture is Austro-
German with recognizable echoes in France and England, the music is
primarily vocal/orchestral, and in every case the larger picture, as I understand it, has never been drawn.[1]

The Sound of Light

April 29, 1798, marks the first time that we know a composer deliberately kept secret a special effect before the premiere. The introduction
to Haydn's oratorio *The Creation* represents the "idea of chaos"—before
anything is formed, as Haydn said—so the music is obscure, meandering
around a dark-hued C minor, until the chorus finally sings, very quietly,
"And God said 'Let there be light,' and there was LIGHT!" A nearly in-
audible pizzicato chord serves as the signal, the switch thrown, the snapping of divine fingers; we sense the languid synapse between God's and

Adam's fingers on the Sistine Chapel's ceiling now filling with an ener-
gizing neural impulse whose echo is the flooding of the entire created
world with light. Baron van Swieten, who prepared the libretto, famously
suggested that Haydn set these words only once. Both van Swieten and
Haydn surely knew the contemporaneous discourse on the sublime—
the aesthetic category accounting for overwhelmingly powerful effects,
vividly described and theorized by Edmund Burke in 1757 and Imman-
uel Kant in 1790. Both the dread of darkness and the sudden shock of
brilliant light were felt to contribute to the overpowering effect of the
sublime, and a tradition dating to antiquity held that the biblical phrase
"And there was light"—short, sudden, simple, and powerful—was the
ultimate source of feelings of transport and awe.

But how was one to render the visual shock of light in music? Via the
sonic shock of overpowering loudness, a sudden tremolo conflagration
of the entire orchestral ensemble in fortissimo, in C major, the Masonic
key of light. Haydn's "Light motif," adapted from Handel, skips up a
fourth, dominant to tonic, landing on the downbeat; in short: arrival,
resolution, order, light. The blazing, even raucous light in *The Creation*
reveals nothing less than the beginning of historical time—an effect
emphasized by the magnificence of its Handelian cadence. Its further
history is demonstrated by Haydn's return to the motif in fully four cho-
ruses, three of which end parts 1, 2, and 3. The radiant light of creation
radiates through the work. The materiality of the sonic shock invites us
to consider the cultural importance of dynamics in the history of music,
and evaluate the reception of music's sublime, at the time attached
almost exclusively to works with massed instruments and voices, in dynamic terms.

The Castle as Island

We imagine eighteenth-century composers grappling, at their writing
desks, with patrons and publishers—often in the most imploring and
obsequious terms; or at their keyboards, with pupils and paper—where
they are masters. Yet despite the preservation (and veneration) of birth-
places and dwellings, we have not fully taken the measure of the spatially
material—places and spaces, landscapes and décor—in the temporal
imagination of the composer. Haydn worked in the Esterházy palaces
of Eisenstadt and Eszterháza from 1761 to 1790, where the princes had
a long-standing, even dynastic, interest in astronomy, collecting celes-

tial globes, telescopes, and such curiosities as an equatorial sundial table in the form of a "noon-day cannon," which would create an explosion when the sun's noon rays ignited a bit of gunpowder concealed in it. Yet Haydn's "times-of-the-day" symphonies of 1761, and the astronomical and meteorological "painting" in his late oratorios *The Creation* and *The Seasons,* not to mention his London visit to Herschel's telescope (through which the planet Uranus had been discovered in 1784) in 1792, have never been associated with princely collecting, nor with his own interest in the remarkable astronomical events of his era. Oddly, critics were contemptuous of musical painting, even of the sun, moon, and stars, perhaps because it was so popular. Indeed, the apparent necessity for critics to revisit this subject frequently suggested that the public simply refused to find brilliantly evocative and sometimes hilariously accurate tone pictures trivial. (A cultural history of music in the material world that deals with cultural histories of music's representation of the material world would be something to see.)

Haydn passed nearly every day for nearly twenty-five years through the symmetrically encircling arms of isolated and remote Eszterháza Palace, behind which Prince Nicolaus Esterházy landscaped his immense grounds with a deer park, pavilions to the sun, Diana, fortune, and Venus, and a labyrinth modeled on the one at Versailles. Responsible for hundreds of opera productions at the palace theater from 1776 to 1790, Haydn seems to have made a subspecialty of producing operas situated on islands, and when the prince turned sixty-five in 1779, Haydn wrote one himself, offering the venerable Imperial court poet Metastasio's celebrated libretto "The Uninhabited Island" (*L'isola disabitata*), imagining the benevolent side of the "island" of Eszterháza, as his prince would recognize it. This island sustains life without effort—perfect for the abandoned wife and her baby sister to subsist on for thirteen years, before her husband returns. In the creation of a new—if miniature, and temporary—society, Metastasio had set out the paradox of the ruler-less existence designed to appeal to the sovereign as reflecting his "natural" empire, showing how the sovereign "creates" nature on the "island" of his inherited lands. For the Spanish king traveling by riverboat to the royal theater in Aranjuez—the original commission of the libretto in 1753—as for the Esterházy prince viewing with satisfaction his nearly completed remote Eden, the libretto conjoins Enlightenment philosophy, colonial exploration, and social relations in an imaginary natural world, in which animal, vegetable, and mineral abundance share the stage with human understanding as it unfolds against the accidental, the contingent, and the enduring.

Metastasio's island is a garden: it is nature tamed and softened and turned to the use and enjoyment and sustenance of its human inhabitants. But the island is also dominated by a large stone, into which the abandoned heroine has been chiseling her epitaph for thirteen years, and stone imagery is everywhere in the libretto. The stone symbolism is the first indication that we are dealing with a labyrinth; the garden has been marked as a test, an emblem of circular wandering and the melancholy it engenders, of seeking to avoid the possible evil or trauma—or truth—that lies in the center. Haydn's operatic structure appears to understand this, and his tormented heroine must sing in the rare key of A-flat major, the key of the "Plutonian realm" (Vogler), as well as present her bleak vision in keys a tritone apart, the "diabolical" interval suggestive of the devil lurking at the heart of the Christian labyrinth, and garden.

Musical labyrinths—a topic predating the eighteenth century, but newly associated with wandering harmonic relationships—also make vivid music's correlation with movements of the soul, of the nerves, and of the psyche: they map an interior geography only hinted at by the material garden. The labyrinth is the ultimate paradoxical emblem, embodying chaos and order, circle and thread, the infinite and the bounded. In Gluck's *Orfeo ed Euridice* of 1762, a touchstone work for the era and quoted by Haydn, the dark rock-strewn cave of the "tortuous labyrinth" marks the space between the underworld and the living from which the hero and heroine must escape. The interpretation of actual and conceptual physical spaces joins a revaluing of musical representation as a desideratum for cultural historians of music.

Don Giovanni's Mandolin

Operatic characters are only infrequently called upon actually to sing on stage; mostly they speak to each other in song. Serenades and self-consciously sung offerings as such must be marked in some way. When Cherubino sings his charming "Voi che sapete" to the Countess in act 2 of *The Marriage of Figaro*, he is accompanied by Susanna on guitar, rendered in the orchestra by pizzicato strings playing accompanimental broken chords, while winds forecast and then entwine with the vocal melody. In Don Giovanni's act 2 serenade to an unseen woman, however, he accompanies himself on the mandolin. The most celebrated engraving of the first production (Prague, 1787) shows this scene, with the handsome young star Luigi Bassi holding the mandolin and gazing at a lighted window.

The so-called canzonetta, "Deh! vieni alla finestra," is full of importunate imperatives. With images of sweetness, sugar, and honey very similar to those in his wooing of the peasant Zerlina on her wedding day, he expresses not only his pains and longing, but a come-on so direct that one wonders how Zerlina would have reacted: "Tu ch'hai la bocca dolce più che il miele, / tu che il zucchero porti in mezzo core" ("You who have a mouth sweeter than honey, you who have sugar at the core of your heart [inside you]"). With fully three endearments in eight lines of text—*o mio tesoro* (line 1), *gioia mia* (line 7), *mio bell'amore* (line 8)—Don Giovanni alternates flattery with urgency. With the simplest tonal means, he creates a great wheel of desire. The first two lines of each stanza present basic tonal progressions in the tonic and toward the dominant. The second two lines, however, see melody and bass moving together rhythmically, but in contrary motion melodically with a sudden upward reach and the sense even of overshooting the return home. The circular shape of the chord progression, after a heart-stopping move to minor and flatside harmonies, gives the text a surge of momentum no woman on stage could resist.

But what of the mandolin? The orchestra accompanies a real mandolin with pizzicato strings. Its melody is ornate and plays continuously throughout the two-strophe song. Three of its four lines stretch upward questioningly or questingly; the fourth drops down. The grain of sound of this archaic instrument is at once tinkly, and hence unthreatening, and thickly tactile, every note clearly the sound of finger stroking against string. It is virtuosic where the voice is declarative, suggesting the perfect combination of skill and ardour. Where Cherubino and Susanna together create a love song that conjures up a sweetly diffident pastoral, Don Giovanni is deceptively double-tracked between mouth and hands. The pointed appearance of *concertante* instruments in an aria, an instrumental counterpoise to the voice set apart from the rest of the orchestra—as also in Susanna's idyllic but duplicitously sensual "Deh vieni non tardar" —may be understood in embodied terms that then carry over into genres without voice, where cultural topoi like the gestures of social dance, pastoral, learned style, *Sturm und Drang,* and lament maintain their communicative power.

Of these three case studies, each turns on the materiality of music in and as performance, on culturally resonant texts, and on interpretations available to their initial audiences. In emphasizing musical issues that cultural history can entail, musicologists may set new terms for debate in the cultural territory they have long inhabited. The ideas sketched here are offered as part of that initiative.

NOTE

1. These case studies draw respectively on my recent essays: "The Voice of God in Haydn's *Creation,*" in *Essays in Honor of László Somfai: Studies in the Sources and the Interpretation of Music,* ed. Vera Lampert and László Vikárius, 139–53 (Lanham, MD, 2004); "Haydn's Solar Poetics: The *Tageszeiten* Symphonies and Enlightenment Knowledge," *Journal of the American Musicological Society* 66/1 (Spring, 2013, 5–102); "Fantasy Island: Haydn's Metastasian 'Reform' Opera," in *Engaging Haydn: Culture, Context, and Criticism,* ed. Mary Hunter and Richard Will, 11–43 (Cambridge, 2012); "The Marriages of *Don Giovanni,*" in *Mozart Studies,* ed. Simon Keefe, 163–92 (Cambridge, 2006).

TWENTY-ONE

A Cultural History of
the Material World
of Islam

Jonathan M. Bloom

I am not quite sure what a cultural history of the material world is, but as a historian of Islamic art I am taking it to mean how studying the things men and women have made might tell us something about the shape of the times in which they were made, and how the activities and institutions associated with these things might have—or have not—changed over time. In that sense, historians of Islamic art have been doing just that for a long time, inasmuch as many historians of other kinds of art would dismiss much, if not most, of what we study—among them pots, pans, plates, rugs, and curtains—as decorative art or material culture rather than real art.

Assuming that one accepts that such a field exists at all, Islamic art tends to have a broader definition than many other disciplines of art history, which are generally limited to the fine arts—painting, sculpture, and architecture—in a particular place (France, Italy) at a particular time (Romanesque, Renaissance).[1] As it is generally understood today, Islamic art is said to range geographically from the Atlantic coast of Spain to the Pacific islands of Indonesia, sometimes including the recent Muslim diaspora to Western Europe and the Americas. Chronologically, Islamic art begins with the revelation of Islam in the early seventh century and continues to the eighteenth, nineteenth, twentieth, or even twenty-first century, depending on one's point of view. Some radicals say that it ended—if indeed it ever existed at all—around 1500 with the emergence of the great empires (Alawi, Ottoman, Safavid, Uzbek, and Mughal); most scholars, however, would say it ended with European colonialism or the emergence of nation-states around 1800. In that view, Iranian Islamic art, for example, was succeeded sometime in the nineteenth or twentieth century by a distinct Iranian art. Others, of course, claim that artists from Seattle to Singapore are still producing Islamic art by virtue of their religion.[2]

Most importantly for the purposes of this chapter, Islamic art is also thought to comprise an extraordinary variety of media, ranging in scale from monumental architecture to exquisitely fine jewelry, in durability or permanence of medium from cast metal and carved stone objects to gossamer textiles and works on delicate paper, and in function from deeply religious to straightforwardly secular, and even humorous or bawdy. Finally, Islamic art also includes a wide range of patronage—from imperial and royal commissions from famous artists to anonymous works made by or for sale to nomads, peasants, and the bourgeoisie of merchants, tradesmen, scholars, etc. In short, virtually none of the traditional hierarchies developed for the study of Western art applies to Islamic art in general, although they may be applied to particular subfields within it.

Indeed, such a broad definition raises the reasonable question whether Islamic art is a valid category at all: Walk into any museum with a collection of Islamic art and try to explain what, say, an illustrated leaf from a fifteenth-century Persian copy of the *Shahnama* (Book of Kings) has to do with a ceramic dish from twelfth-century Syria, let alone a nomad tent hanging from nineteenth-century Central Asia. Although all were produced in societies where Islam is the dominant religion, none of them has anything to do with the actual religion of Islam, and none of them has very much to do with the others. Objects on display that do have an Islamic religious component, such as leaves from a Koran manuscript or prayer carpets, tend to form a relatively small part of collections of Islamic art, even in such "Islamic" settings as the new Museum of Islamic Art in Doha, Qatar. No wonder that visitors to such exhibitions are often mystified. Nevertheless, after some forty years of studying and writing about Islamic art, I have come to the conclusion that "Islamic art" is the worst term to describe the subject, except for all the alternatives that have been tried.

Many scholars of Islamic art, particularly those working in the later periods, have chosen to follow a logocentric or text-based approach to their research, in which they use documents and texts to help explain works of art. Although this kind of approach can occasionally be used in the earlier periods, it is often more successful for the later ones because of the greater numbers of documents, texts, and works of art that have survived from this period. Yet this logocentric approach, which is by no means unique to Islamic art, tends to minimize the special contributions that the study of the material world can make.

I learned this lesson in the 1970s when I was a student in Cairo. I rashly purchased a ten-volume set of folio books entitled *Stèles funéraires,* which cataloged a collection of about 4,000 inscribed tombstones in the Cairo Museum of Islamic Art.[3] I had no particular need of the books, but as they were incredibly cheap, I thought the matched set would look good in my modest library. A year later, while writing my dissertation, I found that I needed to learn something about the funerary practices of Egyptian women in the ninth and tenth centuries, and discovered that nothing pertinent had been written on the subject, since most scholarship about funerary practices—if it had been done at all—had been written by and about men. Much to my surprise, however, I discovered that my ten volumes contained a wealth of information about the funerary beliefs and practices of women, since approximately half of the epitaphs commemorated them. What I learned from this experience was that a study of material culture (one could hardly call many of the epitaphs art) could tell me things that are inaccessible from text-based research.[4]

I see a cultural history of the material world working from a perspective exactly opposite that favored by a text-centered approach to art history, which tends to envision culture in terms of texts with the physical remains serving as illustrations. People, however, have always expressed themselves in various media: some people express themselves through words or sounds; others through making things. A cultural history of the material world puts the emphasis on the things people made, and it assumes that objects can tell us things that texts may not be able to. To follow such an approach, one should, I believe, start with the thing itself and work through a series of questions. What was it made from? How was it made? Who made it? When was it made? Where was it made? And finally, why was it made?

Let me give two examples of how I might apply this approach. The first is a ceramic bowl in the David Collection, Copenhagen (fig. 1).[5] This earthenware bowl, measuring 10.5 inches (26.5 cm) in diameter is covered with a white engobe, and painted in brown and red slip under a transparent lead glaze. Probably made in northeastern Iran or Central Asia in the tenth century, it is one of a relatively large group of earthenware bowls and plates attributed to the cities of Samarqand and Nishapur, which are decorated elaborately and often exclusively with Arabic inscriptions. The inscriptions are like puzzles, written in a decorative

Fig. 1. Earthenware bowl covered with a white engobe, and painted in brown and red slips under a transparent lead glaze. Northeastern Iran or central Asia, tenth century. Diameter: 27 cm. Copenhagen, David Coll. 22/1974. (Photo courtesy of the David Collection.)

angular script embellished with extraneous knots, bumps, and flourishes that make the texts extremely hard to read. The inscription on this bowl, written clockwise starting from six o'clock when looking down into the bowl, records a well-known saying that "He who believes in recompense [from God] is generous with gifts" (*man ayqana bi'l-khalaf jada bi'l-'atiya*). The proverb is a *hadith* or tradition attributed to the Prophet Muhammad, as well as to his cousin and son-in-law Ali, the fourth caliph and a major figure in Shia Islam.

A cultural history approach to this piece might begin with an examination of the materials from which the bowl was made. Whence did the clay come? How was it collected, transported, and refined? (Recent developments in petrographic analysis began to allow scholars to ask such questions.[6]) Were the engobe and slips collected and refined in the same way? What about the lead oxide for the glaze? Where was that found? How was it extracted and how was it transported to Samarqand, assuming that is where the piece was made. How were materials ground into a powder? Once the materials were assembled, one might begin to think about how the piece was formed: how many people were involved in the production? Was the decorator the same person as the potter? Was the decorator literate in Arabic, or did someone else provide him a design to copy? If he was copying a design, on what material was that design done? Was this a unique piece or one of many with the same decoration, but of which only this one has survived? What kind of kiln was used to fire the bowl? With what was the kiln fired? How and where was the fuel collected? Was this bowl commissioned or made on spec for sale in the market? How much might it have cost? Was it part of a set with matching or complementary examples? Was it used for food, and if so, what kind of food? The cultural history approach might also ask questions about why and how it was preserved for centuries, and why and how it ended up in the David Collection in Copenhagen.

Having considered—if not answered—such questions, we might then turn to the more traditional art-historical questions about the style of the writing and the content of the inscription. The style is comparable to the new scripts that were being developed in the tenth century for copying manuscripts increasingly written on paper. The same saying is found on several other pieces of different shape, but does its presence here represent the veneration of the Prophet, a particularly Shii milieu, or merely conventional platitudes? The inscription allows us to place the piece within a milieu in the midst of Iranophone Central Asia that was comfortable enough in Arabic so as to take pleasure in deciphering complex Arabic script as something appropriate to do after a meal. The writing on the interior invites a person holding the bowl to empty it of food, and then turn it in his or her hands to read it. While the art-historical questions are interesting indeed, the first set of questions appears much more wide-ranging and likely to tell us more about the history of culture.

My second example is the minbar (pulpit) from the Kutubiyya Mosque in Marrakesh, Morocco, which we know to have been commissioned by the Almoravid ruler of Spain and North Africa on New Year's Day in 1137 in Cordoba, Spain, for a mosque in Marrakesh (fig. 2). Now in a museum in Marrakesh, the minbar is the subject of a handsome monograph put

Fig. 2. Minbar from the Kutubiyya Mosque, Marrakesh, Morocco, now in the Badiʿ Palace Museum, Marrakesh. Photo from Jonathan M. Bloom et. al., *The Minbar from the Kutubiyya Mosque* (New York, 1998), fig. 25.

together under the auspices of the Metropolitan Museum of Art, which was responsible for a project to restore it.[7] A triangular wooden structure measuring nearly 12 feet (3.86 m) high, the minbar comprises a frame of cedarwood onto which was glued an extraordinary marquetry of colored woods and bone. The entire visible surface of the minbar was completely enveloped in this web of carved and inlaid decoration, although much has fallen away. Each of the minbar's triangular sides is decorated with a geometric strapwork pattern exactly coordinated to the minbar's stepped profile, in which marquetry bands of bone and colored woods separate hundreds of small carved panels (fig. 3). The

Fig. 3. Minbar from the Kutubiyya Mosque, detail. (Author's photo.)

risers and backrest are similarly decorated with panels of vegetal decoration, and the edges and sides of every other surface were once covered
with magnificent carved or inlaid ornament, comprising several million
individual pieces of wood.

Conservators from the Metropolitan Museum of Art were able to examine the minbar closely and identify the woods with which it was made
and decorated, as well as the various techniques and tools used (although
one of the techniques used to make miniscule inlaid tiles remains completely unexplained). The woods included African blackwood, box, and
jujube; what was first thought to be ivory turned out to be bone. From
where were these woods imported? Why was bone used instead of ivory
when no other expense was spared to make this minbar? The nature of
certain cuts led the conservators to discern the use of the fretsaw—a tool
that had previously thought to have been invented only three centuries
later in the Italian Renaissance. The quality of the carving of the individual panels is so exquisite that is it equal to or finer than the carving on
the famous ivory boxes produced in Cordoba about 150 years earlier—
perhaps the reason that the first scholars to study the minbar thought
that the panels were carved not from wood but from "darkened ivory."

The minbar is one of the great masterpieces of Islamic art, and it is about as different as possible from the bowl discussed earlier. It was a unique object produced by and for the highest levels of society, being a royal commission for a royal mosque from the most able artisans around who, even as a team, probably took several years to complete it before shipping it in pieces 500 miles over mountains and the Straits of Gibraltar for assembly in Morocco. Since the minbar is firmly localized and dated, it provides a fixed point for the understanding of the cultural history of the period, and a close examination of it turns on their head many of the accepted facts about the period, most of them derived from reading the historical sources.

For example, historians normally say that the Almoravid patrons of the minbar were uncouth Berbers from North Africa who had no interest in the visual arts. Wrong! Art historians normally say that that the art of carving ivory and all the other arts declined after the fall of the Umayyad caliphate in the early eleventh century when the ivory carvers were forced to move to Cuenca. Wrong! The minbar clearly shows that Cordoba must have remained a great cultural center despite the textual laments of contemporary chroniclers. Historians have also tended to separate Spain from Morocco, but the minbar shows how the two regions were linked in a single cultural realm. Historians have speculated how artisans worked out geometric designs in advance, but the minbar's missing panels show that designs were scribed directly on the wooden structure, showing that paper had not yet become common for preparatory sketches. Some historians have recently speculated that an Islamic interest in geometric decoration was directly linked to a "Sunni revival," and that geometric decoration spread from east to west.[8] Wrong! One could go on and on, but the point is made: a close examination of the minbar from the perspective of material culture begins to reveal many aspects of history that would not appear otherwise.

In terms of Islamic art, I envision a cultural history of the material world treating the artifact as a product of human endeavor equivalent to the written text. Just as written documents cannot tell us everything about every aspect of society, so too a study limited to material culture will not tell us about every aspect of society, but the two approaches can be combined to provide a fuller, more nuanced picture. As material culture was not necessarily produced by the same milieux that produced written culture, it may provide access to different aspects of society that are not necessarily revealed by written documents—including women, nonliterates, nonelites, or nonurbanites such as nomads and villagers.

Texts and documents are wonderful things, and the Islamic world has produced more than its share of them, thanks to its early adoption and spread of paper and papermaking technology.[9] But not all human activities are conceived with words, and so a cultural history of the material world might help to put some art back into the venerable field of art history.

NOTES

1. For a general introduction to the issues related to the delineation and study of the field, see Sheila S. Blair and Jonathan M. Bloom, "The Mirage of Islamic Art: Reflections on the Study of an Unwieldy Field," *Art Bulletin* 85, no. 1 (March 2003): 152–84.

2. For modern Iranian art, see, for example Hossein Amirsadeghi, ed., *Different Sames: New Perspectives in Contemporary Iranian Art* (London: Thames & Hudson, 2009); for modern Islamic art, see Wijdan Ali, *Modern Islamic Art: Development and Continuity* (Gainesville: University Press of Florida, 1997).

3. Hasan al-Harawy, Hussein Rached, and Gaston Wiet, *Stèles funéraires,* 10 vols. (Cairo: Musée Arabe, 1932–1942).

4. Jonathan M. Bloom, "The Mosque of the Qarafa in Cairo," *Muqarnas* 4 (1987): 7–20. The irony does not escape me that previous text-based scholars had basically ignored the texts of the epitaphs not only as texts, but also as material culture.

5. 22/1974. Most recently published in Sheila Blair and Jonathan Bloom, *Cosmophilia: Islamic Art from the David Collection, Copenhagen* (Chestnut Hill, MA: The McMullen Museum, 2006).

6. Robert B. J. Mason, *Shine Like the Sun Lustre-painted and associated pottery from the medieval Middle East* (Costa Mesa, CA: Mazda Publishers, in association with the Royal Ontario Museum, 2004), chapter 6.

7. Jonathan M. Bloom et al., *The Minbar from the Kutubiyya Mosque* (New York: The Metropolitan Museum of Art, 1997).

8. Gülru Necipoğlu, *The Topkapı Scroll: Geometry and Ornament in Islamic Architecture, Topkapı Palace Museum Library MS. H 1956* (Santa Monica, CA: Getty Center for the History of Art and the Humanities, 1995); and Yasser Tabbaa, *The Transformation of Islamic Art During the Sunni Revival* (Seattle: University of Washington Press, 2001).

9. Jonathan M. Bloom, *Paper Before Print: The History and Impact of Paper in the Islamic World* (New Haven, CT: Yale University Press, 2001).

TWENTY-TWO

Franz Kugler and the Concept of World Art History

Horst Bredekamp

Kugler's History of World Art

The art historian Franz Kugler had an astonishing career. In 1831, he earned his doctorate at the University of Berlin with the theme of medieval book illuminations; his habilitation followed three years later with writings on the architecture of the Middle Ages, Islam, the Egyptians, and India.[1] Kugler had thereby completed his habilitation at the age of twenty-five, but without receiving a professorship; he became a professor at the *Kunstakademie* (Art Academy) in 1835,[2] but taught continuously at the university; the course catalogs from 1833/1834 to 1842/1843, when he took a position as an art expert in the Prussian Ministry of Culture, show a total of nineteen semesters of teaching.[3] The emphasis of his research and instruction was on the Middle Ages in Europe, but Kugler reached out as far as India as if this were a matter of course.

He made special reference to the *Kunstkammer* in Andreas Schlüter's *Berliner Schloß* (Berlin's City Palace), which still housed lavish stocks of art and handicrafts, though objects had been transferred out several times, giving birth to Karl Friedrich Schinkel's first autonomous museum—the Altes Museum—as well as the Berlin University and its collections.[4] Kugler expresses his liberal understanding of these works, which do not fall within the category of high art, in his *Beschreibung der in der Königl. Kunstkammer zu Berlin vorhandenen Kunst-Sammlung* (Description of the art collection present in the Berlin royal art cabinet), published in 1838. It was devoted to the collection's carvings, enamel, seals, medallions, statuettes, reliefs, drawings, ivory carvings, glass apparatus, goldsmithing, and cabinetmaking—i.e., to the core of the inventory found today in Berlin's *Kunstgewerbemuseum* (Museum of Arts and Crafts).[5] Of special interest is that, in the foreword to the work on the works of art in the *Kunstkammer,* Kugler refers to the stocks of the ethnographic collections, whose treasures he at least summarily underscores with a view to the art of India, China, Persia, Australia, and Mexico.[6]

The material in the art cabinet offered Kugler the basis upon which he could construct his universal history of art.[7] Published in 1842, this *Handbuch der Kunstgeschichte* (Handbook of art history) opened to view a history of world art that did not restrict the concept of "art" to Europe, but described it as a possibility of all peoples. The *Kunstkammer*, with its works of European handicrafts offered the model for opening up the art of all times and all peoples from prehistory to the present, lacking almost any hierarchization. His developmental-historical pattern employed categories that, from the start, pointed beyond Europe: the preliminary phase of non-European and pre-Hellenic art, the classical phase of Greek and Roman antiquity, the Romanesque phase of the Middle Ages and Islam, and the modern phase from the Renaissance to the present.

Among the sources Kugler used in addition to the *Kunstkammer* of the *Berliner Schloß* is Alexander von Humboldt's collection of ancient Mexican sculptures, which made a strong impression on Kugler.[8] But Kugler's approach differed markedly from Humboldt's. Humboldt found the Mexican idols interesting in terms of cultural, not of art, history; for Kugler they possessed a genuine art-historical value. Kugler thereby had his own standards, inasmuch as he compared all the world's pictorial cultures without giving Europe and the Mediterranean world a privileged status. Kugler regarded the Mexican finds as standing higher than the art of Egypt.[9]

Equally as impressive as the horizontal line of art history's globalized panorama is the vertical temporal stratification that Kugler undertook. With no mention of the hand axe, Kugler not only begins his history of art in planet-spanning vastness, but also at the origin. The first pictures in the illustrated edition of Kugler's *Handbuch*, compiled by Ernst Guhl and Joseph Caspar and published in 1851, show the outlines of the material; Stonehenge, for example, is relatively clearly recognizable (fig. 1).[10]

According to Kugler, the mental penetration of material that leads to form has already crystallized in this earliest prehistory: "In the selection of the variously shaped stones as given by nature (as detritus or in the quarry), in the particular manner of their presentation, their ar-

Fig. 1. Joseph Caspar, Monuments of the North European Antiquity, 1845. (Photo: Ernst Karl Guhl/Joseph Caspar, Denkmäler der Kunst, Bd. I, 1851, Taf. 1.)

rangement, they were at any rate already able to achieve the more general impressions of sublimity, proportion, and even harmony."[11] With an impressively matter-of-course approach, Kugler begins his art history with intentionally hewn and collected stones, continuing with the monumental testimonies known to his time, like the stones of Carnac and Stonehenge.

The Problem of Prehistoric Art

In a remarkable article in 2007, Ulrich Pfisterer used the lectures from the Warburghaus to reconstruct how, as early as the 1830s, a comprehensive concept of art history was developed that ranged from the first artifacts to the present.[12] At the center of his article, however, stands the shock of the discovery of Altamira in 1879 and 1880. After doubts about the authenticity of these paintings were allayed, these objects were soon accepted as part of art history—especially because of their formal proximity to the art of impressionism.

The art history that focused on European post-ancient art was paralleled by an art history focusing on the legacy of prehistory. Pfisterer convincingly shows that its strict lining up of objects in comparisons resembled the forms of comparative analysis employed by the Hamburg School around Aby Warburg. Along with this widening of the gaze, a temporally vertical viewpoint also developed, finding a high point in Herbert Kühn's book of 1923, *Die Kunst der Primitiven* (The art of the primitives): "Our age—rich and poor at the same time—stepped out of the narrow confines of European contemplation of art; the view is expanding immeasurably; the first steps are taken toward a world history of art . . . Winckelmann's and Goethe's concepts no longer suffice to interpret the art of the primitive or natural peoples. An age for which the pinnacle of art apparently means doing the same thing and solely the Renaissance and for which every stylistic invention seems a decay cannot understand the art of primitive peoples."[13]

But then Pfisterer traces the squandering after 1900 of the opportunity to turn art history and its methods into the kind of all-encompassing leading field of study that Kugler had striven for. The idea that the first artifacts are to be seen not as art, but as a kind of pictorial language, and not as objects made for their own sake, but as magical tools, played a decisive role in separating the entire field of prehistory and early history from art history. The art of the so-called *Naturvölker* (natural peoples) was thereby no longer part of an expanded art history.

Three problems that have been ever more heatedly discussed in recent years show that this separation from art history created an unsolved problem. They all focus on the question of the phase of human development that marks the beginning of what we can genuinely speak of as art. That is, we can add, at what point art history in Kugler's sense begins.

In 2010, an exhibition in Stuttgart was devoted to the development of art up to the end of the Ice Age. In it, a wealth of stone axes and their further development to blade tips was displayed. The hypothesis that they can be entirely subsumed under their practical function is countered by the no less vehemently argued interpretation that, from the beginning, they were suffused with form-conscious semantics—i.e., that homo faber's creation of form can be equated with becoming human.[14] In this sense, Kugler's handbook would be a book on the history of man as the form-conscious producer of artifacts.

Gottfried Boehm has long been using the reflection of the stone axe in its character as "image," producing an "iconic difference."[15] Just over ten years ago, Heinrich Klotz took the excavations of the ruins of Catal Höyük—a Stone Age urban complex in Anatolia—as the occasion to attempt to characterize the human species as homo faber. During the founding phase of the Karlsruhe *Zentrum für Kunst und Medientechnologie* (Center for Art and Media Technology), he presented an interpretation of the stone axe as the primal matter of modernity, as if paralleling the transformation of a prehistoric man's flying weapon into a space station in the initial sequence of Stanley Kubrick's *2001: A Space Odyssey*. He provided a succinctly condensed motto—a bridge between modernity and the art of humanity's early period. Klotz said what is captivating about the stone axe is "its artificiality, its harmonious regularity, and its symmetry, which indicate the intensity of human shaping. We can even call this form beautiful and ought to see confirmed what was considered a doctrine of modern functionalism: a form that thoroughly serves its utility must also be beautiful."[16]

The following proclamation shows the methodological dilemma, but also the possibilities, inasmuch as he defines the art of Homo erectus as more modern than modern art itself: "Even if not all designed shape can be recognized in the functional aesthetic of Modernism and if that aesthetic's generalization leads to dogmatism, it can nevertheless be applied to the first object created by a human being. The artificiality of the stone axe is also art, and its functionality is also beauty."[17] This statement holds a concentrate of the entire problematic. Modernism sees itself in the art of prehistory, just as categories are taken from the perspective of this prehistoric art to explain modernism.

One could smirk at this anachronism, but the material immediately has its revenge. That people were conscious of an "iconic difference"[18] more than 100,000 years ago is shown by collections of fossils that a framing design accentuated as a picture within the picture.[19] Stone axes like these have been found in numbers that rule out coincidence. The Stuttgart exhibition showed one such fossil piece from England.[20] The finesse with which the fossils were recognized as special, and apparently also prized and centrally emphasized, reveals that these predecessors of the—anatomically—modern human being were such highly sensitive and skillful humanoids that the distinction becomes problematic.

In 2008, the press was full of the photo of a series of shells that are supposed to be among the earliest art forms from the Indian Ocean.[21] The individual pieces all have holes in the same spot; they were created by pressure or a blow. Two or three similarly designed objects could have come about by chance, but the number of six shells assures the critical observer that these are the components of a jewelry chain. A fundamental condition for proving that something was conceived as an object to be viewed is the assembly of a sample large enough to rule out coincidental formation, and that is the case here. Based on investigations carried out primarily in South Africa and Morocco, a small, triumphant group of researchers is currently shifting the question of the birth of the individual from the fifteenth century back by about 80,000 years.[22]

Figures of the Ivory Age

But the real sensation unfolded over the last five years in the Swabian Alb. Widely perceived up to now only in the examples of spectacular individual items, finds in this region have led to a new revolution in our image of the development of humankind.

Sculptures have been found that are 20,000 years older than the pictorial culture of Altamira and the associated sites in France, which are themselves about 20,000 years old. These sculptures cast doubt on the current theory of development because they are shaped completely in the round and their three-dimensionality displays a stupendous mixture of mimesis and abstraction. Thus, the approximately 3-cm mammoth-ivory figure found in the cave Vogelherd (fig. 2) is an astounding presentation of the contours of this extinct animal, situated somewhere between individual characterization and abstraction. It shows the plastic modeling of the massive body in the swelling surface, under which the shoulder blades and hip structure are both visible. Peculiar rows of x-shaped crosses cover the back and belly.[23]

Also, humanoid figures have been found in the last years. Up to now, the Venus of Willendorf has been the undisputed star among prehistoric figures, with her emphasized sexual characteristics, her corporeal ostentation, her enigmatically covered head, and her hand-fitting dimensions.[24] But in 2008 in the cave of Hohle Fels, a 6-cm ivory statuette was found; aged about 35,000 to 40,000 years old, it is 5,000 years older than the Venus of Willendorf. This could be the earliest figurative sculpture yet found.[25] But what is probably the most impressive figure from the

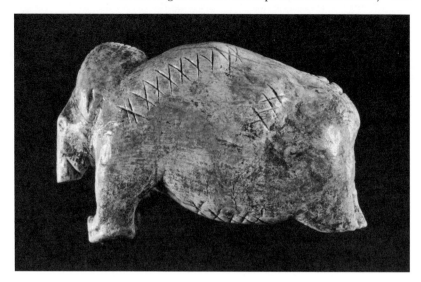

Fig. 2. Mammoth-sculpture, made of mammoth ivory, 5 cm. long, 3 cm. tall, carved notch, discovered 1931 near Vogelherd, ca. 32,000 years old. (Photo: H. Jensen, © University of Tübingen.)

cave in Hohlenstein-Stadel, conspicuous for its height of almost 30 cm, was created about 32,000 years ago (fig. 3). The legs seem to belong to a predator standing on its hind legs, while the arms are those of a human. The head has mutated into a lion's. Together, the tension in this figure's body and the body components fused into a chimera have a mysterious effect.[26]

The Material Iconology

Against the background of the most recent finds, the image of the history of art is changing—both in terms of its objects, and its disciplinary history. The finds on the Swabian Alb turn Kugler's magnum opus into what it equally declamatorily and futilely claimed to be: a handbook of art history. As in a picture puzzle, this work—with its liberal gaze plunges into the world's cultures, and its concept of art tracing back to the stone axes—moves from the periphery to the center of the discipline.

This process is not just a vision born from the occasion; rather, it is the product of processes developing from both sides, from art history

Fig. 3. "Lion-man," made of mammoth ivory, ca. 35,000 years old.
Ulmer Museum. (Photo: Thomas Stephan © Ulmer Museum.)

and from pre and early history. The walls of the Stuttgart exhibition were covered with definitions of art from Pablo Picasso to Marcel Duchamp. They intend to make these artifacts, some of them 40,000 years old, understandable as parts of modern art. People like to speak of objects of modern art as having been created by a type of person who is to be regarded as modern him or herself. The real conceptual problem here is swept under the rug, of course. It is that antiquity lies like a blocking mountain range between the modernism of early history and the modernism of the nineteenth and twentieth centuries, formally eluding this system of relations.

One way to subvert or integrate this barrier lies in the power of the material. The figure with the lion man (fig. 3) seems to develop its own semantics of material, inasmuch as the skill acquired in stone is used for unimagined ways of ensouling matter in the soft, organically produced material of the mammoth tusks (fig. 2). As long as stone was the only material for sculpture, there could be no iconology of the material. Only in the contrast between various working materials are their specific qualities visible as such. Taking everything currently known into account, ivory therefore represents the first condensed field of a material iconology, as it was developed by Gottfried Semper[27] and others, up to Monika Wagner in our day.[28]

Among the first was Kugler, who made a comprehensive claim to understand art history as a universal human history of artifacts. His *Handbuch* is the implementation of this goal. The material and its iconology lie at the beginning of a development from which art history can be understood as a history of humankind and its disconnection from the animal kingdom.

The epochs of early history are customarily divided in accordance with materials: the Stone Age, the Copper Age, the Bronze Age, and the Iron Age. We have seen how ivory and its first known figurative forms force their way into the Stone Age. This is the research result of the last three years that can only be called spectacular. The Ivory Age—the millennia between 40,000 and 30,000 BCE—should be inserted between the other prehistoric epochs named for materials.

This has consequences, because in this material, even more than in the other name-giving materials, we see that, considering the organic softness of the material, art history's form-specific methods, oriented toward aesthetic appearance, themselves appear as the objects' *desideratum*.

Fig. 4. August Friedrich Stüler, stairway hall, Neues Museum. (Photo: BPK/Neues Museum, Berlin/Art Resource, New York.)

Museums and Material Iconology

As Peter N. Miller has shown, the second founding father of this approach is Gustav Friedrich Klemm. His ten-volume *Allgemeine Cultur-Geschichte der Menschheit*, whose first volume came out in 1843, breathes the same spirit as Kugler's *Handbuch* from 1842.[29] Klemm added a small text on the founding of a museum for all cultures of mankind,[30] and his own collection became the core of the Ethnology Museum of Leipzig.[31]

In a parallel movement, Kugler's concept was also realized at least approximately embodied as a museum: August Stuler's *Neues Museum* in Berlin. Its conceptualization began in 1843—i.e., one year after Kugler's *Handbuch* was published (fig. 4).[32] This museum, which was reopened after Chipperfield's removal of war damage in 2010, can be regarded as the vessel of a universal claim to found a general history of art—from the stone axe, through Egyptian objects, to Mexican book illumination—that grasps the entire pictorial inventory of human artifacts as one cosmos in which, from the beginning, form is tied to semantics: in which, in a universal Aristotelianism, the intrinsic connection is emphasized in such a way that the art-historical methods are applied in genuine self-evidence, and not merely in coincidental bridge-building.[33]

The study of material culture could take a starting point in rethinking Kugler's and Klemm's epochal trials to create a universal art and cultural history.

NOTES

1. Jörg Trempler, "Franz Kuglers Promotion und Habilitation oder die Zeichnung als Prüfungsgegenstand," in *In der Mitte Berlins: 200 Jahre Kunstgeschichte an der Humboldt-Universität,* ed. Horst Bredekamp and Adam S. Labuda (Berlin: Akademie Verlag, 2010), 55–65.
2. Kilian Heck, "Die Bezüglichkeit der Kunst zum Leben: Franz Kugler und das erste akademische Lehrprogramm der Kunstgeschichte," *Marburger Jahrbuch für Kunstwissenschaft* 32 (2005): 7–15.
3. Horst Bredekamp and Adam Labuda, "Kunstgeschichte, Universität, Museum und die Mitte Berlin 1810–1873," in *In der Mitte Berlin: 200 Jahre Kunstgeschichte an der Humboldt-Universität,* 25–54, 33f.
4. Christoph Martin Vogtherr, "Das Königliche Museum zu Berlin: Planung und Konzeption des ersten Berliner Kunstmuseums," *Jahrbuch der Berliner Museen* 39 (1997); Bredekamp and Labuda, "Kunstgeschichte, Universität, Museum und die Mitte Berlin," 27–29.
5. Franz Theodor Kugler, *Beschreibung der in der Königl. Kunstkammer zu Berlin vorhandenen Kunst-Sammlung* (Berlin: Carl Heymann Verlag, 1838).

6. Franz Theodor Kugler, *Handbuch der Kunstgeschichte*, 2 Bde. (Stuttgart, 1842), ix-xi. See Henrik Karge, Franz Kugler, and Carl Schnaase, "Zwei Projekte zur Etablierung der 'Allgemeinen Kunstgeschichte,'" in *Franz Theodor Kugler: Deutscher Kunsthistoriker und Berliner Dichter*, ed. Michel Espagne, Bénédicte Savoy, and Céline Trautmann-Waller (Berlin: Academie Verlag, 2010) 83–104.

7. Franz Theodor Kugler, *Handbuch der Kunstgeschichte*.

8. Henrik Karge, "Welt-Kunstgeschichte: Franz Kugler and die geographische Fundierung der Kunsthistoriographie in der Mitte des 19. Jahrhunderts," in *"Kunsttopographie:" Theorie und Methode in der Kunstwissenschaft und Archäologie seit Winckelmann* (Stendal: Stendal Verlag, 2003), 29–31.

9. Franz Theodor Kugler, *Handbuch der Kunstgeschichte*, 35.

10. Ernst Guhl and Joseph Caspar, eds., *Denkmäler der Kunst zur Übersicht ihres Entwicklungs-Ganges von den ersten künstlerischen Versuchen bis zu den Standpunkten der Gegenwart*, vol. 1 (Stuttgart: Ebuer and Seubert, 1851) A., plate 1.

11. "Bei der Auswahl der verschieden geformten Steine, wie sie die Natur (als Gerölle oder im Steinbruche) gab, bei der eigenthümlichen Weise ihrer Aufstellung, ihrer Zusammenordnung konnten immerhin schon die allgemeineren Eindrücke der Erhabenheit, des Maases, selbst der Harmonie erreicht werden." Franz Theodor Kugler, *Handbuch der Kunstgeschichte*, 4.

12. Ulrich Pfisterer, "Altamira—oder: Die Anfänge von Kunst und Kunstwissenschaft," in *Vorträge aus dem Warburg-Haus*, vol. 10 (Berlin: Academie Verlag, 2007), 13–80.

13. "Unsere Zeit—arm und reich zugleich—tritt heraus aus dem engen Rahmen europäischer Kunstbetrachtung, ungemessen erweitert sich das Bild, die ersten Schritte werden getan zur Weltgeschichte der Kunst (. . .). Die Begriffe Winckelmanns und Goethes reichen nicht mehr zu, die Kunst der Urvölker, der Naturvölker zu deuten. Eine Zeit, die das Griechenland und Renaissance allein als die Höhe der Kunst erscheint und jede stilisierte Richtung als einen Verfall, wird kein Verständnis haben für die Kunst der primitiven Völker." Herbert Kühn, *Die Kunst der Primitiven* (München, 1923) 7; cited in Ulrich Pfisterer, "Altamira," 63.

14. Thomas Wynn, "Archaeology and Cognitive Evolution," *Behavioral and Brain Sciences* 25, no. 3 (2002): 389–402.

15. Gottfried Boehm, "Die Wiederkehr der Bilder," in *Was ist ein Bild?* (Munich, 1994), 11–38, 30; Gottfried Boehm, *Wie Bilder Sinn erzeugen: Die Macht des Zeigens* (Berlin: Berlin University Press, 2007), 34–38.

16. "Wir erkennen an ihm seine Künstlichkeit, seine Ebenmäßigkeit und seine Symmetrie, die auf die menschliche Gestaltungsintensität verweisen. Wir können sogar diese Form als schön bezeichnen und müßten bestätigt sehen, was dem Funktionalismus der Moderne als Lehrsatz gegolten hat: eine Form, die konsequent ihrer Nützlichkeit dient, müsse auch schön sein." Heinrich Klotz, *Die Entdeckung von Catal Höyuk. Der archäologische Jahrhundertfund* (München: C. H. Beck, 1997), 13.

17. "Wenn sich aus der Funktionsästhetik der Moderne auch nicht alle gestaltete Form erklären läßt und deren Verallgemeinerung zu Dogmatismus

führt, so läßt sie sich doch auf den ersten, vom Menschen geschaffenen Gegenstand anwenden. Die Künstlichkeit des Faustkeils ist auch Kunst und seine Funktionalität ist auch Schönheit." Heinrich Klotz, *Die Entdeckung von Catal Höyük. Der archäologische Jahrhundertfund*, 13.

18. Gottfried Boehm, *Was ist ein Bild?*, 11–38.
19. Michel Lorblanchet, *La Naissance de l'Art. Genèse de l'art préhistorique* (Paris: Éditions Errance, 1999), 82, 89ff.
20. K. P. Oakley, "Emergence of higher thought 3.0–.2 Ma B.P.," *Philosophical Transactions of the Royal Society of London, Series B. Biological Sciences* 292, no. 1057 (1981): 205–11, fig. 2.
21. Francesco d'Errico, Christopher Henshilwood, Marian Vahaeren, and Karen van Niekerk, "*Nassarius kraussianus* Shell Beads from Blombos Cave: Evidence for Symbolic Behavior in the Middle Stone Age," *Journal of Human Evolution* 48 (2005), 3–24. Ulrich Bahnsen, "Das Geheimnis der Gravuren," in *Die Zeit. Welt- und Kulturgeschichte*, vol. 1 (Hamburg: Die Zeit, 2005) 543–47, 547.
22. C. Henshilwood and Francesco d'Errico, "Being Modern in the Middle Stone Age," in *The Hominid Individual in Context. Archeological investigations of Lower and Middle Palaeolithic landscapes, locales and artefacts*, ed. Clive Gamble and Martin Porr (New York: Routledge, 2005), 244–64, 251f, 257f.
23. Reinhard Ziegler, "Nilpferde im Rhein, Affen auf der Alb. Die Säugetiere aus dem Eiszeitalter in Süddeutschland," in *Eiszeit: Kunst und Kultur* (Ostfildern: Thorbecke Verlag, 2009), 43–50, 43.
24. Nicholas J. Conard, "Die erste Venus," in *Eiszeit: Kunst und Kultur*, 268–71.
25. Harald Floss, "Kunst schafft Identität. Das Aurignacien und die Zeit der ersten Kunst," in *Eiszeit: Kunst und Kultur*, 248–57, 249.
26. Ulmer Museum, *Der Löwenmensch. Geschichte—Magie—Mythos* (Ulm, 2005); see Kurt Wehrberger, "Der Löwenmensch von Hohlenstein-Stadel," in *Les chemins de l'Art aurignacien en Europe / Das Aurignacien und die Anfänge der Kunst in Europa, Actes du colloque 2005 d'Aurignac / Tagungsband der gleichnamigen Internationalen Fachtagung*, ed. Harald Floss and Nathalie Rouquerol (Aurignac: Éditions Musée—forum Aurignac, 2007), 331–44.
27. Gottfried Semper, *Der Stil*, 2 vols. (1860/1863).
28. Monika Wagner, *Das Material der Kunst: Eine andere Geschichte der Moderne* (Munich: C. H. Beck, 2001).
29. Gustav Friedrich Klemm, *Allgemeine Cultur-Geschichte der Menschheit*, 10 vols., (Leipzig, 1843–1857). See Peter N. Miller, "The Missing Link: 'Antiquarianism,' 'Material Culture' and 'Cultural Science' in the Work of G. F. Klemm," in *Cultural Histories of the Material World*, ed. Peter N. Miller (Ann Arbor: University of Michigan Press, 2013).
30. Gustav Friedrich Klemm, "Fantasie über ein Museum für die Culturgeschichte der Menschheit," Supplement vol. of *Allgemeinen Cultur-Geschichte der Menschheit* (Dresden: B. G. Teubner, 1841); see Peter N. Miller, "The Missing Link."
31. Peter N. Miller, "The Missing Link."
32. Elsa van Wezel, "Die Konzeptionen des Alten und Neuen Museums zu Ber-

lin und das sich wandelnde historische Bewußtsein," *Jahrbuch der Berliner Museen* 43 (2001); Elke Blauert and Astrid Bähr, eds., *Neues Museum: Architektur, Sammlung, Geschichte* (Berlin: Nicolai, 2009).

33. Horst Bredekamp, "Der lange Atem der Kunstkammer: Das Neue Museum als Avantgarde der Vorvergangenheit," in *Museale Spezialisierung und Nationalisierung ab 1830: Das Neue Museum in Berlin im internationalen Kontext*, ed. Ellinor Bergvelt, Debora Meijers, Lieske Tibbe, and Elsa van Wezel (Berlin: G + H Verlag, 2011) 25–36.

TWENTY-THREE

The Missing Link: "Antiquarianism," "Material Culture," and "Cultural Science" in the Work of G. F. Klemm

Peter N. Miller

Gustav Friedrich Klemm (1802–1867) is well and truly forgotten. The last stand-alone piece devoted to him made him into a prophet of Nazi racial theories and was published in a volume of essays cheerfully entitled *Kultur und Rasse*.[1] And yet, it is in his work that the concepts of "material culture" (*Materiellen Cultur*) and "cultural science" (*Culturwissenschaft*) were first developed. In a way, then, our steps toward the reuniting of material culture and the cultural sciences lead back to Klemm. But, because he placed himself at the end of a long line of collector-scholars originating in the early modern period, our steps back to him take us back still further, to antiquaries like Ole Worm and Peiresc. Klemm, then—last of the antiquaries, first of the cultural scientists, around whom pivots premodern and modern epistemologies of material culture.

Klemm explained in later life that his interest in realia was first aroused by the sight of the different armies passing back and forth through Chemnitz in the Napoleonic wars, with their weapons, gear, uniforms, and different ethnic composition. He fell in love with Greek and Latin at the gymnasium, while the tercentenary celebrations of Luther in 1817 focused his attention on to the Middle Ages in Germany. Intellectually, the key text for him was Ebert's *Bildung des Bibliothekars* (1820)—not a book that figures largely in our conception of key texts of the later *Goethezeit*—which showed him how a collection could function as the foundation for encyclopedic learning.[2] He read Herder and Voltaire, from whom he realized for himself the "goal of studying human conditions in family, state, war, religion, science and art." He took to excerpting medieval historians and travel writers, but especially found it useful to concentrate on Germany. During his school vacations, he wandered through Saxony and Thuringia with a sketchbook, drawing weapons, tools, buildings, and tombstones. With help from Montfaucon and Moller when necessary, he turned his own drawings into the basis of "a collection of antiquarian illustrations." By 1825, his collection was already giving him a general sense of the history of human conditions.[3]

In the summer of 1830, Klemm worked in Leipzig with the famed naturalist Hofrath Tilesius—and then went back to old German monuments, comparing them, as a scientist might. By then he was appointed to his position in the Royal Porcelain Collection in Dresden, with whose reorganization he was charged. This gave him the opportunity to study more about China and about the history of technology. His earliest publications—on porcelain and old Germanic Europe—followed.[4] This, in turn, led him to wide-ranging reading "of the most important travel works of old and more recent times."[5]

1.

In these works of the mid-1830s, Klemm explicitly identifies himself with a tradition of early modern scholars and scholarship which he called "antiquarian." In the preface to his *Handbuch der Germanisches Alterthums-kunde* (1836) Klemm explained that he realized that his "antiquarian studies" contained sources and supporting evidence for the cultural history of the oldest Germanic period.[6]

With his next publication, also of 1836–1837, Klemm distinguished himself. *Zur Geschichte der Sammlungen für Wissenschaft und Kunst in Deutschland* is, or would be if it were known, one of the pioneering treatises in the history of early modern learned collecting. With its detailed information about *Kunst- und Wunderkammern* and libraries, it could have been the model book that Julius von Schlosser's *Die Kunst- und Wunderkammern der Spätrenaissance. Ein Beitrag zur Geschichte des Sammelwesens. Ein Handbuch für Sammler und Leibhaber* (1908) became.

The table of contents reveals the volume's early modern center of gravity: it begins with libraries from the fourteenth century, then churches as medieval museums, then sixteenth- and seventeenth-century *Kunst- und Raritätenkammern*—with probably the first serious effort to understand the treatises of Samuel Quiccheberg and Lorenz Hofmann—and concludes with eighteenth-century museums. The main thrust of the argument about early modern cabinets is establishing the link between the study of antiquities and the study of nature. Travel plays a central role here. Klemm recognized the triangular relationship that Momigliano revived in our own time between *antiquitates,* nature, and ethnography.

Klemm devotes no space to non-German collections, and his study of the German ones really gains traction only in the mid-seventeenth century. But we ought not to assume that Klemm had not thought about the earlier period. Long quotes from Einckel's *Museographia* make plain that the history of the earlier period and, indeed, the literature on it (such as existed), was completely familiar to him. Indeed, it is very much the earliest period in the history of the *Kunst- und Wünderkammern* that directly inspired him. Here, however, it is Ole Worm who figures as the key.

Worm's *Museum Wormianum* (1653) represented for Klemm, as it does still for historians of collecting, the moment when a mature literature on collecting the man-made met a mature reflection on the study and collection of nature. The *Museum*'s frontispiece is famous (there is a reconstruction of the frontispiece in the Danish National Library, and a performance artist re-created it in 2005 for a temporary exhibition at Harvard's Peabody Museum of Anthropology). Its principle of inclusiveness puts the human inside the natural, and sees human history as part of nature's history. Klemm devotes a long passage to ekphrasis of Worm's frontispiece. It served as his own model.[7] Thus, he made space in his account for "Geschichte, Alterthümer und Ethnographie" and placed tools and scientific instruments alongside natural, artistic, and historical materials. For Klemmn, the eighteenth century marks the great leap forward in museum organization and content, especially in the natural sciences. Klemm is deeply committed to the details of this history: he even provides the opening hours for the Berlin Museum, as if recognizing that access—and sensitivity to the importance of access—denotes a wholly changed attitude to the purpose of collecting and its audience.[8]

As he was finishing his history of German collections, he was selected as tutor to accompany the Saxon heir on his Italian trip in 1838. As with Bachofen a few years later, this trip would trigger an explicit shift; in his case from antiquarianism to cultural history. "A few months after the end of my travel, the plan of a Cultural History and Cultural Science was sharply outlined in paper I sent to my friend A.B. v. Lindenau."[9] It was at this point that he took to organizing his own collection: to broaden in new directions, to renew in older ones. He purchased a complete collection of South Sea materials (*Gewerbszeugnisse*), followed by objects from

Africa and the Arctic, and worked diligently on their disposition.[10] By 1840, his collection numbered 1,257 objects, and was distributed through five large rooms divided into fourteen sections, by function: tools and weapons/jewelry/clothing/vessels/dwellings and furniture/writing materials and writing/coins, weight and measure/vehicles/musical instruments/the sacred/ arts/history of writing. In terms of origin, the objects were distributed as follows: 700 from Africa, 500 from America, 600 from Russia, 350 from the Arctic, 600 from China/Japan, 600 from the Near East, 500 Greco-Roman, 400 early German, and 1,200 from the medieval era.[11] Klemm explained that the "goal of the collection is none other than to bring to understanding the creation of various human artistic and manufactured products out of naturally found materials and their further development, and with that to ground a *Culturwissenschaft* whose foundations the ten volumes of my *Cultur-Geschichte* illustrate."[12]

In 1841, the first volume of that *Allgemeine Cultur-Geschichte der Menschheit* was ready for the press. As he had done in his earlier work, Klemm begins at the beginning: volume 1 is devoted to the history of the earth. What follows is a march through space and time, beginning with the peoples whom he considered most natural ("passive") and progressing by stages through those who were most cultured—culture understood here in its fully anthropological sense as referring to those who made increasingly complex interventions upon the natural world. The categories of analysis became increasingly complex, too. They can be used to chart the way cultural history can be written from the material world in a way that acknowledges differences of culture. For example, the "passive" folk, or the "Wild men in the primeval forests, on the sea coasts or the arid plains," under one heading which encompassed basics such as food, drink, weapons, tools, decoration, shelter, family, religion, and warfare.[13] The major expansion of categories comes with the discussion of China and Japan—the first advanced societies. Klemm introduces after food, beverages; after dwelling: shipping, pack animals; after commerce, cattle breeding, agriculture and horticulture, crafts, mining, pottery; after family life: acting, political organization, government, provincial administration, urbanism, finances, legislation, penal code, public transport; after religion: Confucius, science and literature, art.[14] Finally, for the most modern societies of medieval and early modern Europe the categories expand still further, to include: the constitution of the body, clothing, abodes, ugly furnishings, ways and means, commercial activities, family life, social life, games, funerary rites, public life, political organization, classes, constitutions, state administration, head of state, laws and judiciary, military affairs, defensive weapons, attacking weapons, religion, holy places, worship, sciences, history.[15]

Klemm's introduction to the project takes the form of the prehistory of what he was calling cultural history. He begins, conventionally, with the Greeks and Romans, but his story only takes off with a long discussion of historical *renovatio* in the sixteenth century, and then a survey of antiquarianism, emphasizing the Dutch-German tradition from Lipsius and Cluverius through Conring before turning to the mass of historical critique in the eighteenth century. From antiquarianism he turns directly, and with no felt need for justification, to cultural history. Voltaire is presented as its pioneer (this too was conventional). With the French Revolution, politics reasserted itself as the centerpiece of universal history.[16] Against the political tendency of the age, Klemm enlisted science as a way of bringing the cultural world back into the story.[17] It was this scientific perspective, Klemm asserted—not the political nor the literary, artistic, antiquarian, or technological—that provided him with his vantage point. He would follow the development of mankind from wild childhood to the division into social bodies, and by reference to specific conditions of existence.[18]

The sources for such a project were as comprehensive as the project itself. What distinguished them was not their content but how they were examined—namely, as historical evidence. "Coins, coats of arms, medals and reliefs, statues and figural groups, entire buildings dedicated to war or peace, sacred or profane use are, like art objects, important sources for the historians, above all if they contain information about the time or the place of their creation or their creator."[19]

Klemm then insists that the source base for understanding the past needs to move well beyond the confines of the image or the art work. "Those image-less, often style-less things, tools, clothes, weapons, models of vehicles, buildings etc. which managed to survive to us from a distant time or space are of no little worth." Up until now, Klemm continued, descriptions and representations of such objects were incomplete or poor. "As in Mineralogy, Zoology, Botany, Archaeology, Numismatics and Paleography, so too in History, direct perception of objects is the best aid (*Hülfsmittel*) to correct understanding."[20] As in all these other fields, so too in history the best supporting science was the direct encounter with the evidence. In the case of nonfigural objects, this meant extracting information from their material constitution and form.

Klemm's vision of human history, as sketched out in his book by categories, was a collector's vision. In fact, to the first volume of the *Cul-*

turgeschichte, Klemm appended a startling text, a "Fantasy of a Museum for the Cultural History of Mankind" (*Fantasie über ein Museum für die Culturgeschichte der Menschheit*).[21] Here Klemm retraces the narrative of cultural history laid out across the ten volumes proceeding not through time, but space: as if through the rooms of a museum, with each room mapping a volume of the *Culturgeschichte.* Since Klemm did, in fact, build the diachronic narrative out of the study of the material artifacts rather than the other way around the "Fantasy" is no daydream, but the blueprint for the actually completed project.

Klemm noted that since Buffon there had been recognition that museums were linked to *Bildung,* and, specifically, that the cabinets of curiosities of the sixteenth and seventeenth centuries needed to be seen as the ancestors of modern scientific collections.[22] But the idea of establishing a collection to illustrate "the progress of Mankind and its Cultural history" had never been scientifically attempted since those early modern collections.[23] It was only now that so much material had been gathered to one place that it was possible to launch the cultural historical enterprise that Klemm was thinking about. He describes it thus: "From now, however, fundamental historical research no less than natural scientific could be based solely on the perception of monuments and was possible through comparison and evaluation of the evidence."[24]

At the heart of this project lies the argument that static artifacts contain within themselves information relevant to dynamic change. Klemm acknowledges that an embodiment of cultural history makes the choice of illustrative objects of paramount importance.[25] And since not everything could be illustrated, the focus had to be on the illustration of disjunction—which also meant that if there were periods of little change these would not be illustrated.[26] Klemm's vision was of a museum as a "*Codex probationum der Wissenschaft.*"

If there was danger in having too many individual pieces, there was also danger in having too few. The curator could not omit what he did not like, or was not interested in. Paraphrasing, and perhaps poking fun at Ranke, Klemm declared that "this is the real impartiality and justice of the Historian" (*Dieß ist die wahre Unpartheilichkeit und Gerechtigkeit des Historikers*), and separated him from the "Kunst-dilettante" who, for instance, would never include the carvings of the Eskimos, or images of the Mexicans and Chinese, alongside the Medici Venus or a Raphael Madonna. Just like the student of nature, the student of the human past could not treat some artifacts with more seriousness and care than others. They were all evidence.[27]

Behind this fantasy, as behind the table of contents for the project as a whole, lay Klemm's own collection. He described it as containing the smaller objects, of little worth, that others would have no interest in, but which worked for his argument.[28]

2.

Present in this vast cultural historical narrative, and brought to exquisite clarity in his "Fantasy of a Museum of the Cultural History of Mankind," is the idea that cultural history can—and in some cases can only—be written from objects. Klemm soon gave a name to this idea. In 1851, he delivered a a lecture in Vienna to the Anthropological Society, entitled "Foundations of a General Cultural Science" ("*Grundideen zu einer allgemeinen Cultur-Wissenschaft*").

Klemm sets up his argument in terms of the opposition between nature and culture. *Cultura,* for the Romans, was what humans do to change the world. A cultural science would have therefore to do with food, clothing, and shelter, but also with vessels, tools, and machines. Studying their origin and development, he writes, constitutes the first axis of a future *Culturwissenschaft.*[29] The second was to explore objects through human relations: from man and woman to family, children, clan, tribe, city, state. The third examined the spiritual life of man through his creation of art and science. With this, Klemm succinctly plotted archaeology, anthropology, the history of religion, and art history on to *Culturwissenschaft.* Klemm summarized all this very clearly.

> Cultural Science begins with the material foundations of human life, with the representation of bodily needs, the means of their satisfaction and the products arising from that. It then represents human relations within the family and their broadening into the state. The final section of it, however, deals with the results of human exploration and experience, and displays the spiritual creations of mankind in science and art.[30]

Klemm's major treatment of this subject is his *Allgemeine Culturwissenschaft* of 1855, with its fantastic cross-cultural discussions of fire, food, drink, narcotics, tools, and weapons. The work is a remarkable achievement in terms of vision and scope. Its introduction, too, is fascinating. In it, Klemm contextualizes his own work in the history of encyclopedism, seen from the perspective of the organization of knowledge—obviously written in the light of both his own *Allgemeine Culturgeschichte* and his fantasy of a museum of human history. Klemm then turned directly, and without pause to collections, and the history of collecting.[31] This lead directly in to a brief survey of the history of cultural history via a survey of the late seventeenth-century genre of *historia literaria,* citing Lambeck and Morhof, up through Voltaire. It is at that point, he writes, that *moeurs,* family life, religious forms, art, and science began to become independent subjects for inquiry. The great subsequent step forward was driven by the work of Linnaeus and Buffon, and the arrival of new materials from the South Seas, the Americas, China, and Siberia. Finally, it became possible to envision a global human science.[32]

Culture meant for Klemm something like a civilizing process: "the improvement or refining of the entire spiritual and bodily force of men or of a people." But it also referred to the broadest range of human interventions in nature: when someone turned a tree branch into a spear to throw at an animal, or to rub two branches together to make a fire to cook that animal, or when using fire to burn down the hut once inhabited by his father and now housing his corpse, or when he painted his body whether for war or decoration. "These are all signs of drives and properties that distinguish him from animals."[33]

Like the natural sciences, the cultural sciences were a "science of experience" (*Wissenschaft der Erfahrung*), based on the appearances of things. Its object was not one part of the human race, or one state, or one part of the earth (neatly acknowledging, while still rejecting, the overarching claims of ethnology, *statistik,* and geography), nor one of the many activities and achievements of man, neither commerce, nor war, nor law, nor literature. *Culturwissenschaft,* according to Klemm "had the task of representing human nature as a whole, as an individual." Whereas *Culturgeschichte* treated this individual in his developmental aspect, making progress in his circumstances, *Culturwissenschaft* showed him in his varied fundamental postures, in family life and society, in war and in peace. "In a word: Culturwissenschaft had the task to bring into view the whole of human activity and their monuments at all times and places."[34]

Klemm expanded upon the three axes laid out in his Vienna lecture. This meant starting with the fundamental transformation of natural into human products. "Food, Clothing and Ornament, Tools, Shelter, vehicles and tools, these are the material foundations of human culture." Explaining their origin and development constituted the first task of *Cul-*

turwissenschaft.[35] The second part of any future *Culturwissenschaft* would, in turn, focus on the relations between people. The priest-king combination produced organs of society; commerce created new relations; the king was paterfamilias; everywhere, religion and politics begin and blend together. The second task of *Culturwissenschaft* was then to represent the connectedness of these phenomena and their development toward the state.[36] The third and final task was to narrate the "achievements of human inquiry and experiment, as well as the spiritual creations of peoples in science and art."[37] Thus, what his younger contemporary Burckhardt defined as cultural history was for him but a part—and the last at that—of a much bigger project.

Not included as a specific chapter in the *Allgemeine Culturwissenschaft,* clothing, nevertheless was exactly one of the kinds of subjects amenable to such a treatment. In 1854, Klemm delivered a lecture to the "Gewerbvereins" of Dresden on its twentieth anniversary, with the title *Die Menschliche Kleidung: Culturgeschictliche Skizze.*[38] Also in 1854, "The Hat" (*Der Hut*) was the subject of a stand-alone piece. Both of these essays were transhistorical and geographical in scope. In the event, no further parts of the *Allgemeine Culturwissenschaft* seem to have been undertaken. Klemm's large project of the period 1854–1858 was historical: a six-volume encyclopedia of women's history, *Die Frauen: Culturgeschictliche Schilderungen des Zustandes und Einflusses der Frauen in den verschiedenen Zonen und Zeitaltern* (1854–58). After this, he eyes seem to have begun to fail, and his prodigious scholarly production began to diminish.

A significant, even defining, feature of Klemm's intellectual profile was the role allotted to objects not merely as foci of investigation, but as their stimuli as well. This is the role of his own collection. After his death—through a circuitous path—it was purchased for the city of Leipzig, and became the core of its Ethnology Museum.[39] Historians seem not to have paid much attention to Klemm.

But others did. Edward Tylor, for example, introduces Klemm's concept of culture history on the very first page of his *Researches into the Early History of Mankind and the Development of Civilization* (1865).[40] Augustus Pitt-Rivers cited Klemm frequently, and borrowed his approach of classifying by forms. The disposition of the museum bearing his name, to this very day reflects the principle of the *Allgemeine Culturwissenschaft.* Klemm's biggest impact was in the United States. Otis Mason, a professor at Columbia University, read the report on Klemm's collection that had appeared in a Leipzig newspaper and translated it into English while incorporating Klemm's vision into his instructions to agents of the newly founded Bureau of American Ethnology. They were, he wrote, to seek out artifacts to "present savage life and condition in all grades and places," without leaving anything aside "because they are either rude or homely."[41]

The "dog that did not bark," however; the reception that did not occur, might be the most fascinating of all: Karl Marx. There is no indication that Klemm read Marx, or that Marx read Klemm. Yet Marx, who was not interested in things, at exactly the same time that Klemm provided the most comprehensive contemporary presentation of material life, provided the most compelling contemporary discussion of the meaningfulness of material culture (the *German Ideology* was written in 1845–1846; the *Allgemeine Cultur-geschichte*, in 1843–1852). Moreover, like Klemm, Marx provided an account of the development of society in which change was geared to material life. What separates the two is that Klemm was interested in the material; Marx, in the materiality; Klemm, in the details of ever-intensifying material culture; Marx, in the changing political forces driving it. The chronological proximity of their arguments tells us a great deal about the 1840s and 1850s in Germany. Their conceptual proximity, however, helps clarify not only the later disciplinary parting of the ways of anthropology and political economy, but also the earlier intertwining of cultural history and political thought in the preceding period.

One crucial source might be Moritz von Lavergne-Peguilhen's *Grundzüge der Gesellschaftswissenschaft* (2 vols., 1838 and 1841).[42] The second volume of this largely forgotten work is devoted to "Die Kulturwissenschaft." Lavergne-Peguilhen devotes an entire section to "General Laws of Culture" (*Allgemeine Kulturgesetze*), which begins with a section devoted to "Kulturwissenschaft." The use of the term, he explains, has nothing to do with the formation of artists or scholars or individuals in general, but with the population as a mass.[43] The goal was the integration of "Production, Cultural and Political activity" for the perfection of the "mass of the population."[44] This could only be achieved through what he called "Kulturwissenschaft."[45]

Dedicating the first volumes of his study of Gibbon's world to Momigliano and Venturi was the way John Pocock acknowledged the early modern heritage of enlightenment social process.[46] Thinking about the relationship of Klemm and Marx as mediated through the term *Kulturwissenschaft* suggests that the further exploration of the worlds of antiquarianism and social thought might well be worthwhile.

3.

What might it mean that material culture and cultural science were born twins? This is a huge question. Even outlining what an answer might look like extends far beyond the scope of this chapter. For one thing, it antedates the serious reflection on the *Kulturwissenschaften* by Dilthey by several decades and, significantly I think given Dilthey's *geistesgeschichtlich* orientation, shows us that originally the material world was seen as a crucial part of its armature. In the German tradition, materiality and the *Kulturwissenschaften* would not begin to be reintegrated until Warburg, and this process was interrupted, in quick succession, by his death in 1929, and the disruption of German academic life after January 30, 1933. In France, where so much of the impetus of the *Annales* was anti-Diltheyan in its fullest sense, neither material culture nor the *Kulturwissenschaften* were terms to conjure with, and it remains the case to this very day. In the Anglophone world, material culture returned in the 1960s, but totally cut off from this nineteenth-century story, and severed from any link to the *Kulturwissenschaften*.

We can even date this story precisely. In his *Einleitung in die Kulturwissenschaftliche Bibliographie zum Nachleben der Antike,* published in Leipzig in 1934, Warburg's then heir apparent Edgar Wind devoted a section to explaining Dilthey's conception of the *Geisteswissenschaften* and Warburg's rejection of it for its lack of historical specificity. The latter's invocation of the *Kulturwissenschaften* was intended as making an alternative pathway.[47] The English translation of this volume, published in London that same year (the Institute having relocated there in 1933), begins with an apologia for retaining, even in the title, the "untranslatable" German term *Kulturwissenschaft.*[48] Wind explained that Warburg's entire project was unintelligible without it.[49] In elaborating on Warburg's foundation in the work of Burckhardt and Usener, spanning the realm of evidence from art, to anthropology, to folklore, to religion, to science, Wind offered the first self-conscious justification of *Kulturwissenschaft* since Klemm, but only as valedictory.[50] The section on Dilthey, which put all this in context, was dropped from the English edition, leaving *Kulturwissenschaft* well and truly marooned.[51] Ernst Cassirer, Warburg's close colleague, himself responded to the outbreak of the Second World War with a call to action entitled, *Der Logik der Kulturwissenschaften.* But by the time he, too, came to an English-speaking world (Yale) and offered the book for publication, it had become *The Logic of the Humanities*—which, ironically, would have translated back into German as *Geisteswissenschaften*—

precisely the Diltheyan notion that Klemm *avant la lettre* and Warburg *après* both opposed. A half-century further on—"cultural science," or "the cultural sciences"—still have not made it into English usage.

Arnaldo Momigliano pointed to the years around 1870 as the breaking open of the humanistic disciplines and the beginning of their reshaping into something resembling our own—or at least the beginning of our own. He pointed to Tylor, Bachofen, Nietzsche, and Burckhardt as key figures in this change. Karl Lamprecht, in the generation that followed, was fascinated by social psychology and art, and deeply committed to integrating material evidence into cultural history. But he had no working concept of *Kulturwissenschaft*. Reflecting on the history of this kind of history, Braudel looked from Klemm to Burckhardt, and wondered if perhaps our received view of center and periphery in the practice of cultural history needed some correction.[52]

Finally, that Klemm self-consciously and repeatedly presents his work as emerging out of early modern antiquarianism brings the history of early modern antiquarianism much closer to the threshold of modern historical practice than we might have thought. That Klemm may have been the "last of the antiquaries" might seem uninteresting, but if the last of the antiquaries is also the first of the *Kulturwissenschaftler,* and first of the anthropologists, then things become more intriguing. And, *pace* the gap between Klemm and Lamprecht (in point of fact, barely a decade), putting Klemm back into the picture makes visible a long and unbroken chain of scholars who used material evidence to explore the history of human culture—a chain that extends back at least to Cyriac of Ancona, and moves through Pirro Ligorio to Peiresc, Leibniz, Caylus, and Schlözer to Barthélémy, and on; beyond Klemm, to Lamprecht, Pirenne, Bloch, and Braudel. If the "counter-history" includes so many key historical thinkers, and all periods up to the present, then we may need to rethink the more familiar narrative of history's history in which writing from things plays no significant role.

NOTES

1. M. Heydrich, "Gustav Klemm und seine kulturhistorische Sammlung," *Kultur und Rasse. Otto Reche zum 60. Geburtstag,* ed. Michael Hesch and Günther Spannaus (Munich and Berlin: J. F. Lehamnns Verlag, 1939), 305–17.
2. Friedrich Adolf Ebert, *Bildung des Bibliothekars,* 2nd ed. (Leipzig: Steinaker and Wagner, 1820). Ebert was secretary of the Royal Library of Dresden, and therefore Klemm's predecessor.

3. Gustav Friedrich Klemm, *Allgemeine Culturwissenschaft*, 2 vols. (Dresden: Romberg, 1854–55), 31–34.

4. Gustav Friedrich Klemm, *Die Königlich Sächsische Porzellan-Sammlung* (Dresden: Walther, 1834); Klemm, *Handbuch der Germanisches Alterthumskunde* (Dresden: Walther, 1836).

5. Gustav Friedrich Klemm, *Allgemeine Culturwissenschaft*, 35.

6. "Bei meinen antiquarischen Studien sah ich mich seit mehrern Jahren vergeblich nach einem Buch um, worinnen die Nöthigen Nachweisungen der Quellen und Hülfsmittel zur ältesten vaterländischen Culturgeschichte enthalten." Gustav Friedrich Klemm, *Handbuch der Germanisches Alterthumskunde*, v. This discussion of Klemm is part of a longer project on the history of the study of things from Peiresc to Lamprecht.

7. "Will man sich nun dies Alles recht vergegenwärtigen, so schlage man das *Museum Wormianum* auf, wo das grosse Kupferblatt hinter dem Titel uns einen deutlichen Blick ins Innere einer Kunst- und Naturalienkammer des 17ten Jahrhunderts gestattet. . . ." Gustav Friedrich Klemm, *Zur Geschichte der Sammlungen für Wissenschaft und Kunst in Deutschland*, 2nd ed. (Zerbst 1837, 1838), 165.

8. Gustav Friedrich Klemm, *Zur Geschichte der Sammlungen für Wissenschaft und Kunst in Deutschland*, 300, 228, 239–40.

9. "Wenige Monate nach Vollendung meines Reiseberichts stand auch der Plan zur Culturgeschichte und zur Culturwissenschaft in scharfen Umrissen auf dem Papier, den ich meinem jetzt verwigten väterlichen Freunde A.B. v. Lindenau vorlegte." Gustav Friedrich Klemm, *Allgemeine Culturwissenschaft*, 35.

10. Klemm described his collecting as a salvage project: "die Zeit wohl nicht mehr fern ist, wo die eigenthümlichen Geräthe und Kunstwerke der wilden Nationen gegen europäische Producte vertauscht, und in alle Welt zerstreut sein werden." Gustav Friedrich Klemm, *Allgemeine Cultur-Geschichte*, 27.

11. The figures are given in M. Heydrich, "Gustav Klemm und seine kulturhistorische Sammlung," 312. "Thus emerged," Klemm later wrote, "the collection about which I have already given closer account in my ten volume Culturgeschichte." Gustav Friedrich Klemm, *Allgemeine Culturwissenschaft*, 35.

12. "Der Zweck der Sammlung ist kein anderer, als die Entstehung der verchiedenen menschlichen Gewerbs- und Kunsterzeugnisse aus den von der Natur dargebotenen Stoffen und die fernerweite Entwickellung derselben zur Anschauung zu bringnen, somit aber eine Culturwissenschaft zu begründen, deren Grundlage die zehn Bände meiner Cultur-Geschichte bilden." Gustav Friedrich Klemm, *Allgemeine Cultur-Geschichte der Menschheit*, vol. 10, lii.

13. "Nahrung, deren Erwerb und Bereitung; Die Jagdwaffen; Jagd der Lasthiere und Vögel; Kleidung und deren Bereitung; Schmuck und Zierrathen; Wohnung und Ruhestätte; Werkzeuge, Geräthe und Gefässe; Fahrzeuge; Gestand und Familienleben; Geselliges Leben; Spiele und Festlichkeiten; Tanz; Oeffentliches Leben im Frieden; Kriegswesen; Religiöse Begriffe (Glaube, Gottesdienst, Zauberei); Cultur (sprache, lieder, erzählungen,

Bilderschrift, Brief eines Mandan, Gemalte Robe, Zahlen, Zeiteintheilung);
Geschichte." Gustav Friedrich Klemm, *Allgemeine Cultur-Geschichte*, 19–20.

14. After "Nahrung: Getränke;" after "Wohnung: Schiffart, Lastthiere;" after
"Gewerbe: Viehzucht, Ackerbau u. Gartenbau, Handwerke, Bergbau, Töp-
ferei;" after "Familienleben: Schauspieler, Staatsverfassung, Die Regierung,
Provinzialverwaltung, Stadtwesen, Finanzen, Gesetzgebung, Die Strafen,
Der öffentliche Verkehr;" after "Religion: Kung-tsen oder Confucius, Wis-
senschaft und Literatur, Kunst." Gustav Friedrich Klemm, *Allgemeine Cultur-
Geschichte,* 19–20.

15. "Körperliche Beschaffenheit; Die Kleidung; Wohnstätten; Häsliche Ein-
richtung; Fortbewegungsmittel; Die Gewerbthätitkeit; Die Familienleben;
Das gesellige Leben; Spiele; Todtenbestattung; Das öffentliche Leben; Der
Staatsverfassung; Stände; Verfassungen; Staatsverwaltung; Das Staatsober-
haupt; Gesetze u. Rechtspflege; Kriegswesen; Schutzwaffen der Menschen;
Angriffswaffen; Religion; Die heiligen Orte; Gottesdienst; Wissenschaften;
Geschichte."

16. "Wie früherhin der Theologie, so mußte nun alles der Politik dienen: Religion, Kunst, Poesie, Geographie, Handel und Gewerbe, alles wurde aus
dem Gesichtspuncte der Politik betrachtet; und wie früherhin die Kirche,
so nahm jetz der Staat Alles für sich und seien Zwecke in Anspruch." Gustav
Friedrich Klemm, *Allgemeine Cultur-Geschichte,* 19–20.

17. "So wie die Naturwissenschaft die Rede und die auf, an in und bei derselben
vorkommenden Erscheinungen, die sie umgebende Luft, die Gewäffer, die
Gebirge, die Rinde, die Gesteine, Gewächse, die Thiere und Menschen
als Theile eines und desselben gewordenen und bestehenden Ganzen im
Einzelnen untersucht und im Ganzen betrachtet, eben so soll der historiker die Menschheit als ein Ganzes, auch allen seinen Gliederungen, nach
seiner Entstehung, Entwicklung, seine Wesen, Seyn und Werden, in allen
Beziehungen und Richtungen erforschen und zu erkennen und darzustellen suchen." Gustav Friedrich Klemm, *Allgemeine Cultur-Geschichte,* 21.

18. ". . . in Bezug auf Sitten, Kenntnisse und Fertigkeiten, häusliches und
öffentliches Leben in Frieden und Krieg, Religion, Wissen und Kunst, unter
den von Clima und Lage von der Vorsehung dargebotenen Verhältnissen zu
erforschen und nachzuweisen." Gustav Friedrich Klemm, *Allgemeine Cultur-
Geschichte,* 21.

19. "Münzen, Wappen, Medallien und Reliefs, Statuen und Gruppen, Monumente und ganze dem kriegerischen oder friedlichen, dem hiera-
tischen oder profanen Gebrauche gewidmete Gebäude werden—wie alle
Kunstwerke—für den Historiker wichtige Quellen, wenn sie zumal Angaben
über die Zeit oder den Ortihrer Entstehung, ihrer Künstler enthalten. Sie
sind auch bereits vielfach für historische Zwecke benutzt, und ihre Kunde
in der Archäologie, der Kunstgeschichte zu eigenen Gebieten des Wissens
erhoben worden." Gustav Friedrich Klemm, *Allgemeine Cultur-Geschichte,* 26–
27.

20. "Nicht geringen Werth haben jene bildlosen, oft formlosen Sachen,
Geräthe, Gefäße, Kleider, Waffen, Modelle von Fahrzeugen, Gebäuden
u.s.w., welche aus fernen Zeiten oder Gegenden zu uns gelangen. . . . Wie in

der Mineralogie, Zoologie, Botanik, Archäologie, Numismatik und Paläographie ist eigene Anschauung der Gegenstände auch in der Geschichte das beßte Hülfsmittel zur rechten Erkenntniß." Gustav Friedrich Klemm, *Allgemeine Cultur-Geschichte,* 27

21. Gustav Friedrich Klemm, *Allgemeine Cultur-Geschichte der Menschheit,* 10 vols. (Leipzig: Teubner, 1843–1854), vol. 1. Beilage. "Fantasie über ein Museum für die Culturgeschichte der Menschheit."

22. "dass die Museen der haltpunct der Erfahrungswissenschaften sind, und diese Erkenntniß war die Ursache, daß der Curiositätenkammern des 16. und 17. Jahrhunderts einem ernsten bewußten Streben in Anlage und Pflege wissenschaftlicher Sammlungen weichen mußte." Gustav Friedrich Klemm, "Fantasie über ein Museum für die Culturgeschichte der Menschheit," 355.

23. "Seltsam aber bleibt es immer, daß das Bedürfniß einer Sammlung für die Uebersicht der Fortschritte der Menschheit und ihrer Culturgeschichte sich nicht dringend geltend machen konnte, und zwar um so seltsamer, als es seit früher Zeit an mannichfacher Anregung dazu durchaus nicht gefehlt hat." Gustav Friedrich Klemm, "Fantasie über ein Museum für die Culturgeschichte der Menschheit," 353.

24. "Da nun aber eine gründliche historische Forschung nicht minder auf eigener Anschauung der Monumente beruht, als eine naturwissenschaftliche, da durch sie nur eine Vergleichung und Beweißführung möglich wird, so will ich in der historischen Ueberzeugung, daß jede Idee, welche eine Wahrheit enthält, auch zu seiner Zeit zur Ausführung kommen werde, meine Ansichten über Begründung, Anordnung und Inhalt eines culturhistorischen Museums hier niederlegen." Gustav Friedrich Klemm, "Fantasie über ein Museum für die Culturgeschichte der Menschheit," 355.

25. "Für die Ausführung einer solchen Darstellung, einer solchen Verkörperung der Culturgeschichte bedurfte es allerdings zuvörderst der sorgfältigsten Prüfung des dargebotenen Materials." Gustav Friedrich Klemm, "Fantasie über ein Museum für die Culturgeschichte der Menschheit," 359.

26. "Bei allen Nationen sind uberhaput die Zeitlater, die Ur-anfänge und Fortschritte stets sorgfällig zu sonder und gesondert vor Augen zu stellen." Gustav Friedrich Klemm, "Fantasie über ein Museum für die Culturgeschichte der Menschheit," 359.

27. "Wie der Naturforscher die Bandwürmer, Scolopendern, Kröten und deren Genossen mit derselben Theilnahme betrachtet, wie die Labradorsteine, Magnolien, Argus, Colibri und Gazellen, so bieten dem Historiker die schmierigen Pelze und Geräthe der Bosjesman und Eskimo nicht minder Stoff zum Denken dar, als die Federkleider der Mexicaner oder die Marmorstatuen der Hellenen. Er hat jedem gleiche Aufmerksamkeit, gleiche Sorgfalt zu widemen und beide haben gleichen Anspruch dazu." Gustav Friedrich Klemm, "Fantasie über ein Museum für die Culturgeschichte der Menschheit," 361.

28. "Anstatt nun das Beste und Wesentliche auszulesen und dem Ganzen am gehörigen Ort einzuverlieben, wird oft ein etwas weniger glänzend in die Augen fallendes Stück beseitigt und den neuen Ankömmlingen ein unge-

278 Cultural Histories of the Material World

bührlich großer und passender Platz eingeräumt, nur um mit der Menge prahlen zu können." Quoted in M. Heydrich, "Gustav Klemm und seine kulturhistorische Sammlung," 307. For this same idea of making ugly objects speak historically see Peter N. Miller, "The Antiquary's Art of Comparison: Peiresc and *Abraxas*," *Philologie und Erkenntnis. Beiträge zu Begriff und Problem frühneuzeitlicher 'Philologie,'* ed. Ralph Häfner (Tübingen: Max Niemeyer Verlag, 2001), 57–94.

29. "Nahrung, Kleidung, Schmuck, Wohnstätte, Fahrzeuge, Gefässe und Werkzeuge, das sind die sachlichen Grundlagen des gesammten menschlichen Lebens, und die Betrachtung ihrer Entstehung und Entwicklung, das würde der erste Abschnitt der Aufgabe sein, welche die Culturwissenschaft zu lösen hat." Gustav Friedrich Klemm, "Grundideen zu einer allgemeinen Cultur-Wissenschaft," 175.

30. "Die Culturwissenchaft beginnt mit den materiellen Grundlagen des menschlichen Lebens, mit der Darstellung der körperlichen Bedürfnisse, den Mitteln zu deren Befriedigung und den daraus entspringenden Erzeugnissen. Sie stellt sodann die menschlichen Verhältnisse in der Familie und in ihrer Erweiterung zum Staate dar. Der letzte Abschnitt derselben aber hat die Betrachtung der Egebnisse menschlicher Erforschung und Erfahrung, so wie die geistigen Schöpfungen des Menschen in der Wissenschaft und Kunst zu entwickln." Gustav Friedrich Klemm, "Grundideen zu einer allgemeinen Cultur-Wissenschaft," 184.

31. "Mittlerweile begann man aber auch die Denkmale der menschlichen Kunst- und Gewerbthätigkeit näher zu betrachten, wie man vorher die Naturkörper gesammelt und beschrieben hattte." Klemm, *Allgemeine Culturwissenschaft*, 2:18.

32. "Man betrachtete seitdem die Sitten, das Familienleben, Staats- und Religionsformen, Wissenschaft und Kunst nicht als einzeln neben einander bestehende, selbständige Erscheinungen, sondern man sah ein, daß sie eben unter einander in innigen Zusammenhange und in steter Wechselwirkung stehen." Gustav Friedrich Klemm, *Allgemeine Culturwissenschaft*, 28.

33. "die Veredelung oder Verfeinerung der gesammten Geistes- und Leibeskräfte des Menschen oder eines Volks. . . ." Gustav Friedrich Klemm, *Allgemeine Culturwissenschaft*, 37.

34. "Die Culturwissenschaft aber ist gleich den Naturwissenschaften eine Wissenschaft der Erfahrung, die auf der Anschauung von Thatsachen beruht. Ihr Gegenstand ist nicht die einzelne Menschenrasse, ein einzelner Staat oder einer der Erdtheile, aber auch nicht eine der vielen Thätigkeiten und Erzeugnisse der Menschen, wie etwa die Gewerbstätigkeit, der Krieg, das Recht, die Literatur. Sie hat die Aufgabe, die Menschheit der Natur gegenüber als ein Ganzes, als ein Individuum aufzufassen und darzustellen. Während nun die Culturgeschichte dieses Individuum in seiner Entwickelung nach fortschreitenden Zuständen und in Völker geschieden betrachtet, hat die Culturwissenschaft dasselbe nach seinen Beschäftigungen, z.B. bei der Erwerbung und Bereitung der zur Befriedigung seiner Triebe nothwendigen Bedürfnisse, dann im Familienleben, im Staatsverein, im Kriege wie im Frieden, bei seinem Forschen und Dichten, Träumen

und Denken aufzufassen, mit einem Wort: die Culturwissenschaft hat die Aufgabe, die gesammte Menschenthätigkeit und deren Denkmale in allen Zonen und Zeiten zur Anschauung zu bringen." Gustav Friedrich Klemm, *Allgemeine Culturwissenschaft,* 37–38.

35. "Nahrung, Kleidung und Schmuck, Werkzeuge, Wohnstätten, Fahrzeuge und Gefäße, diese sind die materiellen Grundlagen der menschlichen Cultur, und die Betrachtung ihrer allmäligen Entstehung und Entwicklung, das bildet den ersten Abschnitt der Aufgabe, welche die Culturwissenschaft zu lösen hat." Gustav Friedrich Klemm, *Allgemeine Culturwissenschaft,* 42.

36. "die gesammten im Staatswesen sich darstellenden Erscheinungen zu betrachten, die Anfänge derselben in der Familie nachzuweisen, die allmälige Entwickelung und Gliederung derselben zu verfolgen, die Gestaltung der Verwaltung, der Gesetzgebung, der bürgerlichen und religiösen Verfassung, des friedlichen Verkehrs der Völker und Staaten unter einander, wie auch das Kriegswesen und die Kriegsverfassung nach seiner Entstehung und Ausbildung zur Anschauung zu bringen." Gustav Friedrich Klemm, *Allgemeine Culturwissenschaft,* 52.

37. "Der dritte aber hat die Aufgabe, die Ergebnisse menschlicher Erforschung und Erfahrung so wie die geistigen Schöpfungen der Völker in Wissenschaft und Kunst darzulegen." Gustav Friedrich Klemm, *Allgemeine Culturwissenschaft,* 52.

38. *Die Menschliche Kleidung. Culturgeschictliche Skizze.* Lecture given on the twentieth anniversary of the Gewerbevereins of Dresden, January 31, 1854 (Dresden, 1856).

39. After Klemms's death on August 25, 1867, his son J. Gustav Klemm took over the sale. In 1868, the British Museum bought his German antiquities. The University of Leipzig decided against buying the rest, saying it was not of scientific worth. The materials ended up with a private medical doctor who catalyzed a committee of thirty-eight well-known Leipzigers who published on November 24, 1869, in the *Leipziger Tageszeitungen* an "Aufruf zu Beiträgen für die Erwerbung der culturhistorischen Sammlung des verstorbenen Hofrats Dr. Klemm zur 'Begründung eines allgemeinen anthropologischen Museums.'" They acted both for its scientific use, and to prevent it from all going abroad: they were successful. In 1870, negotiations for the purchase went ahead, and in 1871 the collection was bought for the "Deutschen Zentralmuseums für Anthropologie zu Leipzig." This was the first ethnographic museum on the Continent. The Neues Museum in Berlin (1868) had many ethnographic objects in the collection, but only much later was a dedicated ethnographic museum founded there. In 1904, the Leipzig museum changed its name to "Städtisches Museum für Völkerkunde," and in 1926 moved into a new building—the Grassi Palace—which was destroyed in an air raid during World War II. For more on this history see Alfred Lehmann, "85 Jahre Museum für Völkerkunde zu Leipzig," *Jahrbuch des Museums für Völkerkunde zu Leipzig* 7 (1951): 11–51; and Fritz Krause, "Chronik des Museums 1926–1945," *Jahrbuch des Museums für Völkerkunde zu Leipzig* 10 (1926/1951): 1–46.

40. Edward Tylor, *Researches into the Early History of Mankind and the Development*

of Civilization, ed. Paul Bohannan (Chicago: University of Chicago Press, 1964 [1865]), 1.

41. Robert Rydell, *All the World's a Fair* (Chicago: University of Chicago Press, 1984), 23.

42. Engels rejected the view that Marx could discover "der materialistischen Geschichtsanschauung" via a "Prussian Romantic of the historian school." See Angela Stender, *Durch Gesellschaftswissenschaft zum idealen Staat: Moritz von Lavergne-Peguilhen (1801–1870)* (Berlin: Dunker & Humblot, 2005), 15. Moreover, in a letter to Franz Mehring of September 28, 1892, Engels denied any influence of Lavergne-Peguilhen on Marx, who at the time was interested only in "pure" philosophy, and not in either economics or history: Angela Stender, *Durch Gesellschaftswissenschaft*, 15.

43. "Die Kulturwissenschaft hat es daher nicht mit pädagogischen Untersuchungen zu thun, oder mit den Mitteln zur Bildung von Künstlern und Gelehrten, sie setzt vielmehr die dahin führenden Wege als bekannt voraus, wie denn überhaupt nicht das Individuum, sondern die Bevöllkerungsmasse Gegenstand ihrer Forschung ist." Moritz von Lavergne-Peguilhen's *Grundzüge der Gesellschaftswissenschaft*, 2 vols. in 1 (Leipzig, 1838), 2:3–4. Even Stender, who surveys not only Lavernge-Peguilhen's reception history, but also that of its constituent parts, treats *Kulturwissenschaft*, by contrast, as a term with no history and in need of no further elucidation. See Angela Stender, *Durch Gesellschaftswissenschaft zum idealen Staat*.

44. "Diese allgemeinen Verhältnisse des Wechselverkehrs und der Gegenseitigkeit gewähren der Kulturwissenschaft, deren Aufgabe es ist, die weigen und unwandelbaren Gesetze zu erforschen, die der Vervollkommnung der Bevölkerungsmassen zum Grunde liegen, die wichtigsen Hülfsmittel . . . Es treten demnach die Bewegungs-, Productions- und Staatswissenschaften in den Rang mittelbarer Kulturwissenschaften ein, weil jede gesellschaftliche Bewegung im Allgemeinen und jede Productions- und Staatsthätigkeit im Besonderen, in Folge jenes organsichen Grundgesetzes, eien nothwendige Rückwirkung auf die Kultur erhalten muß." Moritz von Lavergne-Peguilhen, *Grundzüge*, 3.

45. By defining the place of *Kulturwissenschaft* between philosophical and practical learning, Moritz von Lavergne-Peguilhen indicates his triangulation between the positions of Kant and Herder; it is the linking of the term to social process and *Productionswissenschaft* that seems to mark off the start of a new trajectory. Moritz von Lavergne-Peguilhen, *Grundzüge*, 6.

46. J. G. A. Pocock, *Barbarism and Religion* (Cambridge: Cambridge University Press, 1999), vols. 1 and 2.

47. *Kulturwissenschaftliche Bibliographie zum Nachleben der Antike. Erster Band Die Erscheinungen des Jahres 1931*, ed. Hans Meier, Richard Newald, and Edgar Wind (Leipzig-Berlin: B. G. Teubner, 1934), "Kritik des Geistesgeschichte," vii–xi.

48. *A Bibliography on the Survival of the Classics. First Volume. The Publications of 1931*. The Text of the German edition with an English Introduction (London: Cassel & Company, 1934), v: "This word is full of odd connotations. English readers might feel themselves reminded of war-time slogans which

succeeded in rendering the word 'Kultur' altogether disreputable. German scholars will think, with some mortification, of the time when their philosophical professors discovered the difference between natural and cultural sciences and became involved in profound discussions as to which science deserved the name of 'cultural.'—These times are past, and there is, at least on the part of the editors of this book, no intention to revive them. If nevertheless the portentous word 'kulturwissenschaftlich' has been retained on the title page, it is for two distinct reasons."

49. "He [Warburg] used it in order to designate his attempt to tear down the barriers artificially set up between the various departments of historical research. Historians of science were not to work independently of historians of art and of religion; nor were historians of literature to isolate the study of linguistic forms and literary arts from their settings in the totality of culture. The idea of a comprehensive 'science of civilization' was thus meant to embody the demand for a precise method of interaction and correlation between those diverging scientific interests in the humanities which have shown a tendency to set up their subjects as 'things in themselves,'" Wind, *A Bibliography*, v.

50. Burckhardt's *Kultur der Renaissance in Italien* was one model "which, by embracing all phases of culture—science, art, and literature, as well as social customs and superstitions—, became the model for further 'Kulturstudien,' the word 'Kultur' as used by Burckhardt meaning the expressions of a historical period taken as a whole. In a similar way, the work done by Hermann Usener, who applied the comparative methods of anthropology and folklore to the study of ancient rituals and myths, had a profound effect in enlarging the scope of cultural studies, although he never intended any more than did Burckhardt, to give philosophical definition to what he really meant by cultural traditions. Thus, the word 'kulturwissenschaftlich' may also better be explained by reference to these two names, Burkchardt and Usener, than by any abstract definition, and it is in this sense—as a reference to a tradition of research ('Forschungsweise'), rather than as an abstract postulate—that the term is to be understood," Wind, *A Bibliography*, vi.

51. This section, "Kritik der Geistesgeschichte," appears in the German edition at vii–viii.

52. "It would be useful to see how far Jacob Burckhardt fits into the movement of German Kulturgeschichte, projected as early as Herder (1784–91) and popularized by the publication of Gustav Klemm's book (1843–52)." Fernand Braudel, "The History of Civilizations. The Past Explains the Present," in *On History* (Chicago: University of Chicago Press, 1976), 186.

List of Contributors

Glenn Adamson is head of research at the Victoria and Albert Museum, and a specialist on the history and theory of craft and design. He is coeditor of the triannual *Journal of Modern Craft,* the author of *Thinking Through Craft* (Berg Publishers/V&A Publications, 2007); *The Craft Reader* (Berg, 2010); and *The Invention of Craft* (Berg, 2012). Dr. Adamson's other publications include the coedited volumes *Global Design History* (Routledge, 2011); and *Surface Tensions* (Manchester University Press, 2012). His most recent curatorial project is a major exhibition and accompanying publication for the V&A entitled *Postmodernism: Style and Subversion, 1970 to 1990.*

Brigitte Miriam Bedos-Rezak is professor of history at New York University. A specialist of diplomatic media, she has published extensively on medieval seals as conceptual tools, markers of identity, and social agents, including *Form and Order in Medieval France* (Andershot, 1993), "Medieval Identity: A Sign and a Concept," *American Historical Review* (2000), and *When Ego was Imago: Signs of Identity in the Middle Ages* (Brill, 2010). In her book in progress, she considers the technicity of imprinted matter in medieval culture and society.

Jonathan M. Bloom shares the Norma Jean Calderwood University Professorship of Islamic and Asian Art at Boston College, and the Hamad bin Khalifa Endowed Chair in Islamic Art at Virginia Commonwealth University with his wife and colleague, Sheila S. Blair, with whom he has

written and edited many books and hundreds of articles on all aspects
of Islamic art. His book *Paper Before Print: The History and Impact of Paper
in the Islamic Lands* (Yale University Press, 2001) won the Charles Rufus
Morey Award for a notable book in the history of art from the College
Art Association in 2003, and he has just revised his 1989 book, *Minaret:
Symbol of Islam*, for a new, expanded edition to be published in 2013 by
Edinburgh University Press

Philippe Bordes was founding director of the Musée de la Révolution
Française in Vizille, France, from 1984 to 1996, and is currently professor
of art history at the University of Lyon.

Horst Bredekamp received his PhD in art history in 1974. After an intern-
ship at the *Liebieghaus* in Frankfurt, Germany (1974–1976), he became
an assistant professor at Hamburg University, where he tenured as a professor of art history in 1982. Since 1993, he has been a tenured professor
of art history at the Humboldt University of Berlin, and a permanent
fellow of the Institute for Advanced Study in Berlin (*Wissenschaftskolleg zu
Berlin*). Among his awards are the Sigmund Freud Award from the German Academy for Language and Poetry in Darmstadt, Germany (2001),
the Aby M. Warburg Award from the city of Hamburg, Germany (2005),
and the Max Planck Research Award from the Max Planck Society and
the Alexander von Humboldt Foundation (2006).

Bill Brown is the George M. Pullman Professor of English at the Univer-
sity of Chicago. He is the author of *The Material Unconscious: American
Amusement, Stephen Crane, and the Economies of Play* (Harvard University
Press, 1997); *A Sense of Things: The Object Matter of American Literature*
(University of Chicago Press, 2003); editor of *Reading the West: An Anthol-
ogy of Dime Westerns* (Bedford/St. Martin's, 1997); and coeditor of *Critical
Inquiry*.

Jaś Elsner is Humfry Payne Senior Research Fellow in Classical Art and
Archaeology at Corpus Christi College Oxford, and Visiting Professor
of Art History at the University of Chicago. He works on all areas of
ancient and early medieval visual culture, including its receptions both
in its periods of production (for instance, on themes such as viewing,
description, and pilgrimage), and in its receptions in later contexts (that
include collecting, academic historiography, the history of archaeology,
and museum display). His most recent sole-authored book was *Roman*

Eyes: Visuality and Subjectivity in Art and Text (Princeton University Press, 2007).

Juliet Fleming is Associate Professor of English at New York University. Her primary research interests are Renaissance literature and literary theory. She is the author of *Graffiti and the Writing Arts of Early Modern England* (Reaktion Press, 2001).

Ivan Gaskell is professor for cultural history, and for museum studies at the Bard Graduate Center, New York City, where he also runs the Focus Project, coordinating research, teaching, exhibiting, and publishing. His work on material culture addresses intersections among history, art history, anthropology, museology, and philosophy. His many publications include *Vermeer's Wager: Speculations on Art History, Theory, and Art Museums,* and six books coedited with Salim Kemal in the series "Cambridge Studies in Philosophy and the Arts." Gaskell has contributed to numerous journals and edited volumes in history, the history of art, and philosophy. He has curated many experimental exhibitions, most recently *Tangible Things* (with Laurel Thatcher Ulrich) at eight venues at Harvard University, where he taught and curated between 1991 and 2011.

Robert E. Harrist, Jr. is the Jane and Leopold Swergold Professor of Chinese Art History at Columbia University, and a former Slade Professor of Fine Art at the University of Cambridge. His research focuses on Chinese painting, calligraphy, and stone inscriptions, and he has written also about topics such as gardens, clothing in modern China, and the contemporary artist Xu Bing.

Bernard L. Herman is the George B. Tindall Distinguished Professor of American Studies and Folklore at the University of North Carolina at Chapel Hill. Three of his books received the Abbott Lowell Cummings Award as best work on North American vernacular architecture. Herman has published essays on quilts, self-taught and outsider arts, foodways, historical archaeology, vernacular photography, and theoretical approaches to the study and interpretation of objects. Herman teaches courses on visual and material culture, contemporary craft, vernacular art, architectural history, everyday life, and humanities-based community engagement. His recent research projects include *Thornton Dial: Thoughts on Paper,* an exhibition and book at the University of North Carolina's Ackland Museum of Art; *Quilt Spaces,* an oral history exploration of Gee's Bend, Alabama, quilts and quilt makers; and *Troublesome Things: In the Borderlands of Contemporary Art,* for which he received a Guggenheim Fellowship.

Deborah L. Krohn is an associate professor at the Bard Graduate Center. Her fellowships include the American Association of University Women, the American Association of Learned Societies, Peter Krueger–Christie's Fellowship, Cooper-Hewitt, the National Design Museum, the Metropolitan Museum of Art, Harvard Whiting, and Fulbright-Hays. Her publications include *Dutch New York Between East and West: The World of Margrieta Van Varick* (Yale/Bard Graduate Center, 2009); *Art and Love in Renaissance Italy* (coeditor, Metropolitan Museum of Art, 2008); and numerous articles and reviews.

Sabine MacCormack was, at the time of her death, Rev. Theodore M. Hesburgh, C.S.C. Professor of Arts and Letters at the University of Notre Dame, with a joint appointment in the departments of history and classics. Most recently she wrote about the impact of Roman thought and culture in the works of Augustine of Hippo—*The Shadows of Poetry: Vergil in the Mind of Augustine* (University of California Press, 1998), and on the role of the classical and patristic heritage in the formulation of religious and cultural policies in the Spanish empire—*On the Wings of Time: Rome, the Incas, Spain and Peru* (Princeton University Press, 2007).

Lynn Meskell is Professor of Anthropology and Director of the Archaeology Center at Stanford University. She has conducted fieldwork in the Middle East, the Mediterranean, and in Africa. Her most recent books include *Object Worlds in Ancient Egypt: Material Biographies Past and Present* (Berg, 2004); *Embedding Ethics,* coedited with Peter Pels (Berg, 2005); and the edited volumes, *Archaeologies of Materiality* (Blackwell, 2005); and *Cosmopolitan Archaeologies* (Duke University Press, 2009). She is founding editor of the *Journal of Social Archaeology.* Her recent research examines the constructs of natural and cultural heritage and the related discourses of empowerment around the Kruger National Park, ten years after democracy in South Africa. This forms the basis of her book *The Nature of Heritage: The New South Africa* published by Blackwell in 2011.

Daniel Miller is Professor of Material Culture at the Department of Anthropology, University College London. Recent books include *Blue Jeans: The Art of the Ordinary* (with S. Woodward, University of California

Press 2012); *Digital Anthropology* (with H. Horst, Berg, 2012); *Migration and New Media: Transnational Families and Polymedia* (with M. Madianou, Routledge, 2012); *Consumption and its Consequences* (Polity, 2012); *Tales from Facebook* (Polity, 2011); *Global Denim* (with S. Woodward Berg, 2011); *Stuff* (Polity, 2010); and *The Comfort of Things* (Polity, 2008).

Peter N. Miller is Professor and Dean of the Bard Graduate Center in New York City. He is the general editor of *Cultural Histories of the Material World* and in this series has edited *Antiquarianism and Intellectual Life in Europe and China, 1500–1800* (with François Louis) and *The Sea: Thalassography and Historiography*. He has published extensively on the history of historical research.

Ruth B. Phillips is Canada Research Chair in Aboriginal Art and Culture and Professor of Art History at Carleton University in Ottawa, and has also served as director of the University of British Columbia Museum of Anthropology. Her research and writing focus on Native American art history and critical museology. Her books include *Trading Identities: The Souvenir in Native North American Art from the Northeast, 1700–1900* (University of Washington Press, 1998); and *Museum Pieces: Toward the Indigenization of Canadian Museums* (McGill-Queens University Press, 2011).

Alain Schnapp is professor of classical archaeology at the Université of Paris I (Panthéon Sorbonne). His work is dedicated both to Greek iconography and the history of archaeology. He is the author of *Le chasseur et la cité: chasse et érotique en Grèce ancienne* (Paris, 1996); and *The Discovery of the Past* (London, 1996).

Michael Shanks is the Omar and Althea Dwyer Hoskins Professor of Classical Archaeology in the Department of Classics at Stanford University. He is also Visiting Professor of Archaeology at Durham University in the United Kingdom, and Visiting Professor of Humanities at the Humanities Institute of Ireland, University College Dublin, and has also taught at the University of Wales Lampeter in Ceredigion, United Kingdom. He has worked on the archaeology of early farmers in northern Europe, Greek cities in the Mediterranean, has researched the design of beer cans, and the future of mobile media for Daimler Chrysler. Currently, he is exploring the English borders with Scotland in the excavations of the Roman town of Binchester, and investigating the Anglo-American antiquarian tradition as a key to a fresh view of the early history of science.

His publications include *Reconstructing Archaeology* (Routledge, 1987); *Social Theory and Archaeology* (University of New Mexico Press, 1987); *Experiencing the Past* (Routledge, 1992); *Art and the Early Greek State* (Cambridge University Press, 1999); and *Theatre/Archaeology* (Routledge, 2001).

Elaine Sisman is the Anne Parsons Bender Professor of Music at Columbia University. She has published widely on music, rhetoric, and aesthetics of the eighteenth and nineteenth centuries, including *Haydn and the Classical Variation* (Harvard University Press, 1993), *Mozart: The "Jupiter" Symphony* (Cambridge University Press, 1993), and the volume edited for the Bard Music Festival, *Haydn and His World* (Princeton University Press, 1997). A board member of the Joseph Haydn-Institut in Cologne and the Mozart-Akademie in Salzburg, she served as President of the American Musicological Society in 2005–6 and was elected to Honorary Membership, its highest honor, in 2011. Her current project is a book on the music of illumination in the Enlightenment, exploring scientific knowledge, astronomical observation, and art and melancholy within musical conceptions of shadow and light.

Pamela H. Smith is a professor of history at Columbia University, and the author of *The Business of Alchemy: Science and Culture in the Holy Roman Empire* (Princeton University Press, 1994); and *The Body of the Artisan: Art and Experience in the Scientific Revolution* (University of Chicago Press, 2004). She coedited *Merchants and Marvels: Commerce, Science, and Art in Early Modern Europe* (with Paula Findlen, Routledge, 2002); and *Making Knowledge in Early Modern Europe: Practices, Objects, and Texts, 1400–1800* (with Benjamin Schmidt, University of Chicago Press, 2008). In her present research, she attempts to reconstruct the vernacular knowledge of early modern European metalworkers from a variety of disciplinary perspectives, including hands-on reconstruction of historical metalworking techniques.

Nancy J. Troy is Victoria and Roger Sant Professor in Art, and chair of the Art & Art History department at Stanford University. In addition to *The De Stijl Environment* (MIT Press, 1982), she is the author of *Modernism and the Decorative Arts in France: Art Nouveau to Le Corbusier* (Yale University Press, 1991); and *Couture Culture: A Study in Modern Art and Fashion* (MIT Press, 2002). In her current book project, *The Afterlife of Piet Mondrian,* forthcoming from the University of Chicago Press, she revisits the site of her earliest art historical interests—the work of Piet Mondrian—

studying its trajectories after the artist's death through the realms of elite and popular culture, and the ways in which the dominant historical narrative of Mondrian and his work has been shaped by art-market forces.

Ittai Weinryb is an assistant professor for medieval art and material culture at the Bard Graduate Center, New York. He was previously a doctoral fellow at the Kunsthistoriches Institut in Florence, Max Planck Institut. In 2010, he received his PhD from Johns Hopkins University for a dissertation on medieval bronze doors. He is currently revising his dissertation into a book manuscript, and is curating an exhibition on ex-votos at the galleries of the Bard Graduate Center.

Index